CONTENTS

LIST OF CONTRIBUTORS

DAVID COLLARD, University of Bath

R. M. SOLOW, Massachusetts Institute of Technology

AXEL LEIJONHUFVUD, University of California at Los Angeles

F. H. HAHN, University of Cambridge

MAURICE SCOTT, University of Oxford

AMARTYA SEN, University of Oxford

R. C. O. MATTHEWS, University of Cambridge

DIETER HELM, University of Oxford

STEFANO ZAMAGNI, University of Bologna

J. F. WRIGHT, University of Oxford

INTRODUCTION

This volume has been written to mark the eightieth birthday of Professor Sir John Hicks. The authors have all been associated with him in one way or another, though we did not request papers from those who contributed to his previous festschrift.[1] The volume begins with an essay by David Collard on his contribution to economics, which sets the context within which the rest of the essays fit. We have been most fortunate in being able to include the first (annual) Hicks Lecture, given in May 1984 by Robert Solow, under the apt title of 'Mr Hicks and the Classics'.

Given the immense range of Hicks's writings, the themes of the essays here are varied. He received his Nobel Prize in 1972 for contributions to welfare and value theory. He has pioneered ordinal utility theory. He has been a major figure in new welfare economics. His reformulation of Keynes's General Theory is classic, and his ideas on monetary economics have been influential. Hicks has also been an outstanding contributor to economic dynamics, general equilibrium, social accounting, capital theory, scientific methodology, economic history, and the history of economic thought. It is not, of course, possible to deal with so many different areas in a collection like this, but the themes touched on nevertheless do cover a wide range.

Hicks's work and ideas are like the 'Impulse' which, in his Nobel Memorial Lecture, he singled out as the mainspring of economic progress. His ideas have had many 'children' already, and there are still many more to come.

[1] J. N. Wolfe (ed), *Value, Capital and Growth*, Edinburgh University Press, 1968.

THE ASCENT OF HIGH THEORY: A VIEW FROM THE FOOTHILLS

By DAVID COLLARD*

1

THE extended metaphor which I shall employ in this essay is suggested to me by Hicks's own language. I remember first falling under the spell of his style when I chose the *Trade Cycle*, published some four or five years earlier, as a school prize. The style of that book, as of so many of his others, is exploratory rather than (overtly) didactic and even the beginner felt himself to be taken into Hicks's confidence. It was Hicks and I together (he somehow made it appear) who deliberately chose too high a value for the investment coefficient, thereby discovering floors and ceilings. He had already hinted that to follow the usual route would be a mistake. Yet for a while we did so: 'we have a river to cross; while we are thinking about building a bridge on the stretch in front of us, we note that our neighbours have already built a bridge somewhere upstream; it seems only sensible to make a detour in order to use it'. Now, in Chapter 7, we were stuck with too high an accelerator: 'at first sight this alternative looks quite ridiculous; one's first reaction is to reject it out of hand . . . but suppose there is some constraint which prevents any fluctuations from passing outside certain limits. . .'. And the Hicksian theory of the cycle was ready.

Chapter 12 of *Capital and Time* has the same sort of feel about it; 'from the point now reached, several roads open out, several of which look like being worth exploring. I shall do no more than take a few steps on some of them'. So (to give widely differing examples) do Hicks's search for the lag, in 'The Hayek story', his analogy between regional and international inequality in *World Economics*, and his assessment of the production function in *Capital and Growth*. This business of treating the reader as confidant is, of course, an expository trick: but it is more than a trick, it is part of the art of persuasion, for the reader is implicated in what has come to pass. Often, in Hicks, there are choices to be made, alternative paths to be considered, alternatives which are discussed with the reader. He delights in keeping his secrets back until, given enough clues, we may stumble upon them for ourselves. Sometimes even Hicks finds the trick difficult to perform: 'I must confess', he writes in his 'Turnpike' essay (*Essays* iii. 20) 'that when I reached this point in my thinking I was very puzzled, . . . is there another way out? . . . There is another way out, and (knowing the answer) it has been hard to write out the foregoing without revealing it'. (The secret in question here was the long-run tendency to constant cost under no joint supply.)

* I am grateful to Walter Eltis, Dieter Helm and Amartya Sen for comments on an earlier draft.

2

We have not yet reached our central metaphor. Indeed my remarks so far may even have obscured it, portraying Hicks as an enchanter and, even, a tease. Yet there are already hints of the next main strand in the metaphor, that of journeys and explorations. They have been great journeys and Hicks the traveller, guide, and chronicler has allowed the rest of us to travel with him. Images of journey and exploration abound: only a few need be recalled here:

> the present volume is the first systematic exploration of the territory which Slutsky opened up (*Value and Capital*, p. 19).

> we are within sight of a unifying principle for the whole of economics. . . but this is running ahead. Before we can explore these long avenues much preparation is needed (ibid., p. 24).

> major questions lie ahead. . . I shall do more than peer a little into these further regions. (*Capital and Growth*, p. 279).

> it will be a narrow passage, but one must hope that there will be a way through (*Critical Essays*, p. 173).

> we are emerging from our mathematical tunnel: we are coming out into economic daylight (*Capital and Growth*, p. 235).

There are many similar images. I have so far held back those which give too obvious a clue to the main metaphor. Some are explicit. Thus when discussing the Simplex method (*Essays* iii. 19) Hicks remarks: 'if one was trying to climb a mountain (without valleys or saddles), the shortest way of getting to the top would be. . . straight up, from wherever one happened to be'. And in seeking an analogy for Ricardo's theory of rent (*Essays* iii. 13): 'If a mountaineer starts at sea level and finishes the day at the top of his mountain, he must on the whole have been climbing; but it is, of course, not excluded that he had to get over a smaller range on the way, and was descending for a while as he came down from it'. Then, to clinch the matter, there is the whole gamut of terms used in the analysis itself. Starting with the utility analysis of *Value and Capital* and proceeding through *Capital and Growth* to *Capital and Time*, we come across surfaces, slopes, frontiers, balanced growth paths, full employment paths, dismal paths, ups, downs, peaks, traverses, profiles, and perspectives. We frequently deliberate about the route, assess the state of the terrain, and consider the view from the point so far reached. And, almost always, our eye is on the territory ahead.

We now have our metaphor and can set it to work. Hicks is explorer, mountaineer, and guide—hence the title of this paper. The mountain, or range of mountains, which he explores is the subject-matter of economics. It is a strange mountain, subject to avalanches, storms, mists, and other dramatic changes in weather conditions. On each expedition we discover fresh facts about the mountain and we absorb them into our mountain-craft;

some of the old facts have to be discarded as they are no longer true. The mountaineer has to make sense of the facts, to discover how his information fits together. He (or she) has to find routes and guide others along them. Where necessary he must climb sheer rock, devising specialist tools for the purpose. But often a shoulder or ridge route will be available and enable us to make easy progress. Occasionally we reach a summit and get a glimpse of other tops and valleys; for much of the time we are not sure whether the clump of rocks ahead is on a summit (most walkers will be familiar with the 'law of the receding summit' which applies to largely convex hills).

Hicks could be read, it is true, at the fireside, not as guide but as reporter or teller of traveller's tales. This is much easier, much less demanding, much more comfortable. But it is also less rewarding and less useful to those planning expeditions of their own.

3

It is never wise to venture out totally unequipped, even with so sure a guide as Hicks. Yet, surprisingly, a stout pair of boots, and waterproofs to cope with the odd shower, will very often do. There are easy and sunny slopes even in, say, *Capital and Growth* and most fit ramblers are able to cope with *A Theory of Economic History* or *Causality in Economics* if they are careful to keep their wits about them. There are safe, outlying hills suitable for the middle-aged and elderly, but visibility is always in danger of being curtailed, so a map and compass should normally be carried. Once we come to the ascent of High Theory itself this rudimentary gear will no longer do: ice-axe, nylon rope, and survival kit must be included.

Our guide's attitude to the use of artificial climbing aids on difficult rock is a sceptical one. He is not interested in technical accomplishments for their own sake when there are simpler ways up or where progress may be made by avoiding an overhang altogether. Very occasionally pitons, etriers, and the like have to be used. Hicks is certainly capable of using them but has come to regard such activities as something of a side show and to view them (almost) with disdain. In 'Formation of an Economist' he refers to the younger generation of American economists who (in the post-War period) 'with far more skill in mathematics than mine, were sharpening the analysis which I had merely roughed out. But I am afraid I disappointed them; and have continued to disappoint them. Their achievements have been great but they are not in my line.' It may be true, as he writes in 'IS–LM: an explanation', that he had to learn matrix algebra in the fifteen years between the *Trade Cycle* and *Capital Growth*, but the tool-kit used in *Value and Capital* was already a sophisticated one by then contemporary standards.

Hicks has put up an impressive number of 'firsts' on 'severe' or 'very severe' faces using techniques that have proved useful to several subsequent expeditions. Let us consider some of these.

(i) The elasticity of substitution was devised and refined for production functions in the *Theory of Wages* and for utility functions in the Hicks–Allen paper and has become an indispensable part of everyone's equipment. A pioneer from a rather different expedition, Mrs Robinson, was employing the same device at more or less the same time.

(ii) The next 'first', the Slutsky equation, had already been scaled, unobserved, by an obscure Russian climber in 1915 and was soon to be absorbed into the standard curriculum of the training schools. It is interesting that Hicks still prefers the elasticity version of the formula. These two tools, the elasticity of substitution and the Slutsky equation were, for Hicks, the keys not only to the theory of demand but also to the theory of general equilbrium.

(iii) Which brings us to the Hicksian week. Our analogy serves us quite well in the case of the Hicksian week. For, although the general outlines of the whole expedition are reasonably clear, the thing has to be done in stages. At each stage we hold counsel (Hicks's Monday) and decide where to aim for next—another top or, in the case of really major expeditions, another camp. Then the plan works itself out (with given expectations) during the following 'week'. On Monday week we have a further consultation... and so on. It does not really happen quite like this but the temporary equilibrium established each Monday is not too bad an approximation. If the mountain is at all interesting, or if it offers any surprises—which it usually does—a complete and detailed plan is impossible. Something like the Temporary Equilibrium seems to be essential to any interesting dynamics.

(iv) Another major first ascent permitted the integration of monetary and value theory ('A Suggestion for Simplifying the Theory of Money'): from the new ridge one was able to gain fresh and stimulating views of peaks only previously seen from their separate valleys. Others had glimpsed the view but had failed to make sense of it. The work appeared to have a great deal to do with the theory of portfolio selection but, as Hicks was later to argue, portfolio section was only part of the story: (it is) 'an area in which we may try our wings, before we venture (if we dare to venture) upon the more difficult and exciting parts of the territory' ('Portfolio Selection'). Those exciting parts are about uncertainty and have still to be understood; shafts of light from 'rational expectations' can never fully illuminate them. Hence his abiding interest in liquidity and fundamental uncertainty.

(v) IS–LM (1937) is the Hicksian device best known to students of macro-economics. It was sharp tool, subsequently honed in the *Trade Cycle* and in a 1957 paper, 'The "Classics" Again' (*Critical Essays* 8). But Hicks has made it abundantly clear that it was a tool only to be used in training exercises, not on real expeditions.

This catalogue of tools invented by or, at least improved by, Hicks could be greatly extended. Rather than extend the list let us look at references to Hicks, and to Hicksian devices, in two recent textbooks on microeconomics. Deaton and Muellbauer (1980)[1] refer to *Value and Capital* for Hicksian aggregation (the composite commodity theorem), for Hicksian compensated demand functions, and for technical work on the relationship between demand and cost functions; he is a 'pioneer of duality'. They refer to *Revision* for compensating and equivalent variation and to *Value and Capital* again for definitions of substitutes and complements. Layard and Walters (1978)[2] refer to the Hicksian version of the Kaldor–Hicks criterion for an increase in economic efficiency, to the Hicksian formula for the elasticity of the derived demand for labour, to Hicks on substitutes and complements and to the Hicks–Slutsky decomposition of a price change. Hicks is alive and well in the training manuals.

4

So far we have noticed Hicks the instructor, inventor of tools and pioneer of some very tricky rock-climbs. Now we shall spend some time with Hicks the mountain guide. In the ascent of high theory it is important to devise useful rules for making progress. On the long haul it is always easier to find a steadily rising path up a shoulder or along a ridge than to proceed by a series of scrambles: it is easier to find a stationary (or rather a progressively stationary) state, a 'turnpike'. If the mountain was well charted, unchanging and clearly visible, such paths would be obvious and we would take a little trouble to get ourselves on to them. But, given his experience of the mountain, Hicks is reluctant to advise a steady path. It is true that much of *Capital and Growth* and even of *Capital and Time* is devoted to working out steady-state growth paths but in the first he is expounding (and making his own) the then current state of growth theory and in the second he is putting his new 'Austrian' theory through its paces. His first love is still a true dynamics. Notice that any complete path, charted for the whole expedition and rigidly adhered to, is subject to the same sort of criticism as the steady state path. The whole thing is known *ab initio* so there can be no surprises; there is perfect foresight. At any one time we are, in practice, unlikely to be able to plan far ahead.

We must not expect that the whole of this large territory will come into sight at once. I believe that the route we shall pursue is such that it will bring most (if not all) in the end into sight (*Capital and Growth*, p. 76).

The far future is vastly uncertain: it is the near future for which we are always really planning. For the determination of these first steps (even if we are to consider them as an approach to the Turnpike) consideration of the properties of the Turnpike is not much guide (*Capital and Growth*, p. 237).

I am very sceptical of the importance of such 'steady state' theory. The real world

[1] A. Deaton and J. Muellbauer. *Economics and Consumer Behaviour*, (CUP, 1980).
[2] P. R. G. Layard and A. A. Walters, *Microeconomic Theory* (McGraw-Hill, 1978).

(perhaps fortunately) is not, and never is, in a steady state; it has adventures which are much more interesting (*Essays* iii. 8).

And, even if there are steady paths, something is bound to happen to make us change our plan—a detour to catch a magnificent view, a shortage of rations, a storm, or whatever. While, for some stretches, we would expect to regain a steady path, 'there must always be a problem of traverse', ('IS–LM: an Explanation'). So, parts of *Capital and Growth* and much of *Capital and Time* were devoted to analysing the traverse, under alternative assumptions.

> Is it possible (or how is it possible) for the economy to get into the new equilibrium, which is appropriate to the new conditions? We do not greatly diminish the generality of our study of disequilbrium if we regard it in this way, as a Traverse from one path to another (*Capital and Growth*, p. 184).

The whole of Part 2 of *Capital and Time* is devoted to the traverse. 'We should begin with an economy which is in a steady state, and should proceed to trace out the path which will be followed when the steady state is subjected to some kind of disturbance:... such a path must have a finite time-reference.' (p. 81) Two sorts of path are analysed closely, a full employment path, and a fixwage path. The disturbance is technical change and the traverse takes a long time to bring us back to the new steady path. Even then the device is a simplification. For in real life a fresh disturbance will occur while the traverse is working itself out so even the new steady path will no longer be appropriate. Having completed his traverse for the 'simple profie', Hicks sees various ways ahead.

> From the point now reached, several roads open out, several of which look like being worth exploring. I shall do no more than take a few steps on some of them (p. 135).

A particularly interesting road is opened up once technical change is superimposed upon a (pessimistic) Malthusian Dismal path; since it is 'only to be used as reference path, we need not worry about its end—in a Malthusian Apocalypse' (*Capital and Time* p. 148). The mountaineering analogy, rough though it is, brings out very well that our inability to plan depends upon uncertainty, its nature and degree. It also warns us not to overdo our healthy mistrust of steady states or (their equivalent) perfect foresight; for there are very few mountains that fail to offer some sort of steady path at least part of the way up; we know roughly the direction in which we want to go and have some idea of when (with luck) we shall get there. To allow more uncertainty than Hicks does takes us dangerously near to an inch by inch scramble over the scree, avoiding any sort of path whatsover.

5

So far I have avoided the question of what constitutes 'progress.' It must have something to do with gaining height and moving in the right direction.

But it has also to do with views and perspectives. Writing on what he regarded as Keynes's odd methodology Hicks remarks that 'we shall be able to walk around these disturbing considerations, surveying them from several points of view and making up our minds about them' (*Value and Capital*, p. 4). On the central massif of capital theory he writes; 'it is as if one were making pictures of a building: though it is the same building, it looks quite different from different angles. As I now realise I have been walking around my subject, taking different views of it' (*Capital and Time*, preface). On the early sections of *Value and Capital* he recalls 'taking step after step along a road which seemed pre-ordained as soon as one had taken the first step. . . The vistas that opened up were in their way exciting' (*Perspectives*, pp. v, vi). In a review of Scitovsky he remarked that 'it is no criticism of the guide who has helped us over the brow of the hill that he has not yet also led us into the more fertile country which lies ahead' (*Essays*, iii, 11). Thus, for Hicks, the view is not merely a luxury, it is of use, for the task is to understand the whole of the mountain range, not just to climb single peaks.

General equilibrium theory offers, *par excellence*, the possibility, but only the possibility, of perspective. It cannot yield up its perspectives as long as it remains a barren system of formal equations. The guide has to explain how everything hangs together; the nature of the watersheds, the stream courses in wet and dry conditions, the relationship between forestry and animal husbandry, the location of old mineral workings, the stability of the glacier and so on. Hicks laboured in monetary and wage theory (and even in the building industry) before attempting his general equilibrium synopsis. He knew the terrain and was able to make sense of it.

Height is a *sine qua non*, for without it there can be no progress and no improvements in the view. Though it has to do with progress it is not, however, the only measure of progress and Hicks, like all good explorers, takes with him scientific instruments of measurement, some of his own devising. One of them (consumers' surplus) makes use of area and is a measure of gain; it is very useful in deciding whether or not small movements on the surface are worth the costs. It comes in (at least) four subtly different varieties following the much simpler prototype used by Marshall and is closely related to the notion of compensation. Progress clearly has to do with movement in the right direction as well as height and effort, with utility as well as costs.

The analogue of income must be efficient progress along the surface, just as the analogue of capital must be the underlying rock itself. To the beginner the best known of Hicks's practical discussions on measuring income was *The Social Framework*, first published in 1942 and still very widely used (I can testify) in the last 1950s. The appearance of a fourth edition in 1972 and collaborative Japanese and Indian versions in 1974 and 1983 indicate that others have found it useful more recently. The *Value and Capital* discussion of income definition is, of course, standard and was referred to, for example, in the *Meade Report of* 1978. It is matched, on the mountain, by a distinction between progress and sustainable progress. The question of income measurement, particularly its relationship to the theory of index numbers and to the utility–cost duality has long fascinated Hicks. His particular contribution has been theoretical rigour tempered by practical acceptance that rough-and-ready statistical artefacts have to be used. The statistician has to use the cost measure so, argues Hicks, we must see what there is to be said for it (a great deal if we use the opportunity cost rather than the real cost version). Back on the mountain the statistician measures height or distance to chart our progress, but his calculations are unable to reveal how much 'better off' we are at different stages of the expedition or *a fortiori* as between different expeditions: 'the statistical measure of Real Income which we are examining is throughout a simple price-weighted index number of Σ pq type. Our problem is not one of the kind of measure to use, for we have no choice about that: it is a problem of the meaning which we can give to the measures which we have to employ' (*Essays* i, 7).

I have suggested the analogue of mass, for capital. But 'capital' is so all pervasive and so central to Hicks's writing that it cannot be confined within a section simply on measurement. It deserves a discussion of its own. Capital features in the title of three of Hicks's major books and has a (fully justified) reputation for being difficult terrain. One of the controversies surrounding capital (the famous Cambridge controversy) is now an old controversy and not one in which Hicks played a major part; though *Capital and Growth* did contain a discussion of reswitching. On the question of measurement it has been clear, from Walras on, that backward-looking measures (based on historical cost but allowing for depreciation) and forward-looking measures (based on expected receipts) would give the same values in equilibrium. But they do not do so in practice and some sort of compromise becomes inevitable (*Essays*, iii. 9). Another (related) controversial issue is which (if any) concept of capital best fits into the production function. The answer seems to be that if it is not to fit merely tautologically then the backward (or cost) notion is the more relevant. However, this 'backward'-looking idea of capital leads us very strongly in a direction which Hicks was not ready to follow until a revival of his interest in 'Austrian' theory, leading up to *Capital and Time*.

It is here that if our metaphor is to continue to hold at all we shall have to move from the Hicksian week into history. Strictly, it dictates that we move into geological time, but this would be unfortunate. Although a Hicksian week may be a long time in economics (as it was once said to be in politics), it is surely not aeons long? The reason for moving into history is that present capital stock is a mixture of processes based on past impulses for change. Some processes will be new, some not. There are, as it were, a number of geological layers of capital stock. At the surface we are dependent on all of them even though only one or two strata push their way through. In this way, Hicks's theorizing about capital and his theorizing about history come together.

Perhaps it is not entirely surprising that our metaphor begins to crumble in the face of capital theory which provides a severe test of any sort of economic reasoning. Now that it is crumbling it is as well to refer to its other defects of which there are at least two: its ambivalence and its unresponsiveness. It is ambivalent because it seems unable to make up its mind whether it is about progress in economics or economic progress; this is not serious. It is unresponsive (unable to be moved, like rock) because, on the whole, the mountain is totally unaffected by what the climber does. True, there can be avalanches, brought on by noise and human movement and we may cut steps in the ice. But our behaviour makes little difference and this is certainly a defect. For the Hicksian expeditions have had some effect on economics, if not upon economies; the mountain *has* responded.

6

It is clear from the essay on *Industrialism* that the Hicksian impulse which works its way through must (compared with the surface phenomena which we usually analyse) have originated in 'geological' time. At its simplest the impulse comes very close to being the industrial revolution itself. Unless disturbed by further impulses the system eventually converges to a new steady state—Hicks is very sympathetic to classical analysis of the steady state. This approach is a development subsequent to, but not inconsistent with, *A Theory of Economic History*, where, in a flexprice system, the merchant was absolutely essential to economic progress. The impulse ties up economic history not only with the Austrian theory of capital, in which time is of the essence but also with the Ricardian analysis of machinery. For the various phases in the traverse may be seen to correspond with the temporal sequence in Ricardo's *Principles* where machinery may cause initial unemployment but is sure to generate more employment eventually. If capital theory is the central massif of economics Hicks has approached it from every direction. The impulse is an heroic attempt to bring these approaches together at a high level of generality; with Hicks, economic history is not to be confined to the foothills.

These references to Ricardo and to the Austrians reflect a continuing interest in the notebooks of earlier explorers. Among economists. interest in the history of their subject is, I think, at two levels. At one level (a perfectly respectable level) is the history of economic thought as a specialist area of study, with its textbooks, readings, and so on. At another level the great economic theorist often has some feel for what his predecessors have done. He had read the travelogues, diaries, accounts, and maps of earlier explorers and has absorbed their lessons. When Hicks comes across a difficult ascent or sees a new view it is as though he asks what Ricardo, or Mill or Wicksell or Hawtrey (to give examples) would have made of it. How would they have tackled it? Similarly he asks of their own problems; what were they trying to do; where did they go wrong, was there a better route? There is a sense in which Hicks *works with* some of his illustrious predecessors.

Hicks has never written a systematic treatise on the history of economics, but it is a recurring theme in his work, and there are set pieces in *Collected Essays* iii. The first group of economists to be considered is the one with which Hicks was working at the LSE—Robbins. Hayek, Allen, Sayers, Kaldor, Lerner, Bowley, and Ursula Webb (later Mrs, then Lady, Hicks). Of these Hayek casts the longest shadow. 'The Hayek Story' (*Critical Essays*, pp. 13) combines Hicks's confidential style (already referred to) with his desire to relate others' theories to his own. 'There was some inner mystery to which we failed to penetrate. . . something central that was missing.' The key has to be a lag of some sort but 'where is the lag to be found;. . . what . . . was Hayek's lag?'. It turned out to be an (unacceptable) consumption lag, so Hayek's theory could not be about fluctuations, it must be about growth. The fascination with Hayek has been a long and special one. In general the other economists at the LSE had profound technical influences but were essentially taking part in the same theoretical expedition under the encouragement of Robbins.

The second group of economists consists of those whose ascents had a direct effect upon Hicks's early work. Marshall was one of the most remote of these and his routes (old-fashioned though they may be) almost invariably earn respect. Pareto had made brilliant use of contour maps but had lost his way, having been distracted by ideology. Wicksell had, it is true, concentrated on the process of change and had a profound effect on Hicksian monetary theory but was (for Hicks's taste) to much concerned with movement from one steady path to another. Pigou had devised a new measure of progress (an 'income' measure) which Hicks christens the new plutology. He sees the similarities between the *Wealth of Nations* and *Wealth and Welfare* and claims 'a line of descent, from Pigou through (his) own *Theory of Wages* to a great deal of modern growth theory' (*Essays*, ii, 1). Of the other British economists outside of the LSE group the most important direct influences seem to have been Hawtrey, Robertson, and Keynes. Hicks's repeated favourable references to Robertson (e.g. *Essays*, ii. 10) will be perplexing to some; they were earned not just by friendship but by a consistent emphasis on the dynamic aspects of theory. In (*Essays*, ii, 31) Hicks mentions, among the other influences upon him, Myrdal, Taussig, Viner, Mises, Schumpeter, Ohlin, and Lindahl. But the greatest though, of course, indirect influence on his greatest book, *Value and Capital*, came from Walras; not on money but certainly on the structure of general equilibrium systems and even (perhaps surprisingly) on capital.

The third group consists simply of the Classics—mainly Ricardo and Mill. I have already noticed how Ricardo's 'machinery' model fits in with Hicks's view of the world, 'It is instructive to think of each invention as setting up what might be called an "impulse"—which, if it were not succeeded by other impulses, would peter out. Ricardo's theory is a theory of the working of the industrial impulse' (*Essays*, iii, 3). Ricardo gets high marks because although his theory is a static one it is rigorously carried through, and attempts to analyse the process of growth in a series of static pictures. Mill, too, gets high marks for his analysis of 'International Trade' and the 'Influence of Consumption on Production' in *Unsettled Questions* and of money and growth in *Principles*. But, again, his method was static. So the classics are important because they chose the big questions, the important questions; unlike the catallactists (who had other defects) they are of little help in method.

Finally, there is Keynes, who made a spectacularly successful dash for the summit while Hicks was busy preparing himself for the big haul; indeed he was constructing some of the same climbing aids. There is general agreement, I think, that in the weather conditions then prevailing, the Keynesian route was a good one, brilliantly established. But, although well-worn, it is not a safe route in all conditions. Hicks has therefore taken great pains, as one familiar with it, to assess when it may be used without danger and to compare it with other routes. Sometimes the attractions of the short dash may be harmful to the long-run success of the expedition (*The Crisis in Keynesian Economics*).

7

Early in *Value and Capital* Hicks distinguished between the study of theory and the study of institutions (via history). 'It is only when both these tasks are accomplished that economics begins to near the end of its journey' (*Value and Capital*, p. 7). On this journey Hicks is an excellent guide and protects us (even if he teases us a little) from the greatest dangers. 'The trap is in fact not one that it was at all easy to suspect; it would therefore seem that it needs to have a signpost upon it, lest others fall into it also' (*Essays* iii. 20). Hicks is that very rare guide who not only knows his mountain craft but is enthusiastic and imaginative. He offers no 'ism'. Because he is so accomplished a theoretician, it is not always appreciated how deeply sceptical he is about so many of the features of mainstream economics; econometrics (for Hicks econometricians are econometrists), theory for the sake of theory, positivism, and the scientific status of the subject. Circumstances change. A theory appropriate to one set of circumstances will not be appropriate to another (indeed, in *Critical Essays* Hicks notes that surges in monetary theory are generated by monetary crises); our theories must be devised to explain current and recent facts. 'There is, there can be, no economic theory which will do for us everything we want all the time' (*Essays* iii. 1). It is not so much that we make progress; merely that different things engage our attention. Even the discarded theories that litter our route may be pressed into service once again. How important it is, then, to be in the hands of a first-class guide with an open and receptive mind; one who is 'too Open to be an Austrian; for I am an Open Marshallian, and Ricardian and Keynesian, perhaps even Lausannian, as well' (*Essays* iii. 9). In this sense we should all try to be Hicksian.

University of Bath

WORKS BY HICKS CITED IN THE TEXT

The Theory of Wages (Macmillan, 1932).

'A Suggestion for Simplifying the Theory of Money', *Economica* (1935). Reprinted in *Collected Essays*, vol. ii.

Value and Capital (Clarendon Press, 1939).

The Social Framework; An Introduction to Economics (Clarendon Press, 1942).

A Contribution to the Theory of the Trade Cycle (Clarendon Press, 1950).

A Revision of Demand Theory (Clarendon Press, 1956).

Essays in World Economics (Clarendon Press, 1959).

Capital and Growth (Clarendon Press, 1965).

Critical Essays in Monetary Theory (Clarendon Press, 1967), including 'The Hayek Story' and 'The Pure Theory of Portfolio Selection' (Clarendon Press, 1967).

A Theory of Economic History (Clarendon Press, 1969).

Capital and Time (Clarendon Press, 1973).

'Industrialism', *International Affairs* (1974).

The Crisis in Keynesian Economics (Blackwell, 1974).

Economic Perspectives (Clarendon Press, 1977).

Causality in Economics (Blackwell, 1979).

Wealth and Welfare; *Collected Essays on Economic Theory* i (Blackwell, 1981).

Money, Interest and Wages: Collected Essays on Economic Theory, ii (Blackwell, 1982).

Classics and Moderns: Collected Essays on Economic Theory, iii (Blackwell, 1983).

MR HICKS AND THE CLASSICS*

By R. M. SOLOW

I AM grateful to everyone who has come here today to do honour to John Hicks. My gratitude is, however, tempered by the realization that you are all thinking to yourselves how nice it is that you are sitting down there while I am standing up here. You are right. This is indeed a terrifying experience. The realization came too late that giving the first Hicks Lecture with John Hicks sitting here is a little like contracting to give a talk on how to paint water lilies, and then suddenly remembering that Claude Monet will be in the audience.

I promised myself at the very beginning that I would not take this lecture as the occasion for an hour-long encomium on John Hicks. In fact, as you will see, I intend to dissent mildly but firmly from some of Sir John's mature reflections. I shall speak up in defence of one of his targets, a young man whom I shall call J.R. (The J.R. I have in mind is not named Ewing.)

But before I come to that, I have to take account of the fact that there are many economists here who are much younger than I, to whom John Hicks is merely a Presence, a Great Name, a Past Master. I come from precisely the generation of economists to whom, in their student days, *Value and Capital* was more than a breath of fresh air. It was the very air itself. It was what made economic theory seem at last to be a subject with depth and rigour. I had my first course in economics as a freshman at Harvard College in 1940. I can still remember the outside of the three textbooks we read, all written by pillars of the profession. But I can no longer remember the inside of any of them. They were dull; they were anecdotal. There did not seem to be any bony structure underneath the flesh. I remember being bored and unhappy. Between 1942 and 1945 I found other things to do; and in 1945 Wassily Leontief gave us *Value and Capital* to read. All of a sudden economics seemed to be a subject worth studying for its own sake, for its intrinsic intellectual interest, and not merely because the 1930s were still a living memory. *Value and Capital*, the *General Theory*, and Paul Samuelson's *Foundations of Economic Analysis*, were the books that formed the way my friends and I thought about economics. I hate to say this, but I think most of you in this room would be better off if you had had the same experience.

With the publication of *Value and Capital* in 1939 John Hicks had already written three works, two articles and a book, whose influence can clearly be seen even today, almost fifty years later, in the daily practice of economics. The two articles were, of course, 'A Suggestion for Simplifying the Theory of Money' in 1935 and 'Mr. Keynes and the Classics' published in 1937 but written for an Econometric Society conference that took place in September 1936, here in Oxford. (Can you imagine writing a paper in

* The first annual Hicks Lecture, delivered in Oxford on 3 May 1984.

September 1936 and seeing it in print in *Econometrica* in April 1937?) In fact, it is that one, the origin, as everyone knows, of the IS–LM model, that gave me both the title and the subject of this lecture. When I speak of J.R., I mean the author of that article.

Let me get one thing out of the way at once. I am not at all concerned with the question as to whether the IS–LM model fairly represents Keynes, in whole or even in part. No more do I care on this occasion who were the classics and what they thought. I take the firm view that what we loosely call 'Keynesian economics' is a collective product. The analogies I have in mind are Newtonian mechanics and the Darwinian theory of evolution. You ask of a piece of evolutionary biology whether it is right, or useful, or interesting, not whether it copies or contradicts a passage of *The Origin of Species*. To a large extent the IS–LM model for almost fifty years has *been* Keynesian economics, though only a part of Keynesian economics it is fair to say. More recently the IS-LM model has come under attack. One of those who have criticized it is the personage I shall refer to as Sir John. On the whole, I propose to take J.R.'s side.

A methodological standpoint

It suits my argument to start with some general—even methodological—considerations that seem to me very important, and not only in this particular context. They have to do with one's attitude toward economic theory itself. James Tobin once described the IS–LM apparatus as 'the trained intuition of many of us'. That seems exactly right to me. You will have to speak for yourself. If I pick up the morning paper and read that the US Congress may soon pass a package of tax and expenditure measures intended to reduce the Federal deficit by $180 billion over the next three years, I known that my mind naturally draws IS and LM curves and shifts them. The same thing happens whenever I try to interpret routine macro-economic events in an underemployed economy. It goes without saying that some questions force you well beyond the scope of the IS–LM apparatus right away. Almost any serious question will do that if you push its ramifications far enough. Tobin only described this two-equation model as the basis for our trained intuition, not as the complete system of the world.

Why was it precisely J.R.'s paper that wormed its way into our imaginations and our intuitions? At that very same meeting of the Econometric Society in Oxford in September 1936, there were three papers that tried to extract a model from the *General Theory*, not just one. Roy Harrod's was published before J.R.'s, in the January issue of *Econometrica*, and James Meade's appeared shortly afterward in the detailed Report of the Oxford meeting. It is not too far-fetched to say that the same basic equations could be detected in all three versions. At some celestial level of abstraction, they could be described as identical products. But it was the IS–LM model that established itself as our trained intuition. What—since I have mentioned Darwin—was the source of its survival value?

If economics were really a science—in the aggressive sense—as most modern economists think it is, then there would be little or nothing to choose among alternative models so long as one way or another they contain the same equations, and thus have the same implications. Either there would be nothing to choose, or else we would choose on fundamentally trivial grounds. But suppose economics is not a complete science in that sense, and maybe even has very little prospect of becoming one. Suppose all it can do is help us to organize our necessarily incomplete perceptions about the economy, to see connections the untutored eye would miss, to tell plausible stories with the help of a few central principles. Suppose, in other words, that economics is 'a discipline, not a science'. Those are Sir John's words, actually, although he used them to express a different, but only slightly different, thought. In that case what we want a piece of economic theory to do is precisely to train our intuition, to give us a handle on the facts in the inelegant American phrase.

IS–LM survived because it proved to be a marvellously simple and useful way to organize and process some of the main macroeconomic facts. I think J.R. saw it that way too. 'We have invented a little apparatus' he says, and proceeds to 'give it a little run on its own'. That is the spirit in which I want to consider it, and to defend it.

I hope no one will fall into the error of thinking that this low-key view of the nature of economics is a licence for loose thinking. Logical rigour is exactly as important in this scheme of things as it is in the more self-consciously scientific one. The difference is not in the standards of model-building but in the scope and ambitions of model-building. Nor should I have to explain—but I will—that a framework like IS–LM is a container whose contents can evolve. There is always research to be done to refine our understanding of the basic components and the forces that shift them. The answer to old questions changes as economic and social institutions evolve; and new questions appear, partly for the same reason and partly as the counterpart of historical accidents. It is certainly possible—and here the analogy with Newton and Darwin breaks down—that historical change may cause Keynesian or Hicksian economics or the IS–LM model to become obsolete, no longer fit training for our intuitions. My argument is only that it has not happened yet.

When Sir John came to reconsider J.R.'s handiwork some five years ago, he was not entirely hostile to it. But he did suggest that the original construction had some pretty fundamental problems to get over; and the reader comes away with the feeling that Sir John is at best mildly optimistic that the repairs can be done and not especially regretful if they can not. Others, especially Axel Leijonhufvud, who never had much sympathy with IS–LM—as Sir John may once in his youth have done—have made some of the same criticisms and added others. (I am leaving out of the picture those whose main source of dissatisfaction with J.R.'s little apparatus is that it is not about Chapter 12 of the *General Theory*. My answer to them is: No, it's not.) I want to discuss four of those zones of weakness that have attracted unfriendly fire: the fix-price assumption, the treatment of expectations, the stock-flow problem, and—in order to meet Leijonhufvud head on—the 'informational' presumptions. It seems to me that there are interconnections among all of them.

Prices and wages

J.R. was explicitly assuming the IS and LM curves to refer to a unit period within which the nominal wage could be taken as fixed. That does not mean that he believed the nominal wage to be a constant of nature. Hardly anyone could have believed that in 1936. In fact he remarks that most economists of the time had 'a pretty fair idea of what the relation between money wages and employment actually was'. It does mean that J.R. thought it would be a mistake to rely on endogenous wage movements within the period (a year, say) to govern the level of employment. It is not so clear what he was assuming about the price level for goods. Forty-odd years later, Sir John seems to take it for granted that J.R. was assuming that to be fixed too, and goes on to verify that the appropriate version of Walras's Law holds even if the interest rate is the only flexible price in the model. The reason he gives for this presumption—that nominal output is used as an index of real output and employment—is not convincing to me. It would be enough for that purpose if real output were an increasing function of nominal output; proportionality is not necessary.

By itself there does not appear to be much at stake here. For the 'many of us' whose trained intuition is represented by IS–LM, I think the common presumption has been that the price level should or could be taken to be equal to (or more or less proportional to) the marginal cost of output, and therefore rising (relative to the wage) as output and employment rise, at least to the extent that there are short-run diminishing returns to labour. One of the uses of this presumption is that it reinforces the tendency of the LM curve to be relatively flat at low levels of output, when marginal cost is likely to be flat, and to be very steep at high levels of output, when marginal cost is likely to be steep. But the story can equally well be told as if the price level were given too, so that firms as well as workers are 'off their supply curves'. The stylized facts suggest that a more complicated story is needed than either of these.

Obviously this is not a suitable way to model an inflationary economy. (It is curious that the deflation of wages and prices in the 1930s did not leave much of an impression on J.R., or on other theorists of the time. Maybe the explanation is that the deflation was over by 1936 and was regarded as an episode, not as the harbinger of a 'deflationary economy'.) The apparatus is clearly designed to deal with an economy in which *either* the wage and price levels undergo only fairly small and fairly irregular movements *or* there is more substantial, sustained, presumably anticipated, inflation but its behavioural consequences can be taken into account simply by modifying the underlying expenditure ad asset-preference functions. When the macro-economic problem is dominated by partial adjustment to inflation and its aggregative and distributional consequences, IS–LM is not the right model, or is only a part of the right model.

Let me get back to the major issue: J.R.'s assumption that the money wage is given for the market period to which IS–LM applies. At an intermediate date—I am thinking of 'The Classics Again', written in 1957—someone I suppose I could call Professor H. remarked that the IS–LM diagram had 'laid excessive weight on the assumption of fixed money wages'. Well, that is a complicated question. There is the point about inflation: where it is relevant we must either modify IS–LM or supplement it or worse. I do not think that consideration is really decisive. The degree of wage flexibility one needs to allow for will also depend on the time one is allowing for adjustment, on the 'length of the run'. I have already accepted Sir John's estimate that we are talking about a year (by which I mean not a month and not a decade). Barring rapid inflation, I doubt that it violates common observation to suggest that in fact wage rates do not respond very flexibly to economic events on a time-scale less than a year. Most collective-bargining contracts last for a year or more. Even where trade unions are not much of a factor, there are obvious reasons why employers should not try to alter wage rates frequently in response to every moderate change in the economic environment.

Then there is a deeper point. For many purposes it is convenient to carry on this sort of discussion in nominal terms. It is the nominal wage that forms the object of explicit or implicit bargaining. But economic agents, we like to believe, react to real wages and real costs. Whatever the case with nominal wages, there is ample evidence that real wages have no strong endogenous pattern in modern industrial economies. (Some econometricians find real wage rates to be pro-cyclical; some find them to be anti-cyclical. All find the correlation to be small. A reasonable person would stand with my first statement.) One has to be careful about the LM-curve in this story, but that ought not to be too complicated either for the Central Bank or the economist-observer. Once again, labour-market adjustments do not seem to undermine the IS–LM story.

Professor H. in 1957 backtracked a little after his first negative remark about wage-rigidity. He judged that endogenous wage movements might be important at very low and at very high levels of employment, but that in between there might well be a zone where the assumptions of given wage rates—even given nominal wage rates—might be entirely reasonable. J.R. could live with that.

The truth is, I fear, that the profession's disdain for the fix-wage assumption is much less respectable in origin. We have a sort of prior disposition to think that prices equate supply and demand. To say that a price does not do so under ordinary circumstances is seen as too crude, like eating peas with a knife. The accepted putdown is that the assumption of wage-rigidity is *ad hoc*. Perhaps it is, but if the *hoc* it is *ad* is the economy we live in, then there must be worse sins. In that kind of world, the assumption of flexible market-clearing does not even have the merit of being *ad hoc*. If the function of macroeconomic theory is to train our intuitions, J.R.'s path seems like the right one. It will certainly not do for the intuition to react like a society dowager: if that is the sort of economy we have, let us not invite it to tea.

There is an intellectually respectable way out. In all of this discussion the tendency is to personify the wage: *it* moves or *it* does not. But in fact wages are set; they do not just happen. Sir John, in his commentary, is rightly insistent that IS–LM is an equilibrium conception. The trained intuition writes: Supply = Demand. That is an excessively narrow notion of equilibrium. What we really mean by equilibrium in the labour market is a set of wage and employment conventions that no party to the transaction feels impelled to take direct action to change. Price-mediated market-clearing is one concept of equilibrium, but only one and an extreme one at that. As soon as we begin to consider other equilibrium concepts having to do with contracts, bargaining, conventions about eligible strategies, arbitration schemes and all that, the range of possibilities is tremendously enlarged. It is not at all unlikely that convincing stories can be found that will make excellent equilibrium sense of a labour market that converts real shocks (at least) into magnified and sustained fluctuations in output and employment. Primitive examples already exist. J.R. could not have been expected to think in these terms. It is entertaining to see how the modern theory of implicit contracts instinctively starts by finding its way unerringly to those assumptions that make a contract economy just like a spot-market economy. We will outgrow that. Meanwhile I suggest that we practise thinking of the IS curve not as a locus along which 'the goods market clears' but as a locus along which 'the wage-employment bargain is an equilibrium given a goods-market outcome that is an equilibrium given the wage-employment bargain'. Practice makes perfect.

Expectations

I turn now briefly to expectations. J.R. had almost nothing to say about expectations. (One remark he did make in passing is a blockbuster, but I will come to that later.) Presumably he took it for granted that in a short-run model the state of expectations could safely be treated as exogenous. Sir John, of course, is much more sensitive to this set of issues.

There is a minor problem and a major problem. The minor problem is the investment component of effective demand. J.R. wrote the demand for investment as a function of the level of output and the interest rate. Every teacher of macroeconomics has had to squirm a bit and explain to students more or less apologetically that this is altogether too simple. 'The interest rate' has to do duty for a whole complex of credit conditions and other determinants of the cost of capital. And investment decisions, being necessarily forward-looking, can not be reduced to a mere reflex of current output. Expected sales or expected profitability over the lifetime of durable equipment is what we really want. The teacher then goes on to suggest that current output may be a fair indicator of the current state of business expectations, and anyway we will take up more detailed theories of investment next week. For a static model, this may be the best we can do. Sir John says much the same thing.

There is an intermediate step one can take that gives the intuition something to hang on to, without completely overloading the static model. Introduce a separate variable to be thought of as 'expected output', some sort of one-dimensional surrogate for future sales prospects. The demand for investment goods can be written as a function of 'expected output' *and* current output, as well as the interest rate. (I suppose the existing stock of capital goods belongs in there too, because otherwise the partial derivative of investment with respect to current output might have to be negative. One comes close this way to a form of the capital-stock adjustment principle.) Then there is a family of IS curves indexed by the state of expectations (relative to the current stock of capital). That seems reasonable, and simple enough to be useful. To take the next step and endogenize the formation of expectations, at least partially, is probably an inevitable ambition. It will take us well beyond IS–LM and into models that are essentially sequential. One simply has to admit that J.R.'s little biplane will not fly that high. It has not yet been shown that any machine we can build will fly that high, but there is always an Icarus waiting to try.

I call that a minor problem about expectations. The major problem posed by Sir John has to do with the LM curve. J.R. has smuggled a stock into what is otherwise a flow model, and not just any old stock, but a stock of money. If the model is an equilibrium construction with a unit period about a year in length, then the intersection of IS and LM must be describing a situation in which the flows of income and expenditure are in equilibrium during the year, so that at most intended inventory accumulation takes place. But the LM curve represents a stock relation, something that must hold, if it holds at all, at a point in time. The natural counterpart to flow equilibrium throughout the period is stock equilibrium at every instant during the period. Expectations, then, at least the expectations that bear on asset demands, must be confirmed throughout the period. That, says Sir John, is a peculiar foundation on which to build a theory that turns on liquidity preference. The very existence of a demand for money as liquid asset presupposes that expectations may be unfulfilled. The expectations in question can not be point expectations, because we have just seen that point expectations must be confirmed during the period. Then, in a passage that I confess I do not understand, Sir John rejects the option of formalizing the relevant expectations as ordinary probabilistic expectations. He settles, tentatively and uncomfortably, for the very special notion that those expectations relevant to asset demands take the form of a simple range. They are therefore confirmed if observed values fall within the anticipated range. But the instant-by-instant confirmation of such expectations does not eliminate all uncertainty, so the basis for liquidity preference remains.

I think, or at least I think I think, that there are several different mysteries getting in one another's way here. One is the difficulty we always seem to have in integrating stocks and flows. A second is the difficulty we always have in fitting money into equilibrium models. A third is the difficulty that some of us always have in handling stochastic equilibria—the difficulty, namely, that the usual probabilistic formulation seems to make too small a concession, i.e. no concession at all, to 'true' uncertainty. Perhaps this last is what Sir John meant in the passage I said a moment ago I did not understand. If we are willing to accept the now standard sort of stationary expectational equilibrium, I do not see why it is not applicable here. I sympathize with anyone who is not willing to accept it, but I have no constructive help to offer. Anyway, none of these difficulties is peculiar to IS–LM. The only one I want to say more about is the first, the general problem of stocks and flows.

Stocks and flows

The broad issue of integrating stocks and flows merges seamlessly into even broader questions about the strategy of macroeconomic modelling. One extreme approach is to make the unit period vanishingly short, to treat time as continuous in other words. The flow relations determine true rates of flow at an instant. The flow equations have the stocks, measured at the same instant, as parameters. Some of the flows thus determined are rates of change—time derivatives—of the stocks that appear in the model. 'Integration' is the *mot juste* for this sort of model. Stock-flow questions are submerged in existence theorems for solutions of differential equations. There are some circumstances in which this is the right way to proceed: when the focus of attention is on long-run equilibrium, the mutual adjustment of stocks to one another in a stationary or steady state. For instance, the work that Alan Blinder and I did some years ago had explicitly this orientation. We made use of a travelling IS–LM system as the instantaneous part of a model whose real object was to study stock equilibrium. The question was precisely whether these stock equilibrium considerations necessarily upset the intuitions fostered by IS–LM. The substantive analysis has since been much improved by others. But the integration of stocks and flows did not seem problematical in that setting.

Sir John would not be happy to stop here, and neither should I. The Blinder–Solow device is not merely technical. It enforces a commitment with economic content: that the IS–LM mechanism works itself out instantaneously, with the economy being at every instant at the intersection of continuously shifting IS and LM curves. This may be suitable for long-run analysis, but it will not do for someone who cares about the short run, and therefore about the IS–LM outcome itself. Then the interplay between short run and long run, between stocks and flows, becomes complicated, and choices have to be made. The early chapters of *Capital and Growth* contain a careful study of this problem. There Sir John points out that one reasonable definition of flow equilibrium entails that if stock equilibrium rules at the beginning of the short period it will rule throughout the short period. Of course it is also possible that initial stock equilibrium will be upset by the flow developments within the period. There would be something awkard and implausible about a theory which had stock equilibrium being restored, with a jerk, 'between' periods. But if stock disequilibrium is allowed to persist for several periods, the basic data that underlie successive short-period solutions begin to crumble. Some economists may be willing to make strong assumptions about expectations—one or another version of rational expectations, for example, but no doubt other devices would do—to bridge this gap. I have the impression that neither J.R. nor Sir John is among them, and neither am I.

I want only to make a pragmatic point that bears on the usefulness of IS–LM. I think it is unnecessary to make an issue of principle out of stocks-and-flows. All modelling runs into trouble when it has to cope with two or more processes that work themselves out at drastically different speeds, a fast process and a slow process, say. When Bach manages it in a suite for unaccompanied cello, it seems like a miracle. Even on the mechanical level, the representation of such systems is messy; and my experience is that on the conceptual level as well the synchronization of short-run and long-run processes is naggingly obscure. One makeshift that economists—and others—sometimes employ is to alternate. One lets the fast process converge while the variables of the slow process stand still at their initial values. (This is exactly Keynes's procedure, of course; ignore capital accumulation even though net investment is non-zero.) Then one stops the fast process for a moment and lets the slow process take a step, just one step, driven by the outcome of the fast process. Now the slow process is frozen again in its new state and the fast process is allowed to converge once more. And so on. I do not want to make this sound easy. The substantive question is the nature of the interaction of the two processes. This is where expectations come in. That part of the problem has economic content. The timing and meshing is often just a matter of making do with whatever analytical techniques are at hand. Tobin has given an excellent example of the pragmatic approach in *Asset Accumulation and Economic Activity*. Apart from the proliferation of assets, his model is very much like IS–LM. Growth theory should ideally be carried on this way too. What I have been describing is very much like what Sir John calls traverse. That is the easiest part of skiing, but the hardest part of economics.

I would not want to be misunderstood as meaning that stock-flow problems are easy or unimportant or merely matters of finding some catch-as-catch-can technique. It is genuinely hard to analyse interacting fast and slow processes intelligibly; and it can be very hard for the monetary authorities, say, to manage an economy with interacting fast and slow processes. They will have to worry, for instance, whether exploiting the short-run real effects of monetary injection will damage their capacity to control slower price-level effects. That is a fact of life, not of modelling. My point is that the modelling problem is substantive, not philosophical.

'Information' and all that

Finally, I want to take a few minutes to defend IS–LM against a quite different antagonist, Axel Leijonhufvud. My original plan was to keep to the dialogue between J.R. and Sir John, a sort of family affair. My reason for widening the net is mainly that doing so gives me an opportunity to make one or two general points in defence of the modelling tradition in which IS–LM is at home, and against a contemporary tendency to shift the emphasis from market failure to 'information' failure.

I do not want to give the impression that I am hostile to all of Leijonhufvud's thoughts on this subject, root and branch. On the contrary, I think some of the ideas expressed in 'The Wicksell Connection' and in 'What Was the Matter with IS–LM?' are quite wholesome, and would probably have met with J.R.'s approval. Let me give an example, so it will be clear that I am not merely being polite. Leijonhufvud argues emphatically that it is both wrong and unhistorical to lay all the blame for prolonged unemployment on wage rigidity, real or nominal. All that talk about Saving and Investment must have been somehow relevant to macroeconomics. Leijonhufvud maintains that the key to—I do not know if he would settle for 'another key to'—the theory of economic fluctuations is a failure of the interest-rate mechanism. Suppose that the typical macroeconomic shock is a change in the perceived profitability of future investment. A smoothly functioning market economy would adapt to that contingency by shifting resources to the production of, and shifting expenditure flows to the purchase of, consumer goods. When it does not do so, there is trouble. In 'The Wicksell Connection' Leijonhufvud describes—rather sketchily—his own favourite way of analyzing that sort of problem, but there is no need to discuss it now.

J.R. would probably have been glad to agree about the importance of the interest-mechanism. Professor H., in 'The Classics Again', is quite explicit on that score: '... There are conditions in which the price-mechanism will not work—more specifically ... there are conditions in which the interest-mechanism will not work'. In 1936, J.R. put a lot of emphasis on the liquidity-trap case, when the long-term interest rate has reached its practical floor. Twenty years later, Professor H. was at pains to go further. There are other possible malfunctions in the interest-investment mechanism. Today, of course, we are all aware that a developed system of financial intermediaries undermines the independence of the IS and LM curves and makes the whole analysis more complicated. This part of Leijonhufvud's argument has a lot to recommend it. Especially recast in terms of the broader equilibrium concept I was urging earlier, I think it has a place in anybody's trained intuition.

The more characteristic aspect of Leijonhufvud's argument against IS–LM is what I find unacceptable. It traces the difference between IS–LM and other (monetarist or 'new classical') models to different assumptions about the diffusion of knowledge, about 'who knows what'. I find this emphasis misleading.

Leijonhufvud begins by setting up a benchmark that he calls 'full-information macroeconomics'. It need not correspond to complete certainty, but 'in a full-information state, agents have learned all that can (profitably) be learned about their environment and about each other's behaviour'. In effect, this benchmark state is a kind of (more or less Walrasian) growth equilibrium. The real point is that there are no unexploited opportunities for *ex ante* mutually advantageous trades. That being so, macroeconomic malfunctions—at least those that do not, like price rigidities, suggest that the economy is kept from efficiency by *force majeure*—can usually be traced to some 'information failure', something that keeps agents from knowing about mutually advantageous adjustments they could make. Alternative macro-economic models, therefore, are most fruitfully distinguished by their infor-mational assumptions. The trouble with IS–LM is that it has nothing to say about—and in fact hides—the process by which the diffusion of information moves a malfunctioning economy back toward full-information equilibrium. This process inevitably involves shifts in both IS and LM, and that is the main reason why they are inferior tools, undependable guides to the intuition.

My response—I say mine because I do not know how this argument would have struck J.R.—is that the emphasis on information is seriously mislead-ing. ('Co-ordination' is another matter entirely.) It suggests that there is something knowable that, if known, would forestall macroeconomic mal-function. I suppose it would follow that macroeconomic policy could usefully be restricted to the production and dissemination of the missing information. The trouble with this line of argument, I think, is that it fundamentally overworks the concept of 'information'. One could equally say that the Second World War was an example of information failure: if Hitler had known what was going to happen, he would never have invaded Russia, perhaps not even Poland. If Caesar had known what was going to happen, he would not have crossed the Rubicon, or would he?

The point is not merely that the information in question is complex and ill-formed, nor even that it would have to include information about the behaviour of others, including things they do not know about themselves. My objection is deeper. This opaqueness of economic events is not a misadventure of the economic system; it is an intrinsic characteristic of a decentralized market economy, dependent on market signals—prices and quantities—for the direction of individual behaviour.

There is an enlightening difference of approach to be pointed out here. Modern monetarists like to start with a purely nominal disturbance—the famous helicopter drop of money—as the archetypical shock to the economy. I think that is because the purely nominal shock is the one instance where the claim might plausibly be made that if only everyone knew what was going on the economy could go to its new equilibrium—a proportional increase in all nominal prices, with no real change at all—with little or no disturbance. Leijonhufvud is rightly scornful. His choice for the archetypical shock is the one I mentioned earlier: an unforeseen shift in the expected profitability of future investment. But that should alert him to the pointlessness of describing ignorance about the consequences as an information failure. No one could *possibly* know what the new equilibrium would look like after the discovery of electricity. It is a bit like describing an airplane crash as a gravitational failure.

To the extent that the economy tends to return to its equilibrium path after being shocked away from it, the diffusion of information, in the ordinary sense, does not seem to describe and control the process. To my eye, it is much more nearly a matter of the resolution of intrinsic uncertainty, the unwinding of explicit and implicit contracts, and the frictions of imperfect markets. Besides, here and now, in the fifth year of a deep recession (one that the trained intuition finds it perfectly natural to analyse in the IS–LM framework) after only the early stages of recovery and with a long way to go to reach the trend, one is not much impressed by the speed and power of the economy's automatic return to growth equilibrium.

Conclusion

I have been so busy defending J.R.'s construction against slings and arrows that I may have given the impression of mere piety. That is not what I intend. In passing, I have mentioned two developments that do seem to surpass the capacity of so simple a model to comprehend: one is the behaviour of a strongly inflationary economy and the other is the operation of a system of financial intermediaries that tends to link IS and LM together. For reasons of time and space I have not even mentioned a third: the predominance of open-economy forces in many circumstances. (By the way, now I want to mention J.R.'s startling remark on expectations referred to earlier: 'There may be other conditions when expectations are tinder, when a slight inflationary tendency lights them up very easily.' In 1936, remember.)

There is yet another problem with IS–LM that I must acknowledge. Just because the apparatus is so simple, it lends itself to the arithmetization of macroeconomic theory. There is a tendency for even generally subtle people to treat it not merely as a guide to the intuition but as a substitute for intuition, and for more extended and deeper theory. That is undoubtedly a bad thing; and it may be for that reason that Sir John has taken such a jaundiced view.

It would be terribly subversive of macroeconomic theory if a two-equation model could sum up most of what we need to know. There is no serious danger of that. Nevertheless it is remarkable that a simple system like IS–LM has served us so long and so well. There are other examples: Mendel's Laws, the elasticity of demand, the Blackwood Convention, the wheel. The story speaks well both for J.R.'s inspiration, and also for the view of macroeconomic theory not as a branch of physics but as a sort of Blue Guide that points out right directions, rough distances, and excellent places to stop, study the landscape, and enjoy the view.

When I was a small child, probably about the time the *Theory of Wages* was being written, I read a little vignette that has stuck in my memory ever since. A woman against whom Philip of Macedon had given his verdict after drinking more than he ought, declared forthwith: 'I appeal against the decision.' 'To *whom* do you appeal?' thundered the King. 'I appeal from King Philip drunk to King Philip sober' was the reply, and the King, seeing the point, reversed himself. I can not imagine Sir John in any state other than sober, but nevertheless I appeal to him to look with more kindness on this offering from his youthful servant J.R. and from J.R.'s ageing emissary.

Massachusetts Institute of Technology

HICKS ON TIME AND MONEY

By AXEL LEIJONHUFVUD

MODERN macroeconomic theory has been shaped to an extraordinary degree by Keynes and by Hicks. My assignment was to discuss them both, but I have found it too large for a paper. I will confine my discussion of Hicks's role to two related themes: Time and Money.

Even within these boundaries, the following attempt at an interpretation cannot be definitive.[1] Among the several reasons for this, one is germane: I know that I shall learn more from Sir John Hicks in the future. But I cannot know exactly what I shall learn next time I sit down to read or re-read him. Hence today's assessment cannot be my 'optimal' or final one. Rather than commit myself fully, I should retain a measure of 'flexibility'.[2]

In certain types of situations, it is rational to commit oneself fully or contingently. In others, where the future contingencies cannot be enumerated or their nature anticipated, one should retain flexibility. One difference between neo-classical and Keynesian theory is that the former tends to exclude, whereas the latter must include, situations of the second sort.[3] The younger Hicks is remembered for his contributions to neo-classical economics; over the years the elder Hicks has become more insistently Keynesian in this particular sense.

Time and equilibrium

'Every economist is familiar with the accomplishments of Hicks the Younger, whether he has read him or not. That brilliant young man was supremely successful—by reformulating utility theory, by simplifying monetary theory, by interpreting Keynes and the Classics, and by reviving general equilibrium theory—in constructing the moulds into which 40 years of subsequent theoretical developments were to be cast'.[4] It is helpful to try to see the young Hicks in historical context.

What went on at the London School in the early thirties appears in retrospect almost as important as what was going on in Cambridge. At LSE, the world of Anglo-American economics was being won over from the tradition of Ricardo and Marshall to modern neo-classical economics—or, in the terms of Hicks the Elder, from 'plutology' to 'catallactics'. If Cambridge

---

[1] I have made one previous attempt. My 'Monetary Theory in Hicksian Perspective' was written in 1968 but not published until 1981, at which time I was still reasonably content with the paper. Once it was in print my understanding of some of the issues began to change—as I shall explain below.

[2] Cf. Hicks, *The Crisis in Keynesian Economics*, ch. 2, and the antecedent Hart (1942).

[3] In stressing this particular distinction between neo-classical and Keynesian theory over others, I am following G. L. S. Shackle more than my own earlier work. Cf. esp. Shackle (1972).

[4] Quoting my own (1979) review of Hicks's *Economic Perspectives* (1977).

was sufficient unto its British self, Lionel Robbins's London School encouraged the study of the Austrian and the Lausanne schools, of the Americans and the Swedes. ('We were such "good Europeans" in London that it was Cambridge that seemed "foreign".')[5] Robbins brought Hayek to London and assembled a stable of superbly talented junior people: R. G. D. Allen, Marian Bowley, John Hicks and Ursula Webb-Hicks, Nicholas Kaldor, Abba Lerner, Vera Smith-Lutz, Richard Sayers, and G. L. S. Shackle. Most importantly, Robbins wrote the programmatic tract that, highly controversial in its time, has long since permeated the teaching of economics to the point where its main message has become a platitude (thus depriving its author of the Nobel Prize?). His *Nature and Significance of Economic Science* argued the 'scarcity' definition of economics, a definition that fundamentally changed both the scope and the content of Marshall's subject. Robbins made rational means-ends calculation the core of economics.

It was the younger Hicks that demonstrated how this Robbins programme could be realized. The Hicks–Allen 'Reconsideration' recast demand theory in terms of rational decision theory. Hicks's simplification of monetary theory drew Money into the orbit of marginalist calculation. 'Taking step after step along a road which seemed pre-ordained as soon as one had taken the first step' in a few years time led to the 'static' parts (chs. I–VIII) of *Value and Capital*.[6] These were the parts of Hicks's early work that, together with 'Keynes and the Classics', were to have such a profound and pervasive influence on how economics was to be taught in the United States in the era when American economics was becoming strongly predominant. Perhaps it is more accurate to say that these parts of Hicks's work were selected by the generation of American economists led by Paul Samuelson that were re-erecting the structure of economic theory using constrained optimization building blocks.

Pure decision theory, formalized as optimization subject to constraints, is essentially timeless. The choice among the foreseen outcomes of alternative actions[7] is a purely logical calculus that does not involve time in any essential way. Thus was created a durable tension between neo-Walrasian microtheory and Keynesian macrotheory that, decades later, was to culminate in crisis.

This could hardly have been foreseen. As Robert Clower has remarked,[8]

> . . . it was only natural for economists generally to proceed on the presumption that general equilibrium theory had no inherent limitations. . . . That any even moderately 'general' economic model should [be incapable of representing Keynesian

---

[5] Cf. the 'Commentary' to *The Theory of Wages*, (1963), p. 306. 'Plutology' and 'catallactics' are discussed in Hicks, 'Revolutions' in Economics', in Spiro Latsis (ed.), (1976) reprinted in Hicks, *Classics and Moderns* (1983).

[6] *Economic Perspectives*, pp. v–vi.

[7] The foreseen consequences may of course be probability distributions of outcomes. This does not alter the problem.

[8] Cf. Clower (1975), p. 134.

processes] . . . would hardly occur naturally to any but a very perverse mind. That
the elaborate Neo-Walrasian model set out in Hicks' *Value and Capital* might fail
[in this respect] would have seemed correspondingly incredible to any sensible
person at the outset of the Neo-Walrasian Revolution.

The younger Hicks knew that Time was a problem. We find him wrestling
with it in almost all the parts of his early work that did *not* become part of
the American neo-classical canon. It was to become even more of a
preoccupation—an unfashionable preoccupation—for Hicks the Elder.

From the first, it seems, Hicks saw it as a supreme theoretical challenge,
deserving the most sustained effort, to find a mode of process analysis that
would retain a role for equilibrium constructions without denying (or trivializ-
ing) change. In the early going, this amounted to finding a workable way
between Walras and Pareto, on the one hand, and Knight and Hayek on the
other.[9] Thirty or forty years later, the opposed alternatives—Arrow–Debreu
v. Shackle or Lachmann—are clearer and also further apart. In the Arrow-
Debreu construction, the rational choice of each agent is defined over all
dimensions of commodity–time–contingency space; the result is that all
decisions are made once and for all at the origin of time. To obtain a model
in which decisions are made in temporal sequence, agents must be ignorant
of some of the information that is necessary in order to calculate all optimal
allocations at the beginning of time. Thus Shackle poses the issue with
uncompromising force: '. . . the theoretician is confronted with a stark
choice. He can reject rationality or time.'[10]

The American Neo-Walrasians, from Paul Samuelson to Robert Lucas,
have not seen this choice as at all difficult. In general, they have simply
gone whole hog for Rationality, letting Time and Change be trampled
underfoot in the philosophical muck as unfit food for economic thought. If
forced (somehow) to choose, it is possible that Hicks the Younger might also
have opted for rational allocation theory; Hicks the Elder almost certainly
would opt for economic history. In actuality, Hicks fought fifty years to
maintain a conceptual middle ground.

The issue may have come into focus at LSE precisely because all of the
neo-classical schools were to some extent cultivated in the circle around
Robbins and Hayek. Marshall had been aware of the problem[11] and had

[9] Cf. Hicks, 'The Formation of an Economist', (1979*b*, p. 199), now reprinted in id. (1983).

[10] Cf. Shackle (1972), Preface.

[11] Hicks, *Capital and Growth*, pp. 47–8 quotes Marshall (1928), p. 379, n. 1: 'A theoretically
perfect long period . . . will be found to involve the supposition of a stationary state of industry,
in which the requirements of a future age can be anticipated an indefinite time beforehand . . .
and it is to this cause more than to any other that we must attribute that simplicity and
sharpness of outline, from which the economic doctrines in fashion in the first half of this
century derived some of their seductive charm, as well as most of whatever tendency they may
have had to lead to false practical conclusions.' Of course, the second half of the 20th century takes
a generally more permissive attitude to 'seductive charms' than this most eminent Victorian
among economists. Shackle's aptly titled chapter 'Marshall's Accommodation of Time', in id.
(1972), gives a sample of other remarks of Marshall's indicating his preoccupation with the
issue.

devised a method that at least partly evaded it. Hayek had worked on the construction of an equilibrium process 'in time' and had found himself forced back onto 'perfect foresight' assumptions.[12] Robbins had drawn the conclusion that 'The main postulate of the theory of dynamics is the fact that we are not certain regarding future scarcities.'[13]

As matters stood around 1930, the static toolbox of economic theory was strictly applicable only to stationary, perfect foresight processes. It was not at all clear that economic theory provided any foundation for the disciplined analysis of monetary questions or business cycles. Hicks's earliest work dramatized the predicament. In particular, his remarkable 1933 paper on 'Equilibrium and the Cycle'[14] drove home a point made by Knight: that in a perfect foresight equilibrium process, people would not demand cash-balances. This spelt trouble for the most sophisticated cycle theory available at the time. What became of Hayek's notion of 'neutral money' as a criterion for maintaining macroeconomic equilibrium, if in equilibrium there could be no place for money, 'neutral' or otherwise?

The Swedish followers of Wicksell had run into similar quandaries and it was from Myrdal and Lindahl that Hicks got help with the next step.[15] The next step had to be a method of describing economic processes that (a) was not confined to just 'perfect foresight' processes, and (b) still did not force the abandonment of the entire apparatus of inherited static theory. Lindahl's temporary equilibrium method[16]

reduced the process of change to a sequence of single periods, such that, in the interior of each, change could be neglected. . . . Everything is just the same as with the 'static' kind of process analysis . . . save for one thing: that expectations are explicitly introduced as independent variables in the determination of the single-period equilibrium.

Thus, when the *General Theory* appeared, Hicks had been working along these lines for some time. His first reaction gave pride of place to Keynes's use of a similar device: a short-run equilibrium adapting to independently

[12] Cf. Hayek (1928).
[13] Robbins (1932), p. 79.
[14] 'Gleichgewicht und Konjunktur', *Zeitschrift für Nationalökonomie*, iv (1933). This remarkably modern, historically important paper was finally translated and published in *Economic Inquiry* (Nov. 1980), thanks to its then editor, Robert Clower. It is now reprinted in Hicks (1982).
[15] G. Myrdal, 'Geldtheoretisches Gleichgewicht', in F. A. Hayek, (ed.), *Beiträge zur Geldtheorie* (1933), was reviewed by Hicks in *Economica*, (Nov. 1934). The review is reprinted in Hicks (1982). G. L. S. Shackle, also a member of the Robbins circle, testifies to the great influence and importance of Myrdal's contribution in his (1967), Chapters 9 and 10. Of Lindahl's temporary equilibrium concept, Hicks first learned through personal acquaintance. He has discussed temporary equilibrium methods repeatedly, e.g., in *Value and Capital*, esp. chs. IX–X and XX–XXII, in 'Methods of Dynamic Analysis' (1956) now reprinted in Hicks (1982), and in *Capital and Growth*, ch. VI.
[16] Hicks (1965), p. 60.

specified long-term expectations.[17] But the kinship was not all that close. Keynes had applied the 'methods of expectations' to a Marshallian short period. Marshall had invented a kind of analysis ('with some slight dynamic flavouring'[18]) which definitely was 'in time' but that left the line between statics and dynamics unclear. In *Value and Capital*, Hicks developed an alternative line of attack.

The attack starts with the famous definition of 'Economic Dynamics' as those parts of economic theory 'where every quantity must be dated'.[19] This was an important step. The Marshallians, for example, had not taken it.

By itself, the dating of goods only adds dimensions to the commodity space considered in 'timeless' statics. Studies in efficient intertemporal resource allocation following Fisher and Hicks have improved our understanding of capital, growth, and interest theory immensely. But the course of this development became quite similar to what happened to British classical theory, about which Hicks observed: 'The more precise capital theory became, the more static it became; the study of equilibrium conditions only resulted in the study of stationary states'.[20] We have to substitute 'steady' for 'stationary', of course, but otherwise the conclusion holds. It is presumably for this reason that Hicks no longer favours his old static–dynamic distinction but prefers to talk of analysis that is 'out of time' or 'in time'.[21]

Dating brings in future time, but it does not necessarily help in bringing in the passage of time. If the usual (stochastically) perfect knowledge assumptions are made, the end result will be the Arrow-Debreu contingency market model in which all decisions are made at the origin of time. There is no business left to transact at later dates. Money and liquidity can be forced into such a structure only by obvious artifice.

The present-day practice at this juncture is for the theorist to retire behind a smoke screen while intoning some incantation about transactions costs. Hicks, in 1939, did a bit better. What must be done is to weaken the informational assumptions of the model so as to make agents postpone at least *some* decisions 'until they know better'.[22] Hicks discussed several types of uncertainty and decided, I think correctly, that agents' uncertainty about

---

[17] Hicks's 1936 *Economic Journal* review is reprinted in *Money, Interest and Wages* as 'The General Theory: A First Impression'.

[18] Surely, Hicks was thinking of Marshall when (*Value and Capital*, pp. 115–16) he declined to follow 'the usual course of economists in the past ... and give(s) one's static theory some slight dynamic flavouring, (so that) it can be made to look much more directly applicable to the real world . . . . But it will still be quite incompetent to deal properly with capital and interest, or trade fluctuations, or even money . . .'

[19] *Value and Capital*, p. 115.

[20] *Capital and Growth*, p. 47.

[21] Cf. esp. his 'Time in Economics', as reprinted in (1982), e.g. p. 291: '(Steady State economics) . . . has encouraged economists to waste their time upon constructions that are often of great intellectual complexity but which are so much out of time, and out of history, as to be practically futile and indeed misleading. It has many bad marks to be set against it.'

[22] It is for this reason that I have proposed changing the Hicksian definition of dynamics to 'those parts of economic theory where *decisions* must be dated'. Cf. Leijonhufvud (1983b).

their own intentions was the most fundamental[23]

> ... in particular, they know that they cannot foretell at all exactly what quantities they will themselves desire to buy or sell at a future period... and this it is, in the end, which limits the extent to which forward trading can be carried on in practice.

This argument is the bridge by which Hicks made his escape from steady-state capital theory into temporary equilibrium theory. In the temporary equilibrium theory of *Value and Capital*, time is divided into a sequence of 'weeks'. Planned demands and supplies for the week depend on current prices and expected future prices. Current prices are determined on 'Monday' and rule unchanged for the rest of the week. On 'Sunday' (we may imagine), the parameters of the equilibrium system are updated: changes in stocks are accounted for and price-expectations revised. The system is then ready for another Monday morning.

In this story, all markets cleared each Monday. Hicks understood perfectly that this assumption by itself did not preclude periods of subnormal activity in the system. The defence of the assumpton that he suggested is exactly the one so strenuously insisted upon by Lucas, Barro, *et alia* almost forty years later. In Hicksian terms, if price-expectations are inelastic, a fall in current prices will induce intertemporal substitution: supplies will be shifted from this week into next.[24] Market-clearing, however, was equilibrium in a 'limited sense'; in the more fundamental sense of 'Equilibrium over Time', Hicks emphasized, the economic system was 'usually out of equilibrium'.[25]

This temporary equilibrium method is thus clearly distinct both from Keynes's short-run equilibrium, on the one hand, and from the new classical equilibrium method of more recent years. It avoids some of the problems of the alternatives and deserves further exploration, therefore,[26] although of course, it has problems of its own. But, while Hicks has resumed the struggle

---

[23] *Value and Capital*, p. 137. Of course, this way out of the predicament ultimately requires us to formulate a theory of the behaviour of agents who *know* that they are likely to 'foresee their own wants incorrectly' (p. 134). *This* problem Hicks did not tackle in 1939. It is in his *Crisis in Keynesian Economics*, Chapter II, thirty-five years later, that we find it addressed. Decision-making by agents who know that they will know better later (but don't know, even probabilistically, what it is they will learn) will not fit naturally into the usual constrained optimization apparatus. For a comprehensive attack on the problem, cf. Ron Heiner (1983).

[24] Cf. *Value and Capital*, p. 131: 'There is a sense in which current supplies and current demands are always equated in competitive conditions. Stocks may indeed be left in the shops unsold; but they are unsold because people prefer to take the chance of being able to sell them at a future date rather than cut prices in order to sell them now. The tendency for the current price to fall leads to a shift in supply from present to future. An excess of supply over demand which means more than this is only possible if the price falls to zero, or if the commodity is monopolized, or if the price is conventionally fixed'.

[25] *Value and Capital*, loc. cit.

[26] It took more than 30 years for the profession to catch on to what Hicks had been up to in 1939. Grandmont's survey (1975) shows how the crisis of Keynesianism, which was in part a crisis of Keynes's method, had produced a more profound appreciation of the difficulties that the temporary equilibrium approach had been designed to address.

for a systematic 'in time' analysis later—and on more difficult ground even[27]—he chose to abandon the Temporary Equilibrium approach.

Why? The Elder Hicks has given his retrospective reasons. There were problems *within* the 'week' and *between* 'weeks':[28]

> Much too much had to happen on that 'Monday'! And . . . I was really at a loss how to deal with the further problem of how to string my 'weeks' and my 'Mondays' together.

Getting from one 'week' to the next required both a theory of capital accumulation and a theory of the revision of expectations. The first problem by itself was forbidding at the time; only the later development of modern growth theory made it manageable. Forty years have not brought us much advance on the second problem.[29]

In his retrospective evaluation, Hicks does not point to the problems that the temporary equilibrium method would have to overcome in order to provide a 'continuation' theory; instead, he focuses on how the method dealt with events 'within the week':[30]

> . . . I tried to go further [than to work with *given* expectations], to allow for the effects of current transactions on expectations; supposing that these effects could (somehow) be contemporaneous with the transactions themselves. . . . That however was nonsense. . . . It does deliberate violence to the *order* in which in the real world (in *any* real world) events occur.
>
> It was this device, this indefensible trick, which ruined the 'dynamic' theory of *Value and Capital*. It was this that led it back in a static, and so in a neo-classical, direction.

What an extraordinarily harsh judgement this is! Why? Because in obliterating the *sequence* in which things happen, the model comes to ignore the structure of markets. It matters, for instance, whether people commit themselves on quantities and discover their mistakes through price-change 'surprises' or set their prices and see their errors revealed in the behaviour

---

[27] The 'Traverse' problem which Hicks set himself in chapter XVI of *Capital and Growth* and analysed at length in *Capital and Time* adds a forbidding burden of capital theory to the difficulties discussed in the text.

[28] Cf. 'Time in Economics', in Hicks (1982), p. 290. In 1956, ('Methods of Dynamic Analysis'), Hicks distinguished between the problems of *single-period theory* and those of *continuation theory*. Cf. the reprint in (1982).

[29] A 'Robertson lag' in income is yet another possible bridge from 'week' to 'week'. In Leijonhufvud (1968), I tried to get to the *General Theory* by this route: I had a first period in which sales declined because sellers had inelastic price expectations and thus did not cut prices fast enough; in the next week, demand was then 'income-constrained' with consequent Keynesian multiplier-effects, etc. I thought at the time that I had, in effect, got over from *Value and Capital* to the *General Theory* in fairly good order and it puzzled me why Hicks had not tried this route. But Hicks had defined his temporary equilibrium in such a way as to preclude unintended shortfalls in sales. See his comments below on the 'indefensible trick'.

[30] *Economic Perspectives*, p. vii. The sentence in quotes is from *Capital and Growth*, ch. VI, where the matter is also discussed. Compare also Clower (1975) and Clower and Leijonhufvud (1975).

of quantities.[31] It matters, in Hicks's terms, whether the markets in the system are mostly of the *flex-price* or the *fix-price* variety. In this century, 'the unorganized flexprice market, the old type, is on the way out... modern markets are predominantly of the fixprice type..'[32] In Hicks's view, this historical transformation is of major macroeconomic significance. The change in the predominant market form is a change in the way that impulses are propagated through the system. The harsh language becomes understandable—for, of course, Hicks sees the 'indefensible trick' still being practised all over!

IS–LM

The younger Hicks may have had somewhat different reasons for abandoning his temporary equilibrium method. One of them surely was that Keynes had come up with an alternative method of short-period analysis. It was a rough-and-ready sort of short-period method and Hicks the Younger would have realized better than anybody else how rough it was. But it seemed to be adequate to Keynes's purposes and Hicks agreed that Keynes's purposes were the supremely important ones.

Soon after his original review, Hicks returned to the *General Theory* and wrote 'Mr. Keynes and the 'Classics': A Suggested Interpretation'. The IS–LM appartus of this immensely influential paper was not a Walrasian (or Paretian) construction but a hybrid. Keynes's macrotheory was built with Marshallian microcomponents. But the modelling idea was, as Hicks has himself explained,[33] borrowed from *Value and Capital*, where he had worked out a two-dimensional representation of the equilibrium for a Walrasian system of three markets.

The IS–LM model summarized numerous features of the *General Theory* with admirable economy and it was to serve in the deduction of numerous Keynesian comparative statics propositions that Keynes had not thought of. The model became the backbone of instruction in macroeconomics for forty years. Nonetheless, something was just a bit askew with it. In later years, Hicks has several times come back to reassess it and the uses to which it has been put. In brief, (a) he has remained fairly content with it as a synopsis of Keynes' theory;[34] (b) he has become less satisfied with it as a way of portraying the 'classics' and hence as a tool for isolating Keynes's contributon by IS–LM comparisons;[35] and (c) he has grown somewhat sceptical

[31] 'Methods of Dynamic Analysis', section iv.
[32] *Economic Perspectives*, p. xi. Cf. also *Capital and Growth*, Chapter VII. *Money, Interest, and Wages*, pp. 226–35, 296–99, 320–4.
[33] Cf. 'IS–LM: An Explanation', in Fitoussi (ed.) (1983) and also included in Hicks (1982).
[34] Cf. e.g. *The Crisis in Keynesian Economics*, p. 6, and 'Recollections and Documents' in *Economic Perspectives*, this paper also records Keynes's detailed and favourable reaction to the IS–LM representation of his theory.
[35] Cf. *Critical Essays in Monetary Theory*, p. vii: 'But as a diagnosis of the 'revolution', [IS–LM] is very unsatisfactory. It is not a bad representation of Keynes; but it does not get his predecessors (the 'Classics'' as he called them) at all right.'

about it as a general purpose framework for macroeconomic analysis.[36] His several commentaries on IS–LM all focus on the problem of time.

From the early fifties to the mid-sixties, Hicks did not participate much in ongoing developments in economic theory.[37] When he returned to theoretical work full time, he was eager to learn what had been accomplished in growth theory but found himself out of sympathy with the directions taken in macroeconomics and monetary theory. The trouble was that these directions had been set by Hicks the Younger—in those parts of his work that the American economists had chosen to cultivate. Hicks's first dismaying confrontation with his own brain-children—now fully grown and so independent!—came, it appears, in 1957 when he was asked to review Patinkin's first edition. Patinkin's work had been systematically and rigorously built on the basis of the Hicks–Allen 'Reconsideration', the paper 'simplifying' monetary theory, 'Keynes and the Classics', and the first eight chapters of Value and Capital (together with some closely related works by Oscar Lange).[38] But the theoretical structure that Patinkin had erected on these foundations, Hicks thought, threatened to emasculate Keynesian economics.[39] Never a whole-hearted Keynesian, Hicks was nonetheless too much of a Keynesian to stand idly by under the circumstances.

Patinkin's basic model was a Walrasian general equilibrium model, built up from choice-theoretical individual experiments, via aggregation, to equilibrium market experiments. It allowed no Marshallian distinctions between short-run and long-run equilibria. It was either in 'the' equilibrium or not in equilibrium at all. Patinkin used the Hicksian technique for portraying the equilibrium of an aggregative version of the system as the intersection of two reduced forms in interest/income space. It 'looked' exactly like IS–LM—except that this version would not allow for unemployment.[40]

Hicks set out to show that 'classical' and Keynesian theory 'do not overlap all the way'—that all the Keynesian furore had not been pointless. His point

---

[36] Cf. e.g., 'Time in Economics', in Hicks (1982), pp. 289–90: 'All the same, I must say that the diagram is now much less popular with me than I think it still is with many other people. It reduces the General Theory to equilibrium economics; it is not really in time. That, of course, is why it has done so well'.

[37] Approximately, from A Contribution to the Theory of the Trade Cycle (1950) to Capital and Growth (1965). Or, perhaps, for the duration of his tenure as Drummond Professor (1952–65). For his preoccupations during this period, cf. 'The Formation of an Economist', p. 202.

[38] O. Lange (1942) and (1944).

[39] The book, he said, was written not 'to elucidate the 'Keynesian Revolution', but to deny that it is a revolution at all'. Cf. Hicks (1957). This judgement was not fair to Patinkin as Hicks has acknowledged. Cf. id. (1979c), n. .5.

[40] Patinkin understood, of course, that this model would produce unemployment only if one imposed the restriction of rigid (and too high) wages. He also was quite clear on the fact that Keynes had assumed neither rigid wages nor a liquidity trap. (Patinkin (1948) had in any case demonstrated already that a liquidity trap would not by itself lead to unemployment in this type of model). Consequently, he chose to deal with Keynesian unemployment informally, discussing the unemployment dynamics of the system 'off the curves' of his formal model. Cf. Patinkin (1956, Chapter 13).

of departure was the right one:[41]

> The crucial point, as I now feel quite clear, on which the individuality of the
> Keynes theory depends, is the implication. . . that there are conditions in which the
> interest-mechanism will not work.

In the original Patinkin review, Hicks tried to show this in two ways. His
first argument, however, amounted to a reassertion of the liquidity trap
explanation of unemployment and Patinkin had only to repeat his demonstration of how, with flexible wages, the Pigou effect would restore full
employment. Within the IS–LM context, the explanation of unemployment
is thus thrown back unto the 'rigid wages' postulate.[42] Hicks's second and
surviving argument attempted to clarify the relationship between Keynes
and the 'classics' by showing how the parameters of the IS–LM model
depend on the *length of period* assumed. The extent to which wages are
variable, Hicks pointed out, will depend not only on the magnitude of excess
demand (or supply) of labour but also on the length of time allowed for
adjustment. Over a sufficiently long period, the IS-schedule should then be
infinitely elastic (at the 'natural rate' of interest), while the speculative
component disappears from money demand so that the LM-schedule becomes quite inelastic. With a shorter period, the 'classical' dichotomy fails,
and the shorter the period the more 'Keynesian' the picture: IS becomes
very inelastic and LM exceedingly elastic in the very short run.[43]

This defense of Keynes (if such it was) could only focus attention on
Keynes's own treatment of time, however. Hicks's reservations on this score
(as well as those of other 'critical readers') went back all the way to the
thirties: '. . . but we have agreed to suspend our doubts because of the power
of the analysis which Keynes constructed on this (perhaps) shaky foundation.'[44] It could not be left at that indefinitely. In his 1974 effort to address
The Crisis in Keynesian Economics, Hicks left the matter to one side and
simply made no use of IS–LM at all. But in *The Crisis,* he advanced the
theory of liquidity as flexibility as one of the needed cures for the ailing

---

[41] Cf., 'The "Classics" Again', as reprinted in Hicks (1967), p. 143. My reasons for judging
this to be the right point of departure are spelt out at great length in 'The Wicksell Connection'
in Leijonhufvud (1981).

[42] Cf. Hicks (1957), Patinkin (1959).

[43] Alan Coddington (1983) discusses this Hicksian analysis in somewhat more detail, pp.
68–73.

[44] Cf. *Capital and Growth,* p. 65. The particular difficulty ('. . . now lulled to sleep by long
familiarity') mentioned in this context was that '[Keynes's theory] works with a *period* which
is taken to be one of equilibrium . . . and which is nonetheless identified with the Marshallian
"short period", in which capital equipment . . . remains unchanged. The second seems to
require that the period should not be too long, but the first that it should not be too short; . . . It
is not easy to see that there can be any length of time that will adequately satisfy both of
these requirements'. (pp. 64–65). One notes that this observation would seem to threaten the
legitimacy of Hicks's accordion playing with the period in his 'The "Classics" Again'.

Keynesian tradition. In contrast to how it emerges in static portfolio theory,[45]

> ... liquidity is not a property of a single choice; it is a matter of a sequence of choices, a related sequence. It is concerned with the passage from the known to the unknown with the knowledge that if we wait we can have more knowledge. So it is not sufficient, in liquidity theory, to make a single dichotomy between the known and the unknown. There is a further category, of things which are unknown now, but will become known in time.

This, clearly, lends urgency to the question of how time is to be treated in Keynesian models. Immediately afterward, therefore, Hicks turned to re-examine the compromises of Keynes's method and found them, on close inspection, less and less satisfactory:[46]

> Keynes's theory has one leg which is *in* time, but another which is not. It is a hybrid. I am not blaming him for this; he was looking for a theory which would be effective, and he found it ... but what a muddle he made for his successors!

In brief, the 'leg in time' is LM, the 'leg in equilibrium' is IS. (Clearly, this 'straddle', as Hicks called it, was a position that had to become uncomfortable with the passage of time!) Hicks' own temporary equilibrium method[47]

> also was divided; there was a part that was *in* time and a part that was not. But we did not divide in the same place. While Keynes had relegated the whole theory of production and prices to equilibrium economics, I tried to keep production *in* time, just leaving *prices* to be determined in an equilibrium manner.

Production will not be equilibrated in a 'week'. Hicks's 1983 'IS–LM: An explanation' carries the argument forward:[48]

> If one is to make sense of the IS–LM model while paying proper attention to time, one must, I think, insist on two things: (1) that the period in question is a relatively long period, a 'year' rather than a 'week'; and (2) that, because the behaviour of the economy over that 'year' is to be determined by propensities and such-like data, it must be assumed to be, in an appropriate sense, *in equilibrium*.

Product markets are in *flow* equilibrium throughout the 'year'; production plans are being carried through without disappointment or surprise; this, in Hicks's view, is how we must interpret the IS-curve. What about the LM-curve? It is a *stock*-relation and, by itself, could apply simply to a point in time. But to be consistent with the IS-construction, Hicks points out, a more restrictive equilibrium condition should be applied, namely, maintenance of stock equilibrium throughout the 'year'. Expectations and realizations must be consistent within the period. But at this point of his 1983

[45] *Crisis in Keynesian Economics*, pp. 38–9.
[46] 'Time in Economics', in Hicks (1982), pp. 288–9.
[47] *Ibid.*, p. 290.
[48] 'IS–LM: An Explanation', in Fitoussi (1983), p. 57.

argument, we are suddenly back facing the dilemma of that 1933 paper: 'Disequilibrium is the Disappointment of Expectations'—and in equilibrium processes there is no place for money! The 'Equilibrium method, applied to liquidity over a period, will not do'.[49]

Within the IS–LM construction itself, therefore, we find this tension between Equilibrium and Change which I see as a *Leitmotiv* through five decades of Hicks's work. Hicks is 'quite prepared to believe that there are cases' where we are 'entitled to overlook' the potential inconsistency between the ways that the IS and the LM have been constructed. But he clearly no longer regards it as a robust tool for the analysis of almost all macroeconomic questions.[50]

IS–LM served us well for so long (didn't it?). How could we not have run into obvious problems with it, if it teeters on the brink of conceptual inconsistency? IS–LM exercises produce the right answers (most of us will agree) to a large number of standard macroquestions. Yet, it produces the wrong conclusions (some of us insist) on some issues. Hicks leaves us with a general scepticism about the method which does not help us much in determining what uses are safe and what uses are not.

In an attempt to find out 'What was the Matter with IS–LM?', I came to a conclusion very similar to Hicks's judgement on the temporal equilibrium method: as with all equilibrium constructions, IS–LM ignores the *sequence* of events *within the period*. The result can be nonsense:[51]

> IS–LM, handled as if it were a static construction ... produced a nonsensical conclusion to the *Keynes and the classics* debate: namely, that Keynes had revolutionized economic theory by advancing the platitude that wages too high for full employment and rigid downwards imply persistent unemployment. It failed to capture essential elements of Keynes's theory: namely, that the typical shock is a shift in investors' expectations and that it is the failure of intertemporal prices to respond appropriately to this change in perceived intertemporal opportunities that prevents rational adaptation to the shock. The same 'as if static' method produced the conclusion that *liquidity preference versus loanable funds* was not a meaningful issue; that it does not matter whether the system is or is not potentially capable of adjusting intertemporal prices appropriately in response to changes in intertemporal opportunities.[52]

[49] *Causality in Economics*, p. 85.

[50] Cf. 'IS–LM: An Explanation', pp. 60–2. The brief summary in the text fails, I am afraid, to do justice to the sublety of Hicks's argument. The reader who would appraise it should consult also his *Causality in Economics*, ch. VI and VII.

[51] Leijonhufvud (1983b), p. 86. But the IS–LM interpretation of Keynes still has backers who feel that the algebra cannot but lead us right. Paul Samuelson (who has, of course, advocated the sticky wages view as preserving the essentials of Keynes's theory) sees preoccupation with the model's conceptual foundations as revealing some sort of anti-mathematical obscurantism. See his Keynes centennial article in *The Economist*, 25 June, 1983.

[52] The equivalence of the liquidity preference and loanable funds approaches to interest determination was argued by Hicks the Younger in his 1936 review of Keynes and in *Value and Capital*, ch. XII. There the argument was made in a Temporary Equilibrium context but it has been carried over to IS–LM by others. The argument is, I think, misleading—except possibly in

Ignoring sequencing becomes a source of trouble in particular in connection with *comparative statics* uses of the IS–LM model—i.e. the uses that are the stuff which macrotexts have been made of for several decades, but which Hicks did not consider in reassessing the model.

Consider, for illustrative purposes, the analysis of an increase in the supply of money in the common textbook context where the money supply is simply an exogenously fixed *M*. Full adjustment to this parametric disturbance requires a proportional rise in all money prices with no effect on output, employment or other real magnitudes. In an IS–LM diagram with money income on the horizontal axis, *both* schedules have shifted the same distance rightwards. In a Lucas model, if *M* is observable, the system goes to this position immediately. In a Friedman model (of, say, ten years ago), on the other hand, nominal income responds strongly in relatively short order, but part of this is an increase in real output and employment and full adjustment to the neutral equilibrium takes 'longer'. In a Keynesian model (of 20 years ago?), finally, the 'short-run' reactions are that the interest rate falls, velocity declines, investment and employment increase a bit, while the price-level stays about the same.

All three possibilities can be demonstrated with the same basic model. How, then, do they differ? To Friedman, the Phillips-curve is vertical only over the 'long run', not already in the 'short run' as in Lucas. In Friedman's short run, the monetary disturbance has output effects because the people temporarily miscalculate real wages. To the Keynesians, the (approximately) proportional increase in nominal income occurs only over the 'long run', not already in the 'short run' as in Friedman. In the Keynesian short run, the monetary disturbance has only weak effects on nominal income now because people fail to anticipate the effect that it must have on nominal aggregate demand sooner or later; hence the short run effects on income occur only in so far as some firms are induced by a fall in the interest rate to increase their investment even though their expectations of future nominal aggregate demand have not improved.[53]

---

the context of rational expectations models; if the general equilibrium consequences of some parameter change are 'rationally anticipated', all markets would 'open' with the new equilibrium prices already 'posted'. For such a conceptual experiment, it indeed does not make sense to ask which excess demand was responsible for the change in which price. One must (to make sense) consider instances where, once price-setters have posted prices based on their best forecasts, actual trading produces excess demands and supplies thus revealing the 'errors' in the forecasts. The issue of the liquidity preference versus loanable funds squabble is how this error-activated feedback control of price works in the case of the interest rate—specifically, whether the interest rate is '*governed*' by the excess demand for money or by the excess supply for securities. To discriminate between the two hypotheses, one must then consider states of the economy which do *not* have ED for money and ES of securities (or vice versa) at the same time. In a Keynes Model, a 'decline in MEC' produces an example, namely, a state with an ES of commodities and a corresponding ED for securities while—at this stage of the *sequence*—the ED for money is still zero. If the loanable funds hypothesis is true, it is possible that the intertemporal prices mechanism will take care of the intertemporal coordination problem (without a recession); if the liquidity preference hypothesis is true, it is inconceivable.

[53] For a more careful and detailed discussion, cf. Leijonhufvud, (1983*b*), pp. 69–70, 76–80.

So, Lucas's people are assumed to know something that Friedman people do not, and Friedman people something that Keynesian people do not.[54] The temporal order of decisions matters when information is incomplete, when people have to react to situations they did not foresee and when they learn from realizations they did not anticipate. Such learning can be slow or fast or, in some cases, unnecessary.

Note how these knowledge or learning assumptions are reflected in the mechanics of manipulating the IS–LM diagram. In the Keynesian exercise, LM shifts right, IS stays put, and the short-run effects depend on the elasticities of the two reduced forms. In the Friedman case, IS also shifts, although perhaps *not quite* all the way; the elasticities then are practically irrelevant. In the Lucas case, both reduced forms shift in parallel fashion. The IS–LM modelling strategy would seem to presuppose that we have to deal with a Keynesian world of slow learners. Otherwise it does not seem to make sense to adopt the two-stage procedure of, first, deriving the two reduced forms and, second, getting the answers by shifting one and keeping the other constant. The use of IS–LM as if it were a comparative static apparatus involves the lag-assumption that one schedule shifts before the other and that there will be a well-defined 'short-run' solution halfway in the equilibrating process. This sequencing or lag structure rests on assumptions of incomplete information on the part of various agents in the model.[55]

This conclusion we have derived from an illustrative case where monetarist assumptions are made about the supply of money. There is, however, also another possible interpretation of Keynesian IS–LM analysis which we will come to later.

Money and history

In the most exciting chapter of his *Critical Essays in Monetary Theory*, Hicks sought to structure two centuries of monetary writings in a simple, striking, and informative way. His 'Monetary Theory and History—An Attempt at Perspective' was critical of ahistorical monetary theorizing and insisted on the necessity of doing monetary theory in historical and institutional context. It also suggested that the history of monetary controversy could be understood as a running battle between two traditions, a 'metallic money' tradition and a 'credit money' tradition.

The 'metallic money' theorists, in Hicks's schema, focused on equilibrium propositions in their theorizing, dealt analytically with money 'as if' it were a commodity, and strove to reduce monetary policy to obedience to some 'mechanical rule'. Credit theorists, on the other hand, saw money as part of the overall system of debits and credits that extends beyond the banking system to encompass the entire economy; credit expansions and contractions

---

[54] This sounds suspiciously like an IQ ranking for Lucasian, Friedmanian and Keynesian economists. This Keynesian didn't mean it that way!

[55] Cf. Leijonhufvud (1983*b*), p. 87.

were central to their conception of the subject and so obliged them to try their luck at disequilibrium analyses; always aware that credit rests on confidence; finally, writers in this tradition saw monetary policy as an exercise in judgment of contemporary conditions. Hicks named Ricardo the patron saint of the 'metallic' tradition and gave Thornton the same status in the 'credit' school of thought. He saw the Currency School and, later, Hayek, Pigou, Rueff, and Friedman as Ricardo's followers and put the Banking School, Bagehot, Wicksell, Hawtrey, Robertson, and Keynes in line of descent from Thornton.

In insisting on the close link between monetary theory and history, Hicks thought above all of the evolution of credit markets and financial institutions: 'In a world of banks and insurance companies, money markets and stock exchanges, money is quite a different thing from what it was before these institutions came into being.'[56] The metallic money theorists (including the modern monetarists) seemed determined to ignore this historical development. Consequently, Hicks's analysis suggested, time had put an ever-increasing distance between their theory and reality.[57]

The 1967 'Perspective' helps one understand what Hicks regards as the important themes running through his own contributions to monetary theory.[58] Consider, once again, what aspects of the work of Hicks the Younger came to be influential and what aspects ignored. For decades, all graduate students have learned that the modern choice-theoretical money demand function stems from his 1935 'Simplifying' paper. Most will know that Hicks already had the demand for money depending on wealth, on anticipated yields on alternative placements, and on the cost of asset transactions. Some may recall that his analysis was anything but reassuring on the stability of the function in terms of these arguments. Few (I am guessing) will remember that, in Hicks's hands, the theory immediately suggested the beginnings of a theory of financial structure, of the composition of balance sheets and of intermediation. Balance sheet equilibria, he noted,[59]

[56] Cf. *Critical Essays*, p. 158.

[57] I have made a previous attempt at getting Hicks's 'Attempt at Perspective' into perspective—and pretty much failed. Cf., Leijonhufvud (1981), ch. 8. My review shows how influenced I then was by Friedman and Schwartz, Brunner and Meltzer, and particularly by their work on United States monetary history since 1929. (In 1968, American monetarists had hardly begun thinking about small, open, fixed-exchange-rate economies yet). This made me critical, for instance, of Hicks's insistence on the 'inherent instability of credit'. The piece also shows my great fascination for Hicks's daring attempt to put 200 years of tangled controversies in order; for various reasons, the way I saw it, several important writers just would not fit neatly into Hicks's scheme—but I failed completely to suggest a scheme that would do better.

[58] The main line of Hicks's work in monetary theory runs as follows: 'A Suggestion for Simplifying the Theory of Money' (1935); ch. XXIII, 'Keynes After Growth Theory' in *Capital and Growth* (1965); the three chapters on 'The Two Triads' in *Critical Essays* (1967); the chapter on 'Money, Interest and Liquidity' in *The Crisis* (1974); the 60-odd-page-long 'Monetary Experience and the Theory of Money' which is the backbone of the *Economic Perspectives* collection (1977); and 'The Foundations of Monetary Theory' in *Money, Interest and Wages* (1982).

[59] Quoted from reprint in *Critical Essays*, pp. 75–76.

[are] determined by subjective factors like anticipations, instead of objective factors like prices, [which] means that this purely theoretical study of money can never hope to reach results so tangible and precise as those which value theory in its more limited field can hope to attain. If I am right, the whole problem of applying monetary theory is largely one of deducing changes in anticipations from the changes in the objective data which call them forth. Obviously, this is not an easy task, and, above all, it is not one which can be performed in mechanical fashion.

In our textbooks, Hicks's paper is remembered for a money demand function with which any latter-day monetarist could be comfortable. But, clearly, he was in the Credit tradition from the beginning!

Moreover, it is the neglected themes of Hicks the Younger that the Elder has taken up and carried forward. The first step beyond his 1935 position, came three decades later with the sketch in *Capital and Growth* [1965] of a simple financial system, consisting of a bank, household savers, and firms:[60]

> Savers can hold their assets in bank money, or in securities (loans or equities) of the producing firms; . . . Firms have real assets, and they may have bank money; they have debts to the bank, and to the savers. The bank has debts owing to it from the firms; it owes debts (bank money) to the firms and to the savers.

The 'Two Triads' of 1967 introduced the classification of assets into running assets, reserve assets, and investment assets; the specific assets that served these functions would differ between the balance sheets of households, of firms, and of banks; for each type of transactor, the three classes of assets could be matched up with Keynes's Transactions, Precautionary, and Speculative motives; in Hicks's treatment, however, these three were no longer just motives for holding money but for preferring balance sheets of a certain structure. In 'Monetary Experience and the Theory of Money' [1977], the financial structure of Keynes's world was envisaged as three concentric sectors: (1) a banking 'core' with monetary liabilities and financial securities as assets; (2) a financial 'mantle' owing financial securities and holding industrial securities; and (3) an outer 'industry' owning the industrial securities and holding the (hard crust of?) the economy's productive assets (and some financial assets and money). In the 1982 'Foundations of Monetary Theory', Hicks added to this 'monocentric' credit economy model, some analysis also of a 'polycentric' world of multiple central banks (and flexible exchange rates).

What do we get out of this 'Credit' approach that a monetarist supply and demand for 'money' apparatus would not provide with less trouble? Hicks, of course, uses his financial structure model routinely in the analysis of a broad range of questions. In my view, however, the significant advantage of his approach is that it gives a better picture of the financial and monetary consequences of 'real causes': a rise in the anticipated yields on real capital will change the configuration of balance sheets desired by the business,

[60] *Capital and Growth*, pp. 284–5.

household, and banking sectors; the financing of investment will in part be intermediated by the banks; consequently, an increase in income due to a rise in marginal efficiency of capital will normally be associated not only with a rise in velocity but also with an *endogenous* increase in the money supply.

Hicks's insistence on linking monetary theory to monetary history has been echoed in recent years by rational expectations theorists who insist that we must link short-run monetary theory to *monetary regimes*. These modern writers, however, have come to their preoccupation with the conditional nature of monetary theory from an entirely different angle. Their concern has been to keep track, not of slowly evolving financial institutions and markets, but of rapidly changing nominal (price level) expectations. A 'monetary regime' may be defined as a system of expectations that governs the behaviour of the public and is sustained by the consistent behaviour of the monetary authorities.[61] Since the short-run effects of particular policy-actions, for example, depend upon the expectations of the public, it follows that we need a different short-run macromodel for each monetary regime. A regime change occurs when the behaviour rules followed by the monetary authorities change. This 'regime approach' directs our attention to the history of monetary standards, viewed as methods for controlling the level of nominal prices, and to the system of nominal expectations that would (rationally) go with each such method.

Historically, we find two basic but contrasting conceptions of how price level control can be accomplished. I have labelled them the 'quantity principle' and the 'convertibility principle', respectively. Briefly (and perhaps a bit too simply) we may say that the quantity principle dictates that the government should control the 'quantity of money' while the private sector sets the price level; the convertibility principle, in contrast, dictates that the government set the nominal price of some 'standard commodity' while the private sector determines the quantity of money.[62] The logically tidiest version of the first would be a fiat standard with flexible exchange rates, and of the second a commodity standard with 'hard money' still in circulation. Price expectations on the fiat standard are almost entirely a matter of beliefs about what the government might choose to do; price expectations on the commodity standard (conditional on the belief that the standard will be adhered to!) are almost entirely a matter of forecasting 'real' business developments.

The two contrasting systems give the extremes on a more or less continuous spectrum of monetary regimes. The last fifty-odd years have taken us from a position rather close to the commodity standard end (in 1929) all the way to the extreme fiat standard end (after 1971). We could proceed to classify macrotheories according to the segment of the regime-spectrum over which they might claim validity.

[61] I have used this rather informal definition repeatedly. Cf. e.g. Leijonhufvud (1983a).
[62] Cf. Leijonhufvud (1982) and (1983a) for rather more careful explanations.

This classification of theories according to control-regime differs from the Hicksian schema of metallic money theories v. credit theories and may be a useful complement to it. This may be seen, for instance, by considering how the American monetarists fit into Hicks's schema. In a metallic money world, money is a produced commodity and thus not neutral; the price level is determined (in the long run) by the cost of producing the metal; the money stock is endogenous and not subject to policy control; the 'mechanical' policy rule is to maintain the metallic standard. The 'mechanical' rule of the monetarists is to fix the growth rate of some 'M'; it is predicated on the beliefs that 'M' is neutral and controllable (and 'more or less' independent of endogeneous real factors); the object is to control nominal income in the short run and the price level over the longer run; fixed exchange rates are readily sacrificed to this end. When Hicks includes both Ricardo and Friedman in the same 'metallic' tradition these points of contrast are obscured (even as the contrasts between Ricardo and Friedman, on the one hand, and Thornton and the Radcliffe Report, on the other, are brought into focus). Similarly, Hicks has come to prefer Wicksell's 'pure credit' model (of an economy without 'hard money') as his vehicle for explaining the central theoretical message of the 'credit tradition'.[63] But to a monetarist audience, for instance, the main lesson of Wicksell's cumulative process is simply that, on a fiat standard, interest targeting of monetary policy produces *nominal* instability. A model of a system where convertibility anchors the price level—and, therefore, anchors rational price expectations as well—does a better job of fitting credit as a *real* magnitude into monetary theory. It is easier, in such a model, to show both how banking policy can influence investment and employment via the price and volume of 'real' credit and how real income movements can influence the supply of nominal money via the demand for 'real' credit.

Keynesian theory, to take a case in point, seems suited to regimes that behave as if monetary policy were constrained by the requirements of external if not also internal convertibility. The real quantity of money varies endogenously over the cycle in such regimes, nominal price level expectations should be inelastic, and the *numeraire* component of prices correspondly sticky. This brings us back to IS–LM. Clearly, the old textbook repertory of IS–LM exercises will pass muster much better if interpreted as applying to an economy which retains some significant vestiges of convertible money systems. (An open economy with fixed exchange rates will do, for instance, as long as we are not thinking of the dominant reserve currency country). But the textbook should not have specified 'M' as a given parameter, controlled by the central bank.[64] Under convertibility, the

[63] Cf. 'Monetary Experience and the Theory of Money', pp. 61–73, and 'Foundations of Monetary Theory', pp. 237, 264 ff.

[64] On which Hicks can rightly say: '. . . I may allow myself to point out that it was already observed in 'Mr. Keynes and the Classics' that we do not need to suppose that the curve is drawn up on the assumption of a given stock of money. It is sufficient to suppose that there is (as I said) 'a given monetary system—that up to a point, but only up to a point, monetary

monetary authorities do not have the powers to regulate nominal income assumed by Friedman or by Lucas. The Keynesian picture (of LM shifting, IS staying put) of relatively modest effectiveness of monetary policy, transmitted via the price and volume of credit, is nearer to the mark.

Keynesian theory should do fairly well, I have argued elsewhere,[65] as long as the monetary system still resembles the kind of system which Keynes strove for as a monetary reformer. Its lack of attention to inflationary expectations was on the whole appropriate to the Bretton Woods world. When the last vestiges of Bretton Woods were swept away, its neglect of inflationary expectations became a critical flaw. We should not have been so surprised!

Conclusion

In some quarters, Hicks is routinely blamed for the paths we have taken from his path-breaking early contributions. Those who do so blame him have not studied him very closely. 'One of the best reasons for studying the elder Hicks, in fact, is precisely that he is less a prisoner of the younger Hicks's constructions than are most of us.'[66] Among the lessons that Hicks the Elder would impress on us, I have tried to bring out two:[67]

> One must assume that the people in one's models do not know what is going to happen, and know that they do not know just what is going to happen. As in history!

Monetary theory, especially, has to be developed 'in time [with] future becoming present, and present becoming past, as time goes on'.[68] And 'it belongs to monetary history in a way that economic theory does not always belong to economic history.'[69]

University of California, Los Angeles

REFERENCES

CODDINGTON, A. (1983), *Keynesian Economics: The Search for First Principles*, London: Allen & Unwin.

CLOWER, R. W. (1975), 'Reflections on the Keynesian Perplex', *Zeitschrift für Nationalökonomie*.

authorities will prefer to create new money rather than allow interest rates to rise. Such a generalized (LM) curve will then slope upwards only gradually—the elasticity of the curve depending on the elasticity of the monetary system . . .'." Cf. *Money, Interest and Wages*, p. 328.

[65] Cf. Leijonhufvud (1983a).

[66] Leijonhufvud (1979), p. 526.

[67] *Economic Perspectives*, p. vii.

[68] Ibid.

[69] 'Monetary Theory and History', in Hicks (1967), p. 156. But this too is an old Hicksian theme. One finds it in his 1943 review of Charles Rist's *History of Money and Credit Theory*. Cf. Hicks (1982), pp. 132ff.

CLOWER, R. W. and LEIJONHUFVUD, A. (1975), 'The Coordination of Economic Activities: A Keynesian Perspective', *American Economic Review*, May.

FITOUSSI, J.-P. (ed.), (1983), *Modern Macroeconomic Theory*, Oxford: Blackwell.

GRANDMONT, J. M. (1975), 'Temporary General Equilibrium Theory', *Econometrica*.

HART, A. G. (1942), 'Risk, Uncertainty, and the Unprofitability of Compounding Probabilities', in O. Lange *et al.*, *Studies in Mathematical Economics and Econometrics*, Chicago. Reprinted in W. Fellner and B. F. Haley (eds.), (1951), *Readings in the Theory of Income Distribution*, Philadelphia: Blakeston.

HAYEK, F. A. VON (1928), 'Das intertemporale Gleichgewichtssystem', *Weltwirtschaftliches Archiv*.

HAYEK, F. A. VON (ed.) (1933), *Beiträge zur Geldtheorie*.

HEINER, R. (1983), 'The Origin of Predictable Behavior', *American Economic Review*, September.

HICKS, J. R. and ALLEN, R. G. D. (1934), 'A Reconsideration of the Theory of Value: Parts I and II', *Economica N.S.*

HICKS, J. R. (1939), *Value and Capital*, Oxford: Oxford University Press.

HICKS, J. R. (1956), 'Methods of Dynamic Analysis', in *25 Economic Essays in Honour of Erik Lindahl*, ed. by the eds. of *Ekonomisk Tidskrift*, Stockholm.

HICKS, J. R. (1957), 'A Rehabilitation of "Classical" Economics?' *Economic Journal*, June.

HICKS, SIR JOHN, (1965). *Capital and Growth*, Oxford: Oxford University Press.

HICKS, SIR JOHN, (1967), *Critical Essays in Monetary Theory*, Oxford: Oxford University Press.

HICKS, SIR JOHN, (1974), *The Crisis in Keynesian Economics*, Oxford: Blackwell.

HICKS, SIR JOHN, (1977), *Economic Perspectives: Further Essays on Money and Growth*, Oxford: Oxford University Press.

HICKS, SIR JOHN, (1979a), *Causality in Economics*, Oxford: Blackwell.

HICKS, SIR JOHN, (1979b), 'The Formation of an Economist', *Banca Nazionale del Lavoro Quarterly Review*, September.

HICKS, SIR JOHN, (1979c), 'On Coddington's Interpretation: A Reply', *Journal of Economic Literature*, September.

HICKS, SIR JOHN, (1981), *Wealth and Welfare: Collected Essays on Economic Theory*, I, Oxford: Blackwell.

HICKS, SIR JOHN, (1982), *Money, Interest and Wages: Collected Essays on Economic Theory*, II, Oxford: Blackwell.

HICKS, SIR JOHN, (1983), *Classics and Moderns: Collected Essays on Economic Theory*, III, Oxford: Blackwell.

LANGE, O. [1942], 'Say's Law: A Restatement and Criticism', in O. Lange *et al.*, *Studies in Mathematical Economics and Econometrics*, Chicago: University of Chicago Press.

LANGE, O. [1944], *Price Flexibility and Full Employment*, Chicago: Cowles Commission.

LEIJONHUFVUD, A. (1968), *On Keynesian Economics and the Economics of Keynes*, New York: Oxford University Press.

LEIJONHUFVUD, A. (1979) 'Review of *Economic Perspectives* by Sir John Hicks', *Journal of Economic Literature*, June, pp. 525–27.

LEIJONHUFVUD, A. (1981), *Information and Coordination: Essays in Macroeconomic Theory*, New York: Oxford University Press.

LEIJONHUFVUD, A. (1982), 'Rational Expectations and Monetary Institutions', paper presented at the International Economic Association Conference on *Monetary Theory and Monetary Institutions*, Florence, Italy, September.

LEIJONHUFVUD, A. (1983a), 'What Would Keynes Have Thought of Rational Expectations?' in G. D. N. Worswick and J. S. Trevithick, (eds.), *Keynes and the Modern World*, Cambridge: Cambridge University Press.

LEIJONHUFVUD, A. (1983b), 'What Was the Matter with IS–LM?' in Jean-Paul Fitoussi (ed.), *Modern Macroeconomic Theory: An Overview*, Oxford: Blackwell.

MARSHALL, A. (1928), *Principles of Economics* 8 edn., London: Macmillan.

MYRDAL, G. (1933), 'Geldtheoretisches Gleichgewicht', in F. A. Hayek (ed.), (1933).

PATINKIN, D. (1948), 'Price Flexibility and Full Employment', *American Economic Review*, September.

PATINKIN, D. (1956), *Money, Interest, and Prices*, Evanston, Ill.: Row, Peterson & Co.

PATINKIN, D. (1959), 'Keynesian Economics Rehabilitated: A Rejoinder to Professor Hicks', *Economic Journal*, September.

ROBBINS, L. (1932), *An Essay on the Nature and Significance of Economic Science*, London: Macmillan.

SHACKLE, G. L. S., (1967), *The Years of High Theory: Invention and Tradition in Economic Thought, 1926–1939*, Cambridge: Cambridge University Press.

SHACKLE, G. L. S., (1972), *Epistemics and Economics: A Critique of Economic Doctrines*, Cambridge: Cambridge University Press.

WAGES AND EMPLOYMENT

By F. H. HAHN

I, LIKE many others, owe a large intellectual debt to Sir John Hicks. That makes it a pleasure to contribute to this birthday volume. *Value and Capital* was one of three books in economic theory that influenced me most. It showed for the first time how one could proceed from a precise theory of the individual actor to a precise theory of the economy as a whole. This struck me and continues to strike me as exactly the right approach, so much so that I suspect that in this matter I am now more Hicksian than Hicks. What follows, although it has macro-economic implications in mind, is firmly rooted in the methodology of *Value and Capital*.

I

There are numerous textbooks and journal papers in which it is asserted that Keynes either assumed fixed (or downwardly rigid) money wages or that if he did not do so he should have done so in order to justify his whole theory. Both these claims are wrong, and part of this paper is designed to show this. To be more accurate, I propose to refute the second claim. The first one (that Keynes *assumed* that behaviour in money wages) must be self-evidently wrong, since that is precisely the cause to which the economists whom Keynes called 'classical' traced the occurrence of unemployment. As I read him Keynes had something more subtle in mind; if money wages changed more freely then matters would be worse not better for the capitalist economy. This will be considered below.

But before starting the discussion proper I have to re-emphasize a point which I have made elsewhere before (1981). In a great deal of the literature money wages are said to be 'flexible' if at all times they are such as to clear a (competitive) market for labour. On that definition the proposition that there would be no involuntary unemployment if money wages were flexible is not exactly deep. If one then constructs theories based on an axiom of wage flexibility in this sense then one should not use them to discuss Keynesian problems. They will have been *assumed* away. It is puzzling that this is not obvious to many economists.

In what follows I shall avoid the use of 'flexible' altogether since this term now seems to be firmly established in its useless meaning. Instead I shall distinguish between *endogenous* and *exogenous* money prices and wages. In the former these prices and wages are to be explained by the theory, in the latter they are not.

Before I start on the analysis proper it will be useful to give a simple account of it and also a warning.

In this paper I consider a Dynamic Non-Substitution Theorem economy (Mirrlees (1969)). That is I consider an economy of constant returns to scale, no joint production, and two non-produced inputs: labour and 'time'.

Although I consider only circulating capital we know that in suitable circumstances the theorem will apply to durable capital economies as well (Mirrlees (1969)). I adopt these assumptions for the following reasons. Firstly, it leads to a simple theory of prices in a steady state. Secondly, it can also lead to a simple, expectation-based price theory in the short run. Thirdly, it allows one to stick closely to the Neo-classical theory and yet incorporate expectations of demand in current decisions. That is because at the equilibrium prices producers do not have a definite supply (they have a supply correspondence) so that they must predict demand to decide on what inputs to employ. All of this is based on the simple equilibrium condition that when a good is produced its expected discounted price must equal current unit production costs.

I first construct a model in which the money wage is given exogenously. This is an *intermediate* step and does not entail any proposition about money wages being fixed. Given the stock of cash the equilibrium of the economy may be one in which more labour is seeking employment than is being demanded. Since I like to prove what I assert I show that such an equilibrium exists.

I then ask a comparative statics question: will a lower exogenously given money wage be associated with more employment and a lower real wage? I show that real income will be higher but that the real wage will also be higher. The latter result is a simple consequence of a lower interest rate and a negatively inclined factor price frontier. Of course the latter applies to a steady state. This answer shows that the sentence 'unemployment is to be ascribed to the real wage being too high' is false in a leading class of economic models. One reader of this paper countered with the observation that he was convinced nonetheless that the sentence was correct for the British economy in the 1980s. I hope that other readers will understand that my result is to be taken in the context of understanding economic phenomena and arguing about their explanation.

The rest of the paper is concerned with perhaps a more interesting question. Suppose the real Phillips curve governs wage behaviour and suppose that agents have the correct expectations of the dynamics of prices etc. generated by this path, how will the economy develop? Unfortunately this question leads to a rather complicated set of equations whose global properties I cannot capture analytically. But a number of qualitative results emerge. In particular during a phase of falling wages and prices real interest rates will be above their steady-state value and real wages below theirs. Hence from what we already know we can conclude that, even if the economy converges to the full employment steady-state equilibrium, it will not do so monotonically. There is bound to be overshooting. From this and the general difficulty of predicting the path I conclude that if it is maintained that falling money wages will restore full employment then Keynes was *logically* right in saying that policy will do so more certainly and more quickly.

Now for the warning. A great deal of economic theory is concerned with what can coherently be claimed to be the case on the basis of certain agreed assumptions, e.g. rationality and greed. *Value and Capital* was a notable contribution to this enterprise. The present paper also is in this tradition. If I agree to Neo-classical premises do I have to agree with, say, Professor Lucas? The answer is no. That seems of interest. But nothing is here on offer to enable one to give specific advice to Mrs Thatcher.

II

I shall start with a model which is at the same time extremely Neo-classical and Keynesian. In fact it is a somewhat elaborate IS–LM model (1937). But it includes relative prices and expectations. Its purpose is to clarify certain basic ideas.

Consider an economy where l goods are produced by goods and labour and where inputs must precede output by one period. I shall abstract from goods which last more than one period. This at this stage will not be restrictive. All production is carried out under constant returns to scale. Firms are risk-neutral. Hence if $q \in R_+^l$ is a vector of commodity prices in terms of labour, $\hat{q} \in R_+^l$ the expected price vector for next period, $R = 1 + r$, the discount factor, then if there is perfect competition

$$\hat{q} = Rc(q) \tag{1}$$

is a necessary equilibrium condition in the current period if all goods are produced. In (1) $c(q)$ is the vector of unit cost functions in terms of labour. Given history before the current period we can write

$$\hat{q} = \alpha(q) \tag{2}$$

for an expectation function. (I am here concerned with the short period—the dreaded rational expectations will appear later.)

I shall assume that (1) and (2) form a consistent system. It is now well known [Grandmont (1977)] that this requires certain restrictions on the function α, (e.g. one must not have an elasticity of expectations greater or, equal to one). Also R must not be 'too large'. I put this formally.

Assumption A.1   The equations

$$\alpha(q) = Rc(q)$$

have a unique solution $q(R) \gg 0$.

Since production takes time $y \in R_+^l$ the vector of outputs available in the current period is already fully determined by decisions taken in the previous period. That is why inventories always played a large part in Keynesian theory before it was reduced to arithmetic by the textbook writers. However I shall also avoid this important element and I shall do so in the following manner. In the construction y will be treated as an unknown. That is, we shall ask what must decisions in the past have been in order that there should be equilibrium in the current market? Since there was equilibrium in the previous period firms had to forecast demand correctly for the current period, since they did not care how much they produced. So if x is current demand vector I assume it was properly anticipated, i.e.

$$x = y \qquad (3)$$

I consider below when (3) is possible.

Before proceeding let us note some obvious points.

(a) Under constant returns a producer in equilibrium does not know how much to produce unless he predicts demand. Prices are insufficient signals.

(b) Since production takes time the current demand for inputs must at $q(R)$ depend on forecast demand $\hat{x}$. I write

$$\hat{x} = \beta(x) \qquad (4)$$

Let us now consider demand. I write m for current money *stock in wage units*. In the first instance I take m as exogenous and so money wages as exogenous. But not for long.

Let $A(q(R))$ be the input-output matrix induced by A.1. Then $A(q(R))x$ is the demand vector for goods by firms. Let $a(q(R))$ be the vector of labour input coefficients induced by A.1 Then $a(q(R))x$ is the demand for labour by firms. If one unit of labour is inelastically supplied to the economy then

$$a(q(R))\hat{x} \leqslant 1 \qquad (5)$$

is the condition for firms not to be rationed in the labour market.

It will be supposed that firms pay out all their receipts to households from whom they borrow to pay for their inputs. Let $Y = q(R)y$. Then the aggregation of the budget constraints of household yields:

$$q(R)x_H + b_H + m_H = Y + a(q(R))\hat{x} + \bar{m} \qquad (6)$$

where $x_H \in R_+^l$ is the total household demand vector for goods, $b_H > 0$ is the value (in wage units) of household lending to firms. The demand for loans by firms ($b_F < 0$) is

$$-b_F = q(R)A(q(R))\hat{x} + a(q(R))\hat{x} \qquad (7)$$

Eliminating $a(q(R))\hat{x}$ between (6) and (7) yields

$$q(R)[x_H + A(q(R))\hat{x} - Y] + (b_H + b_F) + (m_H - \bar{m}_H) = 0 \qquad (8)$$

which is the Keynes–Clower Walras Law.

Now $x = x_H + A(q(R))\hat{x} =$ by (4) $x_H + A(q(R))\beta(x)$. So given $\bar{m}, q(R), R$, one can write $F(x)$ as the aggregate demand vector. That is current demand depends on expected demand, which in turn depends on current demand. To have a well-defined current demand one needs to ensure that $F: R_+^l \to R_+^l$ has a fixed point.

Assumption A.2
(a) $x_H \gg 0$ when $\beta(x) = 0$

(b) $\beta(kx) < k\beta(x)$ all $k > 1$

(c) $x_H[ka(q(R))\beta(x)\dots] \leqslant kx_H[a(q(R))\beta(x), \dots]$

A.2(a) says that households will consume even when firms do not currently produce. They spend out of money balances and debt repayment by firms. A.2(b) postulates that expectations are conservative ('inelastic') while (c) assumes that the marginal propensity to consume any good does not exceed unity.

Now let $\tilde{x} = \dfrac{1}{\sum x_i} x$ where $\sum x_i > 0$ can be assumed for $m > 0$. Then A.2 ensures that for every $\tilde{x}$ there is a scalar $k(\tilde{x}) > 0$ such that

$$\sum F_i(k(\tilde{x})\tilde{x}) = k(\tilde{x})$$

The diagram below illustrates for fixed $\tilde{x}$

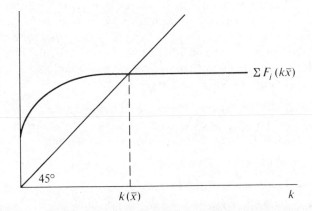

A.2(a) ensures that the curve starts on the vertical axis and A.2(b) and (c) that its slope is less than one.

Now consider the map

$$\psi_i(\tilde{x}) = \frac{F_i(k(\tilde{x})\tilde{x})}{\sum F_i(k(\tilde{x})\tilde{x})} \qquad i = 1 \dots l$$

This map takes the simplex into itself and on the usual preference assumptions is continuous. Hence it has a fixed point $\tilde{x}^*$. At that fixed point

$$F_i(k(\tilde{x}^*)\tilde{x}^*) = \sum F_i(k(\tilde{x}^*)\tilde{x}^*)\tilde{x}_i^* = k(\tilde{x}^*)\tilde{x}_i^* \quad \text{all } i$$

and so $x^* = F(x^*)$ when $x^* = k(\tilde{x}^*)\tilde{x}$.

I shall assume that given the other determinants of demand, x^* is unique. These other determinants are $Y, q(R), R$ and $\bar{m}$. Accordingly, I write the demand function as

$$x^* = X(y, q(R), R, \bar{m})$$

where x^* is the appropriate fixed point. Since I have assumed that firms in the previous period correctly predicted this period's demand, one wants from (3) that

$$y = X(Y, q(R), R, \bar{m}) \qquad (9)$$

For that to make sense (recall that $Y = q(R)y$) we need the following Keynesian assumption.

Assumption A.3
(a) $X(0, q(R), R, \bar{m}) \gg 0$

(b) $\sum q_i(R) \dfrac{\partial X_i}{\partial Y} < 1$

Part (a) corresponds to the postulate of some autonomous expenditure while part (b) postulates a marginal propensity to spend of less than one. It is then easy to see that (9) can be satisfied provided it does not require more labour in the previous period than is available.

Lastly I shall suppose that the demand for money balances (in wage units) depends on Y and R. This could be justified by a transaction demand story on the lines of Baumol (1952) and Tobin (1956) together with the expectation assumption that R remains at its current value over the relevant future. Let $m(Y, R)$ be the demand function for money balances.

Pulling everything together we have

Definition D.1   An *Unemployment Equilibrium* (U.E.) relatively to an exogenously given money stock in terms of labour $(\bar{m})$ is a price vector $q(\bar{m})$, a discount factor $R(\bar{m})$, an output vector $y(\bar{m})$ such that

E.1 $q(\bar{m})$ solves $\alpha(q) = R(\bar{m})c(q)$

E.2 $y(m) = X(q(\bar{m}), R(\bar{m}), Y(\bar{m}), \bar{m})$

E.3 $m(Y(\bar{m}), R(\bar{m})) = \bar{m}$

E.4 $a(q(m))\beta(y(m)) < 1$

One can suppose that U.E. exists for a proper choice of $\bar{m}$ and sensible functional forms. The equilibrium is of the IS–LM variety but less aggregated and with more attention to expectations.

I now proceed to a comparative statics exercise. This is best thought of as a comparison between the $\bar{m}$-equilibrium of a given economy with the $(\bar{m} + \Delta\bar{m})$-equilibrium of another economy, which but for its 'real' balance endowment is the same as the first one. Once again it is postulated that firms in the neighbouring economy had correct expectations in the previous period of demand in the current period.

To keep things as simple as possible let us now assume that

$$\alpha_i(q) = \alpha_i(q_i) \qquad i = 1 \dots l$$

so that the ith firm's expectation of its next period selling price depends only on its own current price. Let $\hat{\alpha}' = \text{diag}\{\alpha_1' \dots \alpha_l'\}$ with $\alpha_i' > 0$ all i.

Assumption A.4   The matrix $[R^{-1}(\bar{m})\hat{\alpha}'(q(\bar{m})) - A(q(\bar{m}))]$ has a positive inverse.

This assumption at once yields

$$\frac{\partial}{\partial R} q(\bar{m}) \gg 0 \tag{10}$$

a result familiar from the literature on the Factor-price frontier.

Let

$$Z = q(\bar{m})X - Y$$

At U.E. using E.1 one can write

$$Z = F(R, Y, \bar{m})$$

so differentiating $Z = 0$ and E.3 with respect to m and solving one finds

$$\frac{dY}{d\bar{m}} = \left[\frac{1}{m_R} F_R + F_m\right] \Big/ \Delta \tag{11}$$

$$\frac{\partial R}{\partial \bar{m}} = -\frac{1}{m_R} [F_m m_Y + F_Y] / \Delta \tag{12}$$

where

$$\Delta = \left[\frac{m_Y}{m_R} F_R - F_Y\right]$$

We have already postulated $F_Y < 0$. If as is usual one assumes[1] $F_m > 0$, $F_R < 0$, $m_Y > 0$ and $m_R < 0$. Then $\Lambda > 0$ and $dY/d\bar{m} > 0$ provided the model applies; that is provided there is unemployed labour in the period before the current one. On the other hand, the sign of (12) is ambiguous. But if $F_m m_Y < |Z_Y|$ which is perfectly possible then $dR/d\bar{m} < 0$.

One concludes.

Proposition P.1   The economy with the larger $\bar{m}$ may have higher real wages (as well as higher income Y and lower interest rate).

The lower interest rate arises because the higher income may not soak up the extra real balances. The lower interest rate in the present construction implies higher real wages. I am aware that I have so far neglected durable (capital) goods and that with such goods the short run story may be different. But if there is excess capacity and one supposes more or less constant average prime costs the proposition may arguably survive for the short period also. I do not pursue this for the following reason. If there are durable capital goods, if the labour force grows at a constant geometric rate, if expectations are correct and if households have linear Engel curves the model which I have constructed can easily be seen to be one of equilibrium growth provided we let $\bar{m}$ grow at the proper rate through time. My exercise then becomes one of comparative dynamics and P.1 will apply to a comparison of steady states. Since so much of the literature claims that economies approach the steady state the proposition continues to be relevant.

[1] $F(\cdot)$ is now a reduced form equation. Hence, for instance, F_R includes the effect on our measure of aggregate demand of the indirect effect of a change in R on q.

Keynes more or less ignored the real cash balance effect ($Z_m = 0$). In that case 'may' can be replaced by 'will' in P.1. Higher output in the neighbouring economy will depend on there being an interest rate effect. Lastly it is obvious that it is differences in $\bar{m}$ in the two economies which make for differences in their real equilibria and that such differences may arise from differences in the money wage or the nominal money stock or both.

The model of this section is a somewhat more elaborate IS–LM construction than is usual but it *is* IS–LM and I do not know why it should be in disfavour. It is, of course, an incomplete account since $\bar{m}$ is exogenous. To that I now turn.

III

The Keynesian argument concerning U.E. is not that it will be permanent. Nor was it maintained that money wages never fall. Rather the contention is that money wage changes are an unreliable cure and that indeed the cure may be worse than the disease. At best the medicine was said to be very slow working.

In examining this matter it is clear that a good deal will turn on expectations and if one is to carry conviction to the modern ear one must postulate that expectations are always correct. This in turn then leads to a puzzle for people like Professor Lucas: if expectations are always correct why are money wages not set at once at that level which is compatible with the clearing of the labour market? But this question is based on a mistake: one can have correct expectations without the economy giving one the means to make an unrestricted choice of the best price. For instance, the employed and the unemployed may not agree on what is best. No one worker can determine the wage for all workers. In addition there may be uncertainty as to the course of the nominal money stock and therefore of the appropriate market clearing money wage (although I shall abstract from this). In what follows I shall simply take the equation specifying changes in the money wage as one of the characteristics of the economy. Individuals with 'true models' of the economy know this equation.

In order to avoid unnecessary algebra I shall modify the model of the previous section to an economy with a single good which can be either consumed or used as an input. I shall also assume a Cobb–Douglas production function. All prices, interest rates, money stock, inputs, and other quantities are now represented by the natural log of their value. For instance, l_t if the log of the labour input at t, m_t is the log of the money stock in wage units at t and R_t is the log of the nominal discount factor. In particular w_t is the log of the money wage and I define the 'real' discount factor by

$$\bar{R}_t \overset{\text{def}}{=} R_t - (w_{t+1} - w_t)$$

Suppose one unit of labour is in inelastic supply. In U.E. then $l_t < 0$.

Given correct price expectations, money wages change so as to satisfy:

$$q_{t+1} - q_t = -\lambda l_t \qquad \lambda > 0 \tag{13}$$

We can transform this to an equation for money wage changes by using the condition E.1 appropriate in this economy;

$$q_{t+1} = \bar{R}_t + (1-a)q_t + c_1 \tag{14}$$

where a is the labour coefficient in the production function and c_1 is a constant, (everywhere c_i will denote a constant). Using this equation and the definition of $\bar{R}_t$ we obtain

$$w_{t+1} - w_t = R_t + \lambda l_t - aq_t + c_1 \tag{15}$$

This can be dubbed the perfect foresight Phillips curve. It is part of the structural specification of the economy.

One can complete the model by an IS and LM function. To do that properly requires that one go back to the decisions of households when they know (14) and (15). But since as we shall see these equations are not required for the main qualitative conclusion which follows I can take a leaf out of the book of much current macro-economic writings and simply postulate:

$$\text{LM:} \quad \bar{m}_t + \mu R - y_t = 0 \tag{16}$$

$$\text{(IS)} \quad b_1 y_t + b_2 y_{t+1} + b_3 \bar{m}_t + b_4 q_t + b_5 \bar{R}_t = 0 \tag{17}$$

where $\bar{m}_t$ in the (log of) the stock of money in wage units. To this if the nominal money stock is constant one can add

$$\bar{m}_{t+1} - \bar{m}_t = -(w_{t+1} - w_t)$$

One now has enough information to write out the system of difference equations which govern the behaviour of the variables of the model.

But fortunately for present purposes we do not need to do the tedious algebra. Let $\bar{m}^*$ be the real money stock which if specified exogenously would give full employment equilibrium ($l_t = 0$). If $\bar{m}_0 < \bar{m}^*$ there is U.E. at $t = 0$, ($l_0 < 0$). We know from the previous section that it is not pathological to have $q_0 > q^*$. That is the equilibrium real wage at full employment may be higher than in unemployment because at $\bar{m}^*$ the rate of interest is lower than it is at $\bar{m}_0$. But by (13) the real wage is falling as long as there is unemployment. Equation (14) shows that this may be brought about by the *expectation* of the falling money wage which raises the real rate. Indeed this rise in the real rate is necessary if labour is to be able to lower its real wage. This in turn means that the nominal rate must not fall too much. In any case if the model is workable it *cannot approach equilibrium monotonically*. That is there will have to be a period of excess demand for labour.

To follow this story in detail one would have to specify the economy with labour rationing. It is not clear that E.1 is now an appropriate condition if firms know that they cannot obtain labour even if they foresee being able to earn the going rate of return. Hence real wages may be rising although R is not falling. For now q_{t+1} may, in equilibrium, exceed production costs plus interest costs. Output will be approximately constant but there may be rationing of demand.

This phase is quite complex, and the analysis of the joint behaviour of the two phases is messy. It can be done, but I shall not attempt it here. Instead I shall suppose that the parameter values allow convergence to the full employment equilibrium. This as we know will involve some 'overshooting' at least once. But by stipulating convergence the wage mechanism is given the benefit of the doubt. However, it should not be overlooked that I am here making an assumption and not using a theorem.

Now consider an alternative scenario. Let $\bar{m}^*$ be the real money balance which had it been specified from 'outside' would have given us a stationary equilibrium with $l^* = 0$ and $y_t = y^*$ all t. By setting $\alpha(q_t) = q_t$, $\beta(q_t) = y_t$ one easily sees that such $\bar{m}^*$ exists. Now suppose the government at t undertakes the following policy:

$$(M_{t+1} - M_t) - (w_{t+1} - w_t) = m^* - m_t \qquad (18)$$

where M_t is the log of the nominal money stock. This policy is known to everyone. With correct expectations it is then known that $l_{t+1} = 0$. Moreover, $q_{t+1} = q^*$ the stationary equilibrium value of the labour price of the good. The demand for the good at $(t+1)$ will be the 'full employment' demand. Hence if we ignore substitution between inputs, today's demand for labour would be the 'full employment' demand. However, the money wage may still change because today's real wage is not the stationary equilibrium wage because $R \neq R^*$. By using the equations already given, $w_{t+1} - w_t$ can be calculated. At $t+1$ the economy is in full employment equilibrium. This has been achieved in one step—at a stroke—and it is clearly superior to a wage adjustment mechanism with a constant nominal money stock.

To this it may be objected that wage earners could have achieved the same outcome at one go with a constant nominal money stock by choosing w_{t+1} to yield $\bar{m}_{t+1} = \bar{m}^*$. This objection misses the distinction between co-operative (co-ordinated) actions and non-co-operative ones. Wage-earners, even if they knew $\bar{m}^*$, may be unable to act co-operatively if for no other reason than that it may be in the interests of some to renege. This objection does not apply to government. Equations like (13) try to capture the imperfect synchronization and co-ordination of workers' actions. Such equations are widely used in the literature. The users therefore should not object to the argument for monetary policy.

It is appropriate at this point to make the following observation. The proposition that a change in the nominal money stock is 'undone' by an equi-proportionate change in money prices applied to the case $l_t = 0$ but not to the case I have been examining. Nor is it true that the development of the real economy is unaffected by the choice between a constant nominal money stock and one obeying (18). For instance, the path of real wages will be

different and there will be no overshooting. By my assumption, both paths
lead to the steady state but the paths differ. (Professor McCallum (1980)
reached a contrary result by treating q_t as a constant and by not allowing for
the time structure of production.) In particular I want to re-emphasize that
the real interest rate is partially governed by the wage mechanism. If indeed
the real interest were constant throughout a wage adjustment process then
in this economy real wages might never change since $q_t = $ constant is a
correct expectation.

It may be worthwhile to nail this point more precisely. Suppose that when
workers know $M_{t+1} - M_t$ they lower (w_{t+1}), (in absolute value) just sufficiently from what it would have been had the money stock been constant to
bring about the same $\bar{m}_{t+1}$. Then unless R_t falls to just keep $\bar{R}_t$ constant, the
real interest rate will be different in the two situations. But if μ is large (a
Keynes answer) that will not happen. Hence the paths of real variables will
differ when M_t is constant from that when it is not.

Of course, (18) assumes a great deal of knowledge on the part of
government, although no more than the correct expectations literature
imputes to agents. But one could try more realistic policies; in so far as they
reduce the necessity for falling money wages and so higher real interest
rates, so much the better. In particular, suppose that workers rely entirely
on the monetary policy to bring about a full equilibrium. Suppose that policy
to be

$$M_{t+1} - M_t = m_{t+1} - m_t = -\lambda l_t \tag{19}$$

Then the real money stock changes in exactly the same way as it did under
(13) but now the real and nominal interest rates coincide. Since with sensible
parameter values the nominal interest rate will be falling and the real wage
rising, one need no longer conclude that the process must overshoot.

IV

The analysis which has been undertaken lacks credibility. That is because it
was purposely constrained to fit currently widely followed ways of theorizing. In particular perfect foresight was assumed. This rules out of court one
of Keynes's most interesting points, namely that the deflationary process of
falling money wages would cause bankruptcies. In the world I have considered everyone knows future prices when they borrow or lend. The second
related point which has been left undiscussed is concerned with durable
capital which I have abstracted from. Rising real interest rates willl reduce
the present real value of old capital and may thus make it unprofitable to
produce it anew. That point, too can be partially brushed aside under
perfect foresight. But I am not sure, since such foresight may lead to
postponement of investment, and this in turn may endanger the existence of
a perfect foresight path. This needs further study. The more sensitive to
unemployment money wages are, the worse the behaviour of the economy,
because, ceteris paribus, the higher are real interest rates and the lower real
wages during the U.E. phase.

It seems to me that at least I have shown that even with modern assumptions Keynes's distrust of the money wage mechanism is not without foundation. Of course, the study of an economy with such a mechanism which is half-way realistic is going to be messy and will probably have to use computer simulation. But that does not seem a good reason for assuming continuous and instantaneous labour market clearing. Nor is it a reason for advocating policies on the basis of such an assumption.

REFERENCES

BAUMOL, W. (1953): 'The Transaction Demand for Cash: An Inventory Theoretic Approach', *Quarterly Journal of Economics*, 62.

GRANDMONT, J. M. (1977), 'Temporary General Equilibrium Theory', *Econometrica*, 45.

HAHN, F. H. (1981), *Money and Inflation*, Blackwell, 1981.

HICKS, J. R. (1937), 'Mr. Keynes and the "Classics"', *Econometrica*.

MIRRLEES, J. (1969), 'The Dynamic Non-Substitution Theorem', *Review of Economic Studies*, 36 (1).

MCCALLUM, B. T. (1980), 'Hahn's Theoretical Viewpoint on Unemployment: A Comment', *Economica*, 47.

TOBIN, J. (1956), 'The Interest Elasticity of Transaction Demand for Cash', *Review of Economics and Statistics*, 25.

MAINTAINING CAPITAL INTACT*

By MAURICE SCOTT

'To intrude upon a controversy being waged by such paladins as Professor Pigou and Professor Hayek seems an act bold even unto rashness; but the question of maintaining capital intact just cannot be left where they left it last summer. The present note will have justified itself if it serves to provoke them to another round' (Hicks (1942)).

Alas, it never did, although the contribution made to the subject by the third paladin himself was of no mean order, as we shall see. The present intruder believes, all the same, that there is still something more to be said. Sir John Hicks showed that each side could justly claim some right, although he mainly came down on Hayek's side.[1] My conclusion, obtained by following up clues provided by Sir John himself, is that, while Hayek's arguments were sound, so were Pigou's, and that from the reconciliation of the two one can learn something which is still not yet generally accepted.

Pigou's great book *The Economics of Welfare* was first published in 1920, and the fourth edition appeared in 1932, almost ten years before the interchange in *Economica* in 1941 to which the above quotation refers. The book opens with a discussion of the meaning of 'economic welfare', and then moves on quickly to the meaning of the 'national dividend', which now (and even by 1932) would more generally be called the national income. This is a key concept for the book, which analyses how this or that policy or institution affects its size (in real terms) and distribution. Its definition was therefore of importance to Pigou, and, following Marshall, he made it the flow of goods and services produced in a given period net of the amounts required to maintain capital intact. But what does *that* mean? This is the subject of a separate chapter in the book, and also of the later controversy.

Before launching into it, let us note that the *purpose* for which the definition was required was to arrive at a meaning of real national income. It was not required for a definition of capital stock for use in a production function, nor for a definition of wealth. These are interesting in themselves, and are matters on which Sir John has shed much light.[2] The purpose was not even to enable the income of an individual person or firm to be defined, as was pointed out by Sir John in his intervention. That, as we shall see, was a very important point.

Pigou's ideas on the subject changed over the years, and I shall confine

* The author is grateful to John Flemming and Geoffrey Harcourt for their comments which led to considerable improvements. They are not responisble for any remaining errors.
[1] Hicks (1974), p. 315 n. 14.
[2] See, for example, Hicks in Lutz and Hague (1961), and also Hicks (1965), (1969), and (1973) on the former, and Hicks (1969), (1971) (as well as earlier editions), and (1974) on the latter.

myself to what seems to have been their final form.[3] He starts with the proposition that, if the quantity of every unit in the nation's capital stock is unchanged over a period, then the total capital stock has been exactly maintained even though its money value may have risen or fallen.[4] In his book he had already argued that changes in the money value of the stock due to changes in the general level of prices should not count as changes in the real capital stock for this purpose.[5] Both there and in his later *Economic Journal* article[6] he had argued that changes in the value due to changes in rates of interest, which would alter the present discounted values of future receipts, should not count either. He also excluded changes in value due to changes in the quantity of labour working in conjunction with the capital stock, as well as changes due to shifts in taste, or to competition from new equipment. 'In fact we may, I think, say quite generally, that all contractions in the money value of any parts of the capital stock that remain physically unaltered are irrelevant to the national dividend; and that their occurrence is perfectly compatible with the maintenance of capital intact' (Pigou (1946), p. 45).

Turning now to changes in the quantity, or physical characteristics, of goods in the stock, Pigou excluded all changes of an extraordinary nature (by 'act of God or the King's enemies' as he put it), but included accidental changes due to, for example, fire, which would be a 'normal' risk to be expected.[7] He then needed to specify some way of adding up the positive and negative changes so as to be able to say whether or not the total stock had been maintained. His preferred method was most clearly set out in the 1941 *Economica* article with the help of an arithmetical example. To paraphrase this, at the risk of some loss of clarity, let us suppose that one unit of good A has become worn out or scrapped on account of obsolescence in the relevant period. Let us ask how many units of good B are required to replace it. By his original proposition, had another unit of A been available, that would have sufficed to replace it. By an extension of that proposition, as many units of good B are required as are expected to yield the same income as one unit of A.

Pigou's method rests, as can be seen, on distinguishing sharply between changes in price and quantity. It is only declines in quantity (including any sorts of physical deterioration, but excluding those caused by extraordinary

---

[3] See Pigou (1935), (1941), and (1946). The last is a reprint of the fourth edition of *The Economics of Welfare* (1932), to which Pigou added a prefatory note in 1938 drawing attention to his 1935 *Economic Journal* article. This leaves his 1941 *Economica* article as his last published statement of the subject.

[4] Pigou (1941).

[5] Pigou (1946), part 1, ch. iv, p. 44.

[6] Pigou (1935), p. 236.

[7] Pigou also excluded, in his 1935 *Economic Journal* article (p. 238) 'physical changes which, while leaving the element as productive as ever, bring nearer the day of sudden and violent breakdown'. The most obvious example of such changes is the ageing of persons or domestic animals. I believe that in wishing to exclude *these* physical changes he was mistaken (see also n. 18 below).

factors) which have to be made good by replacement by new capital whose value is the same, the valuation being made at the time when the deterioration takes place.[8] The national income in any period is then the sum of consumption and gross investment minus that part of gross investment required to maintain capital intact.

Let us now turn to Hayek. Shortly after Pigou's article in the *Economic Journal* appeared, in June 1935, Hayek published an article in *Economica* (August 1935) entitled 'The Maintenance of Capital'. This was long (35 pages) and complex. It examined the evolution of Pigou's treatment in *The Economics of Welfare*, and also included references to his most recent article, just published. It was addressed to the same problem as Pigou's, namely, the relation between changes in the stock of capital and income. However, the argument was more in terms of the income of individuals— whether persons or firms—than of national income. Much attention was given to obsolescence and to uncertainty and changes in expectations. It concluded, amongst other things, that 'the stock of capital required to keep income from any moment onwards constant cannot in any sense be defined as a constant magnitude' (op. cit. p. 269).

Subsequently, in 1941, Hayek published *The Pure Theory of Capital*, in which he said much the same things. Pigou reacted to all this by his article in *Economica* in 1941, in which he undoubtedly misinterpreted some of Hayek's argument (as Sir John pointed out in 1942). Hayek replied in the same issue by a simple example.[9] Pigou had argued that real capital, and so real income, would be maintained as long as capital goods were physically maintained. Consider, then, two[10] businessmen who simultaneously each buy 'equipment of different kinds but of the same cost and the same potential physical duration, say ten years. X expects to be able to use his machine continuously throughout the period of its physical 'life'. Y, who produces some fashion article, knows that at the end of one year his machine will have not more than its scrap value.' According to Pigou, since the physical deterioration of both machines is the same, X and Y should make the same deductions from their gross receipts in the first year to get their net profits (ignoring all other costs). Hence, equal gross profits will imply equal net profits. Yet if X deducts one-tenth of the cost of the machine and saves it, his capital at the end of the year will clearly have been maintained, whereas Y will retain only one tenth of his capital (ignoring the

---

[8] Pigou admitted that there was some imprecision in reckoning the relative valuations of A and B in his example due to the length of the period chosen. This can, however, be avoided in theory, if not in practice, by measuring income over infinitesimally short periods. One then requires to multiply the rates of change of quantities in the stock by their values at a point in time. In his 1941 *Economica* article he did not refer to 'values', but to income yield. He did, however, refer to values in *the Economics of Welfare* (1946), p. 47.

[9] In fact, Hayek had already provided an essentially similar example and argument in his 1935 *Economica* article (see pp. 257–8).

[10] Hayek, in fact, considered a third businessman undertaking a risky investment, but it is sufficient for our purposes to consider only two.

scrap value) if he does the same. 'I find it difficult to conceive that this procedure could have any practical value or any theoretical significance', concludes Hayek, and stresses that foreseeable obsolescence *must* be taken into account. The problem arises when some obsolescence is not foreseen and, in an uncertain world, this is bound to happen. Changes in expectations will then lead to windfall losses and gains and resulting changes in capital value. To calculate income one should not subtract such losses or add such gains in any period. It is the difficulty of separating these from the foreseeable ones that Hayek regards as making it practically impossible to arrive at a definition of the maintenance of capital that can be used in defining income.

In the spring following this exchange between Pigou and Hayek, Sir John Hicks published his 'further suggestion', whose beginning we have quoted. The views he expressed there were reaffirmed over thirty years later in '*Capital and Time*', (1973) (see the note to ch. XIII). After describing Pigou's suggested method, he added 'This principle of Professor Pigou's stands up very well to most sorts of criticism, but it has (I think) been torpedoed by Professor Hayek...Professor Hayek, on the other hand, having demolished the rival construction, fails (in my view) to provide anything solid to put in its place'. Hayek had clung to the definition of income which Hicks himself had described and analysed with such lucidity in *Value and Capital* (1939, ch. XIV) that that has become the standard reference on the subject. The idea of income as the maximum rate of consumption which the recipient can enjoy and expect to continue to enjoy indefinitely is widely termed 'Hicksian income'. In *Value and Capital* Hicks had, all the same, criticized this concept, along with those of saving, depreciation, and investment, as not being 'suitable tools for any analysis which aims at logical precision. There is far too much equivocation in their meaning, equivocation which cannot be removed by the most painstaking effort. At bottom, they are not logical categories at all; they are rough approximations, used by the businessman to steer himself through the bewildering changes of situation which confront him. For this purpose, strict logical categories are not what is needed; something rougher is actually better' (op. cit., p. 171). Nevertheless, he also took the view that 'calculations of social income...play...an important part in social statistics, and in welfare economics' (p. 180). In his *Economica* article he stressed the importance of knowing the purpose for which a definition was required in any controversy about definitions. His purpose was the same as Pigou's, namely, the measurement of net social income, and for this purpose he was prepared, apparently, to abandon the *Value and Capital* 'Hicksian income' the 'constant income stream' income, in order to get something suitable.

His suggestion was as follows. Net income in any year is consumption plus gross investment minus depreciation of the original stock of capital, where depreciation is 'The difference between the total value of the goods comprising that original stock as it is at the end of the year (C_1) and the value (C'_0)

which would have been put upon the initial stock at the beginning of the year if the events of the year had been correctly foreseen, including among those events the capital value C_1 at the end of the year' (empasis as in the original).

At first sight this definition encounters Hayek's objection that it requires the separation of changes in the value of capital due to foreseen events from those due to unforeseen ones (windfalls). However, Hicks suggested that the procedure should not be to attempt to value C_0', which would necessitate such a separation, but rather to attempt to value $C_0' - C_1$, depreciation, by 'distinguishing, of the various experiences which the initial capital goods will have had during the year, which sorts will cause a divergence between C_0' and C_1. These are the things which will cause true depreciation. By applying the rule to each case as it comes up we ought to be able to discover them'. He then mentions wear and tear in the course of production and obsolescence of the kind described in Hayek's example as being true depreciation on this test. On the other hand, he apparently thought that most obsolescence would be excluded by the test, since most of it was due to imperfect foresight. Thus if C_1 was lower than C_0 (the actual market value of the original stock at the beginning of the year, given the expectations then held) because of unforeseen obsolescence during the year, it would *not* be lower than C_0' for that reason.

Hicks thought that this definition of income would give the same results as Hayek's in all cases where both could be employed. It would also *generally* be the same as Pigou's, but there would be exceptional cases (of the kind described in Hayek's example) when they would differ. However, he clearly thought that these differences were likely to be unimportant for Pigou's purpose. Indeed, so far as obsolescence due to changes in tastes were concerned, this could not strictly be allowed in making welfare comparisons, since one had to assume that tastes were unchanged for comparisons to be possible at all.

So far as I know, Pigou never stated whether this suggested compromise satisfied him, and nor has Hayek. In my own view, which I attempt to justify below, it was the right attempt, but did not quite go far enough. Putting myself in Hayek's place I would deny that most obsolescence can be excluded on the grounds that it is due to imperfect foresight.[11] While it is probably true that businessmen cannot predict at all accurately how fast any particular piece of equipment is going to become obsolete, the law of large numbers must come to the rescue when one considers the whole capital stock. Provisions for depreciation ought, for such a large number of heterogenous items, to correspond reasonably well to actual depreciation in value (abstracting from inflation, as did our three paladins). In that case, while the correction made to C_0 to arrive at C_0' may sometimes reduce it, because unforeseen obsolescence has occurred, it may equally sometimes increase it, because obsolescence has been slower than expected. Now there

[11] See Hayek (1935), pp. 257–60.

are many (including possibly Hayek)[12] who take the view that obsolescence is the most important cause of the depreciation of capital, and I do not think it is obsolescence due to changes in tastes which they have in mind, but rather that due to a variety of other causes such as innovations, shifts in demand as income increases, and the erosion of quasi-rents as product wages rise. If that is so, the apparent gap between Hayek's and Pigou's methods becomes very large indeed. All the same, I believe the gap can be closed, and the clue as to how this may be done is the fact pointed out by Sir John himself: whereas Pigou was concerned with net social income, Hayek's examples and arguments referred essentially to individual businesses.

To make further progress it is essential to define the concepts of *investment* and *maintenance* expenditures more explicitly. Only when this is done can one obtain a clear idea of *depreciation*, and relate all three concepts to 'Hicksian income'—which I regard as the best available income concept, despite Sir John's own criticisms above.

I have suggested elsewhere that investment expenditures are best regarded as all the costs of changing economic arrangements.[13] This is a wide definition, which in practice may have to be narrowed. It includes all the usual expenditures on buildings and other construction, machinery, equipment, and vehicles, and increases in stocks of goods and work in progress. It also should include such things as research and development expenditures, and some managerial, and marketing costs and some of the costs of financial intermediations. Although it is not a good description for some of these expenditures, let me call their sum gross *material* investment, to distinguish them from *human* investment, which consists of some expenditures on education and health and the training and movement of workers. In what follows I shall largely neglect human investment, although it is undoubtedly important. This is done just to simplify and shorten the exposition.

How can we distinguish between investment expenditures and maintenance expenditures? It may seem, at first sight, pedantic to point out that the latter, as well as the former, are expenditures incurred to change economic arrangements. Painting a house or oiling and greasing a machine change the house or the machine. Ploughing and sowing change the fields. It would generally be agreed that these should be treated as current costs of production, not investment, but why?

One criterion suggested in the United Nations *System of National Accounts* (1968), para. 6.56, p. 100 and para. 6.102, p. 110, is that all expenditures whose benefits last for longer than a year, the period of account, should be regarded as part of gross investment, whereas other expenditures (such as for ploughing and sowing), should be regarded as

---

[12] See Hayek (1935), pp. 257, 259. '. . . it is obsolescence, rather than wear and tear which is the cause of mortality—homicide to make room for a new favourite, rather than natural death', Barna in Lutz and Hague (1961), p. 85. See also Kuznets in Conference on Research in Income and Wealth (1951), p. 65.

[13] Scott (1976).

current. Unfortunately, this is arbitrary and is not in practice followed. Painting and repairs to buildings last for much longer than a year, but are nevertheless treated as current maintenance costs. Nor is this a trivial matter. Were they to be regarded as gross investment, the latter would be increased very substantially.

Another criterion to be found in systems of national accounts is that of improvement *versus* restoration. Expenditures which restore the physical condition of assets are treated as maintenance, whereas improvements are, at least in principle, included in gross investment.[14] This seems to be the best way of defining the distinction, but it has far-reaching implications which have not been generally realized. This definition at once reminds one of Pigou's starting-point for defining the maintenance of the capital stock. Both definitions are concerned with maintaining the number and physical characteristics of assets unchanged.

Strictly speaking, however, *individual* assets are not and cannot always be kept physically unchanged. In order to make this idea more precise, let us first consider a case in which assets would be kept physically unchanged in a simple sense *in aggregate*. In a static economy, with balanced stocks of all assets, the stock of each type of asset would be kept unchanged. Individual members of the stock (e.g. individual taxis, cows, or houses) would be subject to ageing or decay. However, the whole fleet of taxis, herd of cows, or housing estate would not, since periodic expenditures would be undertaken to repair damage, replace worn-out parts, or replace whole units by new ones. All these expenditures should be classified as *maintenance*, and treated just like any other current cost of production. In such a case we could say that *required maintenance*, no more and no less, was being undertaken, and this expenditure would be a (near enough) constant flow.

For the owner of an *individual* asset, however, some of the actual expenditures to maintain his asset would inevitably be lumpy. In order to estimate his income, he would need to set up a fund to which he would contribute at a constant rate, and out of which he would meet the necessary expenditures, the balance in the fund earning interest (or paying it, when the balance was negative). The correct deduction to be made from his current receipts on account of maintenance would then be his constant rate of contribution to the fund, and not the actual repair and replacement expenditures. If such funds were set up for each and every asset in our static economy, we would find that the rate of the aggregate contributions to them would equal the rate of the aggregate actual expenditures.

Consider now a closed economy in which required maintenance expenditure is undertaken, no more and no less, there being zero gross investment, so that no expenditures to *improve* assets in aggregate, or increase their number, are being made, merely expenditures to keep them unchanged in aggregate. Let us also posit a constant labour force, and no changes through

---

[14] See, for example, Maurice (1968), pp. 361–2.

'acts of God or the King's enemies'. Then this static economy would be capable of producing a constant real flow of consumption goods and services for as long as these conditions persist. That flow is then the static economy's income in the Hicksian sense.

We are now in a position to introduce *depreciation*. It is clear that, in the economy just described, depreciation must be zero. Since gross investment is zero, and income is total consumption, and also equals total consumption plus gross investment minus depreciation, the latter must be zero. This may surprise some, and I shall be accused of changing accepted terminology. I have been able to perform my trick, it will be said, only because I have regarded wear and tear as being covered by maintenance, rather than by depreciation. Replacing junked taxis or dead cows would usually be regarded as part of gross investment, and so these replacement expenditures would have to be covered by depreciation, even in a static economy.

This objection has some force, in as much as it is correct to say that *some lumpy* replacement expenditures are conventionally included in gross investment. Nevertheless, I think the objection cannot be sustained. First, as a matter of principle rather than practice, I must ask the objectors how they propose to distinguish gross investment and maintenance expenditures? We have already seen that the durability of the benefits from the expenditure is an inadequate criterion, and I believe lumpiness is too. Are taxi replacements more lumpy than building repairs and redecoration? What is the critical 'lump' and how is it determined? I do not see how these questions can be answered satisfactorily at a theoretical level. Secondly, as a matter of practice, I believe that the criterion already suggested (i.e. whether the expenditure restores, or improves, and the extent to which it does each) agrees well enough with those generally used and which are discussed below. Admittedly *some* expenditures, which I should classify as maintenance, in practice are included in gross investment (e.g. for replacing taxis), but this helps to offset an opposite error, since there are many expenditures which are treated as current yet ought to be included in gross material investment (research and development etc. listed above) and recorded maintenance expenditures often improve, rather than merely maintain, assets,[15] that is, if they were to be matched by a notional fund, the contributions to that fund would have to grow.

Let us now attempt to move on from a static to a growing economy. If depreciation is zero in the former, can it also be zero in the latter? In my view, and taking the *whole* of a closed economy, the answer is yes, but, I hasten to add, there *is* depreciation then for individual businesses within the economy. The reason why it is zero for the whole economy is that such depreciation is cancelled out by an equal and opposite amount of *appreciation*.

A growing economy is changing, and so investment is being undertaken. Some assets which would have to be maintained in a static economy, and

---

[15] See Barna in Lutz and Hague (1961), pp. 90–1.

which is would then pay to maintain, will now be neglected and perhaps scrapped. Maintaining them will no longer be worthwhile, since they are becoming obsolete. It is worth noting that that is often the direction of causation—from obsolescence to physical decay. Buildings, for example, can be maintained indefinitely, but many are allowed to deteriorate and are finally pulled down because they have becomes obsolete, and the land on which they stand can be better used. In these circumstances, what one might call ordinary maintenance expenditures will fall short of required maintenance, and some of gross investment will merely compensate for the loss of income caused by this shortfall. The question is how much, and how it can be determined.

It is important to note that, in ordinary circumstances, one would not expect that very much gross investment would be needed. The reason for this is that the loss of income due to the failure to maintain is likely to be small, *precisely because of the obsolescence that has occurred.* If some asset were, for example, fully maintained until its quasi-rent fell to zero, through competition with newer assets, and/or as a result of rising product wages, or possibly land rents, then scrapping it would involve no loss of income at all. Failure fully to maintain it during the latter part of its life is also not likely to lose much income, since its quasi-rent will then be small and one can trust the asset-owner to undertake maintenance which *is* worthwhile, and so does appreciably affect earning power. It seems probable that only a minor part of gross investment would thus have to be deducted to bring maintenance up to the required level, and that the problem of estimating how much is not an important one, since not much is involved. Furthermore, I believe that the opposite error of including as current expenditure what should be classed as gross material investment is likely to more than offset the required deduction.

The upshot of all this is, then, that conventionally defined *gross* material investment is more likely to understate than overstate true *net* material investment for the whole of a closed economy. Instead of deducting something (depreciation) from gross material investment to get net material investment, one should probably add something. Reverting to the Hicksian definition of income, the constant income flow, an economy with a static labour force could transfer all the resources engaged in producing the flow of goods and services conventionally labelled gross investment into consumption goods and services production, and expect to be able to continue to consume probably rather more than the resulting total existing consumption plus the value of gross investment indefinitely.[16] Since the transfer would probably still leave a surplus over required maintenance, total sustainable consumption, and so Hicksian income, would probably be rather higher.

So far, if I have carried the reader with me, Pigou is vindicated. But what

[16] This assumes that £X of gross investment could be transformed into £X of consumption. For a variety of reasons, precise equality is not to be expected, even if both are measured at factor cost. However, for simplicity this point is glossed over. Strictly speaking, investment should be measured by its equivalent amount of consumption if we want the sum of consumption and net investment to equal Hicksian income.

about Hayek? He, too, can be vindicated. In a completely static economy there are no relative price changes and no obsolescence. In a growing economy, both occur. Excluding changes in the number of workers, or in human capital (as I have thus far and shall continue to do, for simplicity), all real improvements, and so all increases in real income, are due to material investment. But the *division* of that increase in income amongst different people is determined by changes in relative prices. Because relative prices are changing, some gain and some lose. An *individual's* income cannot be estimated without allowing for present and prospective relative price changes. If, on balance, these are adverse, the individual will have to deduct depreciation from his current receipts to get his net income. If they are favourable, however, he must add appreciation. An example may help to clarify all this.

A business owns assets which it maintains in a physically unchanged state, so that required maintenance, no more and no less, is being undertaken. It employs a constant labour force. The consumer price index in the economy is constant, as are interest rates. The value added in the business (the sum of gross profits and wages, net of maintenance expenditures) is constant in money terms, but, because of investment elsewhere in the economy, wages are rising. If the business continues like this, its gross profits will dwindle away to nothing, and it will then have to close down to avoid making losses. Clearly, then, the proprietor's income from the business is less than its current gross profits. Some of its gross profits must be set aside as depreciation, and invested so as to offset the loss of income which is occurring as a result of the rise in wage rates. Depreciation can, indeed, be defined so as to equal the investment required so that this loss should be just offset. I have distinguished it from maintenance, in that the loss is *due to a relative price change* instead of being due to a physical change of some kind in the assets concerned.

From the point of view of the businessman, this distinction is immaterial. Whether his assets are physically deteriorating, or whether they are becoming obsolete as relative prices change adversely, really makes no difference. In either event there is some expenditure he needs to undertake in order to offset these changes, and it is only after subtracting the cost of this expenditure that he can regard the remainder of his gross profit as Hicksian income or net profit, which could all be consumed indefinitely. Indeed, for the individual businessman the distinction between depreciation and maintenance has been made on different lines. 'Maintenance' has consisted of all those expenditures which are sufficiently small, frequent and regular that one can, without too much distortion, estimate one's income by subtracting the *actual* expenditures instead of by setting up a fund and subtracting contributions to it. It is much simpler to do the former than the latter. 'Depreciation' has been concerned with expenditures which are too large and irregular to be treated in this way, and where a fund has had to be set up if estimates of income are not to be badly distorted. 'Depreciation' then consists of contributions to the fund, and gross investment consists of those expenditures which are *not* subtracted from revenues in estimating income. The distinctions between depreciation, maintenance, and gross investment have thus rested on simple practical grounds of convenience and approximation, and this is why criteria such as the length of the accounting period and the lumpiness of the expenditure have been used which seem quite arbitrary from a conceptual point of view.

So much for the practical businessman, but what of the practical social accountant? As we have seen, there are two important distinctions to be drawn: between gross investment and maintenance expenditures, and between depreciation and maintenance. We have suggested that the first distinction should rest on whether the expenditures improve or merely restore, but we have also admitted that this is not a precise distinction. To achieve precision, we suggested setting up a fund for each and every asset, so that gross investment would then consist of all expenditures which changed assets (or, more generally, changed economic arrangements) without distinguishing improvements from restorations. Required maintenance would then be the sum of contributions to these funds. Unfortunately, this theoretically satisfactory solution is quite impractical, since it would enormously increase gross investment and the deduction for required maintenance. Ploughing and sowing change assets, as do painting and repairing, oiling and greasing, and a vast amount of other expenditure besides. In practice, therefore, we must fall back on the same criteria as the businessman: we avoid setting up funds and include as many actual maintenance expenditures as possible with other current costs of production. The larger the group of assets in our aggregate, and the longer our period of account, the more closely will such actual expenditures approximate to the notional contributions to our notional funds. It is the closeness of this approximation at which we must aim in deciding how to treat this or that item.

If we can cover all, or nearly all, physical deterioration *in so far as it results in a loss of income for society* by actual maintenance expenditures, then we can stick to our definition of depreciation as loss of value due to current or expected relative price changes, and appreciation as the corresponding gain in value. It is then the case that, whereas maintenance expenditures offset a loss which would otherwise occur both to the individual and to society, depreciation is a loss to the individual but *not* a loss to society. Since we have defined it as being due to relative price changes, for every loser there must be a gainer, and so appreciation *should* be equal and opposite to depreciation.[17]

---

[17] Some writers, including Kuznets (in Conference on Research in Income and Wealth (1951), p. 66, but he appears to have modified his stance in Conference on Research in Income and Wealth (1957), pp. 277–9) and Ruggles and Ruggles (1956), p. 114, have questioned the view that obsolescence, which leads to the depreciation of individual assets, results in a loss of income for society as a whole. Their views do not seem to have gained general acceptance, perhaps because they failed to draw attention to the appreciation of some assets which accompanies, and offsets, the depreciation of others.

In the example given above, it is clear that the workers in the business are gaining exactly what the owners of the business are losing. The value added by the business is being redistributed from profits to wages. Workers could, therefore, consume more than their current wages and expect to be able to consume as much indefinitely (ignoring death, that is!). The extra amount is appreciation, and, if we could estimate depreciation and appreciation on a consistent basis and sum them for the whole of a closed economy, they would cancel out. In practice, we cannot hope for consistency, since expectations and rates of discount will differ for different individuals. Some future transfer of income which costs A £X and benefits B by the same amount, and whose present value ought to be the same for each, will not in general be given the same value by each. Indeed, conservative accounting principles teach A to reckon in the cost, so that a suitable depreciation provision is made, but also teach B to ignore the benefit until it is actually realized. Hence it is very likely that individual businesses will exaggerate depreciation provisions (although inflation is a powerful factor working in the opposite direction). In economies growing like those of Western countries since the Second World War, these errors are, however, as nothing to the errors in the accounts of workers, whose incomes as conventionally stated ignore a really vast amount of appreciation.

There is, then, much to justify Hayek's doubts about the practicality of income measurement for the individual, as well as Hicks's warnings in *Value and Capital*, where, *inter alia*, he drew attention to the inconsistencies of different people's expectations mentioned above (Hicks (1939), pp. 177–8). The difficulty of estimating individual incomes does not, all the same, translate into an equal difficulty in estimating national income, since there is much cancelling of appreciation and depreciation when we sum the incomes of all individuals, and this greatly reduces the errors and uncertainties of measurement.

To summarize, let us consider the definition of net social income as consumption plus gross investment less expenditure required to maintain capital intact (which I call required maintenance). I have tried to justify the following propositions.

(1) The definition assumes that the resources used to produce net investment (i.e. gross investment less required maintenance) could be converted to produce an equivalent value of consumption. Alternatively, net investment should be measured as this equivalent value. This equivalence is needed to make the total equal to Hicksian income.

(2) Gross investment expenditures are aimed at improving, while maintenance expenditures are aimed at restoring, economic arrangements.

(3) We can avoid making this imprecise distinction between improvement and restoration by imagining a fund set up for each and every asset, into which contributions are made at a rate which would remain constant in a static economy, and out of which actual maintenance expenditures are paid.

Required maintenance is then the sum of these contributions, and all actual expenditures which change assets are included in gross investment.

(4) Such a procedure would result in enormous rates of gross investment, since even expenditures such as ploughing and sowing, let alone painting, repairing, oiling, and greasing, can be regarded as changing assets. In practice, therefore, we treat actual maintenance expenditures so far as possible as current costs instead of including them in gross investment. The approximation involved becomes better as one lengthens the period of account, or as one aggregates more and more assets together. Actual maintenance expenditures then correspond more and more closely to the notional contributions to the fund mentioned in (3).

(5) In fact, it seems likely that, with two exceptions mentioned below, actual maintenance expenditures included in current costs fall not far short of required maintenance. This is because actual maintenance expenditures counter physical deterioration where it matters—the assets which are scrapped or allowed to crumble away are mostly those which are worthless. One class of physical deterioration which is certainly large for particular countries, and perhaps for the world as a whole, is the extraction and destruction of fossil fuels. Another which may be large is the damage done to the environment by a variety of human activities: deforestation, over-grazing, over-fishing, pollution, etc.

(6) Some expenditures which improve economic arrangements (such as research and development expenditures, etc.) are included in current costs and not in gross investment, and this, for many countries, probably outweighs the shortfall mentioned in (5). It therefore seems likely (apart from the two exceptions mentioned) that gross investment as conventionally measured *under*states, rather than *over*states, true net social investment.

(7) The above all refers to expenditures which change material assets physically. Net social investment should include improvements in human assets. Neither material nor human investment should include changes in the value of assets due to changes in the general level of prices, or to changes in interest rates, or to changes in expectations (windfalls).

(8) Nor should social investment for the whole of a closed economy include changes in the value of assets due to current or expected relative price changes, and this covers nearly all obsolescence. For an individual (or for an open economy) such changes must be taken into account when income is estimated. Adverse expected price changes will result in depreciation of his assets and will lower his income. Favourable expected price changes will result in appreciation and will raise his income. If all asset owners held identical expectations and used identical discount rates, and if all assets, human as well as material, were covered, the sum of depreciation and appreciation in a closed economy would be zero.

The above glosses over some difficulties, including some raised by the protagonists in this discussion,[18] and so there is still more to be said.[19] But if I have succeeded in advancing matters from where they stood more than forty years ago, I shall be satisfied.

Nuffield College, Oxford

REFERENCES

Conference on Research in Income and Wealth (1951), *Studies in Income and Wealth*, XIV, National Bureau of Economic Research, New York.

Conference on Research in Income and Wealth (1957), *Problems of Capital formation, Studies in Income and Wealth*, XIX, National Bureau of Economic Research, New York, Princeton University Press, Princeton.

HAYEK, F. A. (1935), 'The Maintenance of Capital', *Economica*, NS ii, August.

HAYEK, F. A. (1941), 'Maintaining Capital Intact: a Reply', *Economica*, NS viii, August.

HICKS, Sir JOHN (1939), *Value and Capital*, Oxford (1st edn., 2nd edn. in 1946).

HICKS, Sir JOHN (1942), 'Maintaining Capital Intact: a Further Suggestion', *Economica*, NS ix, May.

HICKS, Sir JOHN (1965), *Capital and Growth*, Oxford.

HICKS, Sir JOHN (1969), 'Measurement of Capital—in Practice', paper given to a meeting of the International Statistical Institute and published in its Bulletin, xliii, and republished in *Wealth and Welfare, Collected Essays on Economic Theory*, i (Oxford, 1981).

HICKS, Sir JOHN (1971), *The Social Framework*, 4th edn., Oxford.

HICKS, Sir JOHN (1974), 'Capital Controversies: Ancient and Modern', *American Economic Review*, lxiv, May.

LUTZ, F. A. and HAGUE, D. C. (eds.) (1961), *The Theory of Capital*, London.

MAURICE, R. (ed.), (1968), *National Accounts Statistics Sources and Methods*, HMSO. London.

PIGOU, A. C. (1932) and (1946), *The Economics of Welfare*, 4th edn., London.

PIGOU, A. C. (1935), 'Net Income and Capital Depletion', *Economic Journal*, xlv, June.

PIGOU, A. C. (1941), 'Maintaining Capital Intact', *Economica* NS viii, August.

---

[18] This footnote is confined to three difficult cases which they mentioned. First, Hayek's fashion machinery. The strict answer is that given by Hicks, namely, that real income comparisons must assume no changes in tastes. Nevertheless, as a practical matter the best solution may be to treat the loss in value as if it were a physical deterioration. I rather doubt that this is the thin end of a big wedge. Christopher Gilbert has pointed out that this treatment could also be justified by regarding the demand for changing fashion goods as an unchanging taste for being in fashion. Shifts in demand resulting from income growth do not lead to the same result, be it noted. Secondly, Pigou's case of equipment which, although it approaches nearer to the point of physical collapse, remains as currently productive as ever, my example being the ageing of humans or domestic animals. This *is* a physical change which *does* reduce the assets' present value. I think it needs to be offset by other investment if capital is to be maintained. Hicksian income will otherwise be overstated. Thirdly, Hicks's example in his 1942 article of an asset which remains physically unchanged and which is unused during the period for which we are estimating income. Hicks pointed out that the asset should appreciate in value over this period (given the usual assumptions of no change in general prices, or in expectations or interest rates), and so this appreciation should be included in income. It is not possible to do justice to this in a brief space. I believe the conclusion is correct, and that it would in principle be covered by a careful application of the definitions of Hicksian income along the lines of Scott (1976)

[19] I hope to say a bit more in a forthcoming book.

RUGGLES, R. and RUGGLES, N. D. (1956), *National Income Accounts and Income Analysis*, 2nd edn., New York.

SCOTT, M. FG. (1976), Investment and Growth, *Oxford Economic Papers*, NS xxviii, November.

United Nations (1968), *A System of National Accounts*, Studies in Methods, Series F, No. 2, Rev. 3, Department of Economic and Social Affairs, Statistical Office of the United Nations, New York.

THE LIVING STANDARD*

By AMARTYA SEN

1. Introduction

IN AN illuminating analysis of 'the scope and status of welfare economics,' Sir John Hicks (1975) makes the apparently puzzling remark: '*The Economics of Welfare* is *The Wealth of Nations* in a new guise' (p. 223). In explaining the connection between Pigou and Adam Smith, Hicks shows that Pigou was 'taking over' much of 'the *classical* theory of production and distribution' and 'turning' it into 'the economics of welfare'.

There is, in fact, a remarkable similarity even in the motivations behind Smith's and Pigou's works and their respective views of the nature of political economy and economics. Adam Smith (1776) starts his inquiry by referring to what will determine whether 'the nation will be better or worse supplied with all the necessaries and conveniences for which it has occasion' (vol. 1, p. 1). Pigou (1952) begins by arguing that 'the social enthusiasm which revolts from the sordidness of mean streets and joylessness of withered lives' is, in fact, 'the beginning of economic science' (p. 5). The central place given to the determination of the standard of living is a part of their common view of the nature of the subject.

This paper is concerned with investigating the *concept* of the living standard. The topic falls within 'welfare economics' in a broad sense, but it is a somewhat specialized problem within that subject. In fact, in recent years, there has been a tendency for attention to move a little away from this specialized problem because of greater concern with the analysis of overall social welfare, systematized in the notions of 'social welfare functions' (see Bergson (1938), Samuelson (1947), Arrow (1951)). But the original problem of living standard comparison remains interesting and important—and one of much general interest.[1]

I begin with making two preliminary points about the concept of the standard of living. First, in so far as the living standard is a notion of welfare, it belongs to one aspect of it, not unconnected with what Pigou called 'economic welfare'. Pigou (1952) defined 'economic welfare' as 'that part of social welfare that can be brought directly or indirectly into relation with the measuring-rod of money' (p. 11). Sir John Hicks (1975) notes that 'the distinctions which' Pigou 'draws, on this basis, are unquestionably interesting', but goes on to say, 'yet the concept of Economic Welfare, on which Pigou in fact based [the distinctions], or thought he was basing them,

* For many helpful comments on an earlier version, I am most grateful to David Collard, Dieter Helm, Maurice Scott, and T. N. Srinivasan.
[1] See Kaldor (1939), Hicks (1940), (1958), Little (1950), Graaff (1957). See also Hicks (1983) on the various uses of economic theory.

has nevertheless been very generally rejected' (p. 219). Hicks has clarified, in this essay and elsewhere (see Hicks (1940), (1958), (1959), (1981)), the main issues involved—including Pigou's rationale and the critics' reasoning. He does not provide an overall judgement, but in his own economic analysis, Hicks opts for the 'decision to treat the Social Product as primary, and to banish "economic welfare" ' (Hicks (1975), pp. 230. 230–1).

The distinction between welfare and economic welfare is indeed problematic. But the approach is also, as Hicks says, 'unquestionably interesting'. The function that the distinction serves in Pigou's analysis can indeed be met in many exercises by the concept of the 'social product'. Nevertheless, there are other problems—notably those concerned with individual welfare and individual standard of living—in which a distinction closer to Pigou's own (between economic welfare and overall welfare) may well be necessary.

Let me illustrate. I haven't seen you for many years—since I was chucked out of school in fact. I run into you one day in the West End waving at me from your chauffeur-driven Rolls-Royce, looking shockingly prosperous and well-heeled. You give me a ride, and invite me to visit you at your mansion in Chelsea. I remark that I am pleased to see what a high standard of living you are enjoying. 'Not all all', you reply, 'My standard of living is very low. I am a very unhappy man.' 'Why so?' I have to probe. 'Because', you reply, 'I write poems—damn good ones too—but nobody likes my poems, not even my wife. I am always depressed about this injustice, and also sorry that the world has such deplorable taste. I am miserable and have a very low standard of living.' By now I can see no reason to doubt that you are indeed unhappy, but I feel obliged to tell you that you don't known the meaning of 'standard of living'. So you drop me off at the next Tube station (remarking: 'My standard of living high/What a plebeian lie!', adding to the set of people who don't think much of your poetry).

I think Pigou would very likely be right in maintaining that your 'economic welfare' is high even though you are unhappy and quite possibly have a low overall welfare. That would be right not because welfare or utility or happiness can plausibly be split into distinct self-contained parts, of which 'economic welfare' happens to be one. Rather, it can be argued that 'economic welfare' is an interesting concept of its own, which relates to—but is not necessarily one separable part of—welfare or utility or happiness. A person's sense of material well-being can be a sensible subject of study, without our being able to split the sense of overall well-being into several separable bits, of which the sense of material well-being is one. A 'plural' approach to utility (see Sen (1981)) permits the coexistence of various distinct concepts of utility, which are *interdependent*, without one being a separable part of another. While I shall presently argue that living standard is best seen not as a utility concept at all (roughly speaking, it can be said that it deals with material well-being and not with the *sense* of material well-being), it *is* an 'economic' concept (roughly speaking, being concerned with *material* well-being). More will be said on this presently.

The second point concerns the motivation underlying studies of standard of living. It can be part of the objectives of policy-making (for example: 'we plan to raise the standard of living fastest!'). But that need not be the only motivation. We may be primarily concerned with a cognitive question, e.g. comparing standard of living between two actual persons, or two actual nations, or the same person or nation at two actual points of time. The use of 'counter-factual', if any, may not, therefore, take the rather straightforward form it tends to take in the usual 'virtual displacement' (or marginalist) analysis (e.g. what *would have* happened if this person had a different bundle of commodities at the *same* point of time, with the *same* utility function?). In making comparisons of actual living standards, there may be no reasonable basis for assuming the same utility function—the same desires, wants, temperament, and so forth.

The distinction concerns the contrast between 'comprehensive comparisons' and 'situational comparisons', discussed in Sen (1976), (1979). Comparisons of standard of living need not be confined only to situational comparisons (e.g. 'I am better off this year than I would have been if I had last year's commodity bundle this year'). They may call for comprehensive comparisons (e.g. 'I am better off this year than I was last year'). We cannot, then, just vary the commodity bundles and keep the utility *functions* (and related correspondences) *necessarily* unchanged. If the utility-functional characteristics are indeed unchanged, then this would be a further fact, and not just a part of the standard counterfactual exercise.

2. Alternative approaches

There are at least three general approaches to the notion of the standard of living of a person. The first is to see the living standard as some notion of the *utility* of a person. The second is some notion of *opulence*. The third is to see the standard of living as one type of *freedom*. The former two approaches have been more explored than the third, though—to put my cards on the table—it is the third that I would argue for in this essay.[2] But I begin with utility and opulence.

The utility view of the standard of living is well presented by Pigou himself. In fact, Pigou uses 'economic welfare', 'the standard of living', 'standard of real income' and 'material prosperity' as more or less synonymous (e.g., Pigou (1952), pp. 100–1, 622–3, 758–767). Economic welfare is defined, as was already stated, as 'a part of welfare as a whole' (p. 12), and 'the elements of welfare' are seen as '*states of consciousness* and, perhaps, their relations' (p. 10, italics added).

It is fair to recognize that the notion of 'utility' has, by now, several distinct meanings. Pigou (1962) himself distinguishes between 'satisfaction' and the 'intensity of desire', referring to the latter as 'desiredness' (p. 23).

---

[2] I have tried to do this elsewhere in greater detail, viz., in my Hennipman Lecture (April 1982), forthcoming as a monograph, *Commodities and Capabilities*, Sen (1984a).

As a loyal 'consciousness-utilitarian', Pigou does not dispute the claim of satisfaction to be the *authentic* version of utility or welfare, and defends the desiredness view (and the willingness-to-pay measure) *contingently* by asserting that 'it is fair to suppose that most commodities, especially those of wide consumption that are required, as articles of food and clothing are, for direct personal use, will be wanted as a means to satisfaction, and will, consequently, be desired with intensitites proportional to the satisfactions they are expected to yield' (p. 24).

It would appear that the more dominant schools of utilitarianism today take a 'desire' view of utility rather than the 'satisfaction' view, and put value on the fulfilment of what is desired rather than on the amount of satisfaction it generates (see Sidgwick (1874), Ramsey (1926), Harsanyi (1976), Hare (1981), Mirrlees (1982)).[3] The battle is by no means over (see Gosling (1969), Brandt (1979), among others), and there are indeed many complex issues involved (see Sen (1981), Griffin (1982)). But this need not detain us here, since it is necessary, for our purpose, to discuss *both* the 'satisfaction' view and the 'desiredness' view of utility, and related to this, to examine the two corresponding views of the standard of living (seen in terms of utility).

The identification of the living standard with *overall* utility as such is obviously open to the problem that was discussed in the last section—the problem that had led Pigou to introduce the notion of 'economic welfare' in the first place. If the standard of living has to be seen in terms of utility, then distinctions of Pigou's type would have to be made.

The second approach—that of living standard as *opulence*—goes back at least to Adam Smith (1776). The concern with a nation being 'better or worse supplied with all the necessaries and conveniences for which it has occasion' (vol. 1, p. 1) is a concern with the opulence of the nation. Indeed, Adam Smith thought that the two objectives of 'political economy, considered as a branch of the science of a statesman or legislator' were 'first, to provide a plentiful revenue or subsistence for the people, or more properly to enable them to provide such revenue or subsistence for themselves; and secondly, to supply the state or commonwealth with a revenue sufficient for the public services.' 'The different progress of opulence in different ages and nations has given occasion to two different systems of political economy with regard to enriching the people' (vol. 1, p. 375).

The modern literature on real income indicators and the indexing of commodity bundles[4] is the inheriter of this tradition of evaluating opulence. Since this evaluation is often done with respect to an indifference map, it is tempting to think of this approach as the utility approach in disguise. But

---

[3] There is a third view, quite popular among economists, that definitionally identifies the utility ranking with the binary relation of choice. As an approach it begs more questions than it answers (see Hicks (1958), Sen (1982a)). It is also particularly unsuited for interpersonal or intertemporal comparison so essential for studies of living standards, since people do not actually face the choice of being someone else, or living at some other time.

[4] The literature has been surveyed and critically examined in Sen (1979).

there is an important difference even when the evaluation of real income is done in terms of an indifference map representing preference, since what is being evaluated is not utility as such (in the form either of desiredness or of satisfaction), but *the commodity basis of utility*. The two approaches will be congruent only under the special assumption of constancy of the utility *function* (not to be confused with the constancy of tastes). As was discussed in Section 1, of this paper, this is a bad assumption for measuring the standard of living (even if it is acceptable for rational choice or planning involving counterfactual comparison of alternative possibilities). The distinction will be further discussed in the next section.

The third approach—that of freedom—is not much in fashion in the literature on the standard of living, but I believe it has much promise. Freedom here is interpreted in its 'positive' sense (to be free to *do this* or *be that*) rather than in its 'negative' form (not to be interfered with).[5] In this approach what is valued is the *capability* to live well, and in the specific economic context of standard of living, it values the capabilities associated with economic matters (see Sen (1980, 1984a)).

To illustrate the contrast involved, consider the problem of food and hunger. In the capability approach a person's ability to live without hunger or malnutrition may be valued. This does not amount to valuing the possession of a given amount of food as such, except indirectly through causal links, in a contingent way (since the impact of food on nutrition varies with such factors as metabolic rates, body size, climatic conditions, sex, pregnancy, lactation, and work intensity). Nor does it involve equating the value of the freedom from hunger or from malnutrition with the *utility* (happiness, pleasure, or desire-fulfilment) from that achievement. More will have to be said on these contrasts presently, since some complex issues are involved (see Sections 3 and 4 below).

I should like to assert that focusing on capability as freedom in the context of judging living standard is not a new approach. Its lineage certainly goes back to classical political economy, even though it may not have been explicitly stated in this form. Freedom was very much a classical concern. In fact, even in the statement about opulence that I quoted from Adam Smith earlier in this section, Smith modifies his reference to providing 'a plentiful revenue or subsistence for the people', by the statement, 'more properly to enable them to provide such revenue or subsistence for themselves' (vol. i, p. 375). In a different context (dealing in fact with the value of negative freedom), Hicks (1959) has pointed out that the classical backing for 'economic freedom' went deeper than justifying it on grounds of 'economic efficiency'. The efficiency proposition, as Hicks (1959) notes, 'was no more than a secondary support', and Hicks is certainly right to question the justification for our 'forgetting, as completely as most of us have done, the

---

[5] See Berlin (1969) for the contrast between 'positive' and 'negative' views of freedom. Berlin's own focus is on the 'negative' approach because of his concern with liberty as such. The nature of the contrast is further discussed in Sen (1982b), (1984b).

other side of the argument' dealing with the value of economic freedom as such (p. 138).

When it comes to evaluating what counts as 'necessaries', with the supply of which Adam Smith was so concerned, Smith (1776) does go explicitly into certain quite complex capabilities, e.g. the freedom to appear in public without shame (vol. ii, p. 352):

A linen shirt, for example, is, strictly speaking, not a necessary of life. The Greeks and Romans lived, I suppose, very comfortably though they had no linen. But in the present times, through the greater part of Europe, a creditable day-labourer would be ashamed to appear in public without a linen shirt, the want of which would be supposed to denote that disgraceful degree of poverty which, it is presumed, nobody can well fall into without extreme bad conduct. Custom, in the same manner, had rendered leather shoes a necessary of life in England. The poorest creditable person of either sex would be ashamed to appear in public without them.

Following Smith's reasoning, I have tried to argue elsewhere (Sen (1983)) that *absolute deprivation* on the space of capabilities (e.g., whether one can appear in public without shame) may follow from *relative deprivation* on the space of commodities (e.g., whether one possesses what others do, such as linen shirts or leather shoes in Smith's example). Some of the apparent conflicts in defining poverty (e.g. the 'relative' versus the 'absolute' views) may be avoided by seeing living standard in terms of capabilities and assessing the value of commodity possession in terms of its contribution to capabilities and freedoms.

The possibility of judging advantage in terms of the extent of freedom has been also discussed by Karl Marx (1846), (1858), (1875), and John Stuart Mill (1859), (1869). The roots of the capability approach and freedom-based evaluation of the standard of living, thus, go back to Smith, Marx, and Mill, among others. The standard of living—and economic freedom in the 'positive' sense—can be seen as relating to 'positive freedom' in general in ways that are not altogether dissimilar to the relationship between 'economic welfare' and 'welfare' in general. The standard of living, on this view, reflects the 'material' aspects of freedom.[6]

3. Utility, opulence and material capabilities

The exact distinction between the utility approach and the opulence approach to the standard of living is worth investigating. If the commodity

---

[6] Note, however, that the test of whether something 'can be brought directly or indirectly into relation with the measuring-rod of money' (Pigou (1952), p. 11) may be a misleading one in examining the basis of 'material prosperity'. Many 'public goods' are not purchasable, e.g. a road or a park, but quite important for material prosperity (and presumably for economic welfare). So is the absence of crime or pollution, though none of these things are offered for sale in the market. There are many complicated issues in deciding on what counts as 'material' but it can be argued that the measuring-rod of money is not central to the idea of 'material prosperity'.

bundles under the opulence approach is evaluated not in terms of preference maps but in terms of costs, then the contrast would be straightforward. One of the things we have been taught by John Hicks is the need to recognize that the 'utility' method and the 'cost' method provide two *alternative* ways of evaluating real income, and that each has distinct—and quite different— merits of its own (Hicks (1940), (1958)). And while in 'equilibrium' theory the two work *together*, in the evaluation of commodity bundles, they provide *rival* methods of assessment.[7] If opulence is evaluated by the 'cost method', then that might easily lead to measures quite different from those yielded by utility weighting. This is a straightforward contrast, once Hicks's distinction is noted.

But suppose we do use the 'utility' method to evaluate commodity bundles. Would we then get an index that is an index of utilities? Not necessarily. *Weighting by utilities* (marginal utilities, to be exact) is not the same thing as *measuring utilities*. Consider the following example. A given person has utility function $U_1(.)$ in period 1 when he enjoys commodity vector x_1 and utility function $U_2(.)$ in period 2 when he has commodity vector x_2. The ordering of the four utilities is the following, in descending order:

$$U_1(x_2)$$
$$U_1(x_1)$$
$$U_2(x_2)$$
$$U_2(x_1).$$

There is no change in 'taste', as it is usually defined in economics, as given by the indifference map, or by what is observed in market behaviour. In both periods the person prefers x_2 to x_1. In terms of indexing the commodity bundles—the ranking of opulence—the bundle enjoyed in the second period x_2 is clearly better than that in the first period x_1. But while opulence is greater in the second period, utility is higher in the first, since $U_1(x_1) > U_2(x_2)$. Ranking commodity bundles *according to utility* is not the same as ranking *utilities*.

Pigou seems to get into a bit of a muddle on this issue. 'Considering a single individual', says Pigou (1952), 'whose tastes are taken as fixed, we say that his dividend in period II is greater than in period I if the items that are added to it in period II are items that he *wants more* than the items that are taken away from it in period II' (p. 51). Quite right that, if by 'dividend' we mean some index of opulence. What goes wrong is the belief about 'economic welfare' being 'intimately associated' with the size of this divi- dend. Pigou notices some lack of intimacy when tastes change, or—in the case of national dividend—when the distribution of purchasing power changes, but the problem is present even with individual dividend and even without any change of taste whatsoever. Pigou is quite right in thinking that

[7] See also Fisher and Shell (1968), (1972), and Sen (1979).

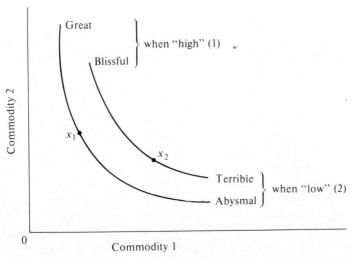

Fig. 1. A person with unchanging tastes and changing utility levels.

with constant tastes, in the case of an individual (when the issue of distribution does not arise), 'this method of definition' (in terms of willingness to pay) 'would be the natural and obvious one to adopt' and 'there would be nothing to set against the advantages of this method of definition' (p. 52). But the definition would not be that of economic welfare (or of the *utility*-view of standard of living), nor necessarily correspond to it. It would be—under the circumstances specified—quite a nice definition of *opulence* (and the commodity-index view of standard of living).

To illustrate the nature of the problem, consider a person who moves from being 'high' (and nearly manic) in state 1 to being 'low' (and quite depressive) in state 2, with an unchanged indifference map. Figure 1 reflects a part of the constant preference map (two indifference curves to be exact).

In both his 'high' and 'low' states (i.e. in both states 1 and 2), he prefers (and gets more utility from) x_2 than from x_1. He is clearly more *opulent* with x_2 than with x_1. But in state 2, when he does have x_2, he is pretty badly off ('terrible', to be candid), compared with what he is in state 1, when he had x_1 (and when he found his position to be 'great'). The ranking of utility is as clear as the ranking of commodity bundles, except that the two go in opposite directions.

This problem would, of course, be avoided had the real utility function (and not just the preference map and the class of its real-valued representations) remained the same. In 'counterfactual' exercises involving 'virtual displacement' *that* would be definitionally guaranteed. That counterfactual exercise may be perfectly sensible for a theory of planning or of rational

[8] See Sen (1979), pp. 12–13.

choice, but—as was argued in Section 1—it is quite inappropriate for comparing *actual* standards of living.

While the example chosen here deals with a purely psychological variation, to wit, between being 'high' and 'low', the utility function can vary for other reasons as well. There could be more pollution in the air, or more crime on the streets, or a touch of '1984' in our daily lives. The commodity bundle x_2 may well be invariably preferred to commodity bundle x_1, and still the person may be in a terrible way in state 2—much worse off than in state 1. It is, of course, possible to go on inventing new '*as if* commodities' (e.g., fresh air, not-being-mugged, non-snooping) to extend the *reach* of the commodity-index view. But such 'extensions' are not easy to reconcile with the uses to which the commodity approach is put. Also, the need for 'inventing' a new commodity always remains so long as there is a functional relation $U(x)$, which can vary, no matter how 'extensively' x is defined.

Which of the two approaches—utility or opulence—is a more appropriate way of seeing the standard of living? I do not know the answer to that question, but I cannot believe that either is very appropriate. In the cases under discussion, the purchased commodity bundle is better *and* utility is lower. If the utility function has changed due to purely emotional reasons (e.g., the person has lost faith in God), and not for any 'material' reason, it is not unreasonable to go with the opulence ranking in pronouncing on the living standard. It is then plausible to say that the standard of living has risen, but the person is more depressed, more unhappy, *despite* that. He may even be able to do many more things in the second period than he could in the first. But he values them less. Bad luck for him, but the badness of the luck is not due to a decline in the standard of living.

But now vary the *interpretation* of the changed utility function. It turns out, let us imagine, that the utility function $U(.)$ has dipped because of pollution in the air, thugs on the street, and snoopers peering through the window. The purchased commodity bundle may be valued higher, but the person cannot do many material things he could do in the earlier period. He cannot breathe fresh air (or avoid some lung disease); he cannot walk around freely after dark; and he cannot have privacy. It would be absurd, in this case, to say that the standard of living of this person has gone up just because the commodity bundle purchased in the second period is higher in both periods.

The message seems clear enough. Neither the utility view nor the commodity-index view will do as a *general* approach to the standard of living. The limited success of each is contingent on certain particular circumstances, which may or may not, respectively, obtain.

Before I end this section, I make two further remarks. First, the difficulties in question with the utility view can arise no matter whether we choose the 'satisfaction' interpretation or the 'desiredness' interpretation. This is easily checked by assuming conditions such that satisfaction and desiredness go together—an assumption that Pigou (1952) did in fact make (pp. 23–4).

The person desires x_2 more than x_1 in each period, and would get more satisfaction from x_2 than from x_1 in either period. But he desires having utility function $U_1(.)$ with commodity bundle x_1 *more than* having utility function $U_2(.)$ with commodity bundle x_2, and he also gets more satisfaction with $U_1(x_1)$ than with $U_2(x_2)$. Everything substantial said before stands, no matter which of the two interpretations of utility we choose.

The second remark concerns the *nature of the argument* that was used to criticize universal use of either the utility view or the commodity-index view of standard of living. We referred to various things the person could or could not do under each circumstances. We invoked the person's capabilities and checked the person's particular freedoms. In the pollution–crime–1984 example, the argument against the commodity-index view rested on noting that in the second period the person could not breathe fresh air, walk around freely, or have privacy. There was, however no corresponding decline in material capabilities in the emotional-variation example (even though the capability to be happy in general was affected), and that is why, in that case, the commodity-view of standard of living seemed tentatively untarnished and certainly more relevant than the utility view. So we have, in fact, already used the capability approach to tell between the contingent appeals of the utility view and the commodity-index view. It seems natural to go on to approach the standard of living directly in terms of capabilities.

It is also worth emphasizing, to avoid ambiguity, that in focusing on particular capabilities in the two contrasting cases, we looked at those freedoms that can be seen as being associated with what Pigou calls 'material prosperity', rather than purely psychological factors. Clearly, in the emotional variation case, there is something the person is obviously not capable of achieving in the second period, to wit, to be happy. But we concentrated on a particular class of capabilities, particular types of positive freedoms, related to *material* living conditions.

The distinction between 'material' and other capabilities is not, of course, entirely clear-cut. Nor is it always very important. Its importance in the context of the analysis of the standard of living lies primarily in the fact that the standard of living figures in common usage in a form that specifically emphasizes material capabilities (e.g., being well-nourished or motorized is taken to be a part of 'the living standard' in a way that fulfilment of poetic ambitions or even being generally cheerful is not). However, even when that usage is granted, it can be asked why should it be appropriate to attach any importance at all to that distinction and regard 'the living standard'—thus conceived—to be particularly worthy of the economist's attention. At this point, a difficult issue of valuation is involved, and the answer may be similar to Pigou's motivation in being concerned specifically with economic welfare. Living standard—seen in terms of material capabilities—may be thought to be more influenceable (certainly, more *directly* influencible) by economic policy. I should emphasize that this justification, which is not without force, is however, a strongly contingent one, and may in some contexts simply not be an adequate ground for being concerned with the material capabilities only (as reflected in the standard of living). In the present—more limited context—we are primarily concerned with *interpreting* the notion of the living standard, rather than examining how important a concept it is.

4. Functioning, capability, and freedom

The distinction between commodities, utility, functioning, and the capability to function, may not be altogether transparent, and call for some explanation.[9] Consider a good, e.g., bread. The utilitarian will be concerned with the fact that bread creates utility—happiness or desire-fulfilment—through its consumption. This is, of course, true. But creating utility is not the only thing that bread does. It also contributes to nutrition, among other things. In modern consumer theory in economics, the nature of the goods has been seen in terms of their 'characteristics'. Gorman (1956), Lancaster (1966) and other economists have systematically explored the view of goods as bundles of characteristics. Bread possesses nutrition-giving characteristics (calories, protein, etc.), but also other characteristics, e.g., providing stimulation, meeting social conventions, helping get-togethers.[10] A characteristic—as used in consumer theory—is a feature of a good, whereas a capability is a feature of a person in relation to goods. Having some bread gives me the capability of functioning in particular ways, e.g., being free from hunger, or living without certain nutritional deficiencies.

Four different notions need to be distinguished in this context. There is the notion of a *good* (e.g. bread); *characteristic of a good* (e.g. calories and other nutrients); that of *functioning of a person* (e.g. the person living without calorie deficiency); that of *utility* (e.g. the pleasure or desire-fulfilment from eating bread or from being well-nourished). An utility-based theory of living standard concentrates on the last item of the four—utility. Analyses of living standard in terms of opulence or 'real income' tend to concentrate on the first item—commodities. Egalitarians concerned with income distribution worry about the distribution of goods, and they too will focus on the first item. These two approaches can be refined by taking explicit note of characteristics, in line with the second item.

'Characteristics' are, of course, abstractions from goods, but they do relate ultimately to *goods* rather than to *persons*. 'Functionings' are, however, personal features; they tell us what a person is doing or achieving. 'Capability' to function reflects what a person *can* do or *can* achieve. Of course, the characteristics of goods owned by a person would *relate* to the capabilities of that person. A person achieves these capabilities through—among other things—the use of these goods. But the capabilities of persons are quite

---

[9] See also Sen (1982a), pp. 29–31, 353–69.
[10] See Scitovsky (1976), Douglas and Isherwood (1979), Deaton and Muellbauer (1980), and other explorations of different types of characteristics associated with consumption.

different from (though dependent on) the characteristics of goods possessed. Valuing one has *implications* on wanting the other, but valuing one is *not the same thing* as valuing the other.

If, for example, we value a person's ability to function without nutritional deficiency, we would favour arrangements in which the person has adequate food with those nutritional characteristics, but that is not the same thing as valuing the possession of a given amount of food as such. If, for example, some disease makes the person unable to achieve the capability of avoiding nutritional deficiency even with an amount of the food that would suffice for others,[11] then the fact that he or she does possess that amount of food would not in any way 'neutralize' the person's inability to be well nourished. If we value the capability to function, then that is what we do value, and the possession of goods with the corresponding characteristics is only instrumentally valued and that again only to the extent that it helps in the achievement of the things that we do value (viz. capabilities).

Consider now one more example, to explain the motivation behind looking at capabilities for assessing the standard of living. Take two persons A and B. A is rather less poor than B, eats rather more food, and works no harder. But he is also undernourished, which B is not, since B has a smaller body size (coming from Kerala rather than Punjab, say), has a lower metabolic rate, and lives in a warmer climate. So A eats more but B is better nourished. However, it so happens that A is religious, contented with his fate, and happier than B, and has his desires more fulfilled than has B, who keeps grumbling about his lot. In the way this example has been constructed, A is doing better than B *both* in terms of commodity-index and utility (in fact, under *each* interpretation of utility: satisfaction and desire fulfilment). That is for sure, but does that imply that A has a higher standard of living? Rickety old A, chronically undernourished, riddled with avoidable morbidity, and reconciled—by the 'opium' of religion—to a lower expectation of life? It would be hard to claim, under these circumstances, that A does indeed have a higher standard of living than B. He may earn more, eat more, and may be less dissatisfied, but he does not have the capability to be well-nourished in the way B is, nor is he free from malnutrition-related diseases. Indeed, it would be hard not to say that it is B who has a higher standard of living despite *both* his unhappiness and lower income than A.

The issue of capabilities—specifically 'material' capabilities—is particularly important in judging the standard of living of people in poor countries. Are they well nourished? Are they free from avoidable morbidity? Do they live long? Can they read and write? Can they count? And so on. It is also important in dealing with poverty in rich countries (as I have tried to argue elsewhere, Sen (1983)). Can they take part in the life of the community (cf. Townsend (1979))? Can they appear in public without shame and without

[11] On the variability of the relation between food intake and nutritional achievements and the existence of multiple equilibria, see, among other works, Sukhatme (1977), Scrimshaw (1977), and Srinivasan (1982).

feeling disgraced (to go back to a question asked by Adam Smith (1776))? Can they find worthwhile jobs? Can they keep themselves warm? Can they use their school education? Can they visit friends and relations if they choose? It is a question of what the persons can do or can be, and not just a question of their earnings and opulence, nor of their being contented. Freedom is the issue; not commodities, nor utility as such.

It is, however, worth re-emphasizing that the thesis here is not that there is no distinction between freedom—even 'positive freedom' in general—and living standard. That would be an absurd claim. It is rather that living standard can be seen as freedom (positive freedom) of particular types, related to material capabilities. It reflects a variety of freedoms of the material kind (e.g. to be able to live long, to be well-nourished, to take part in the life of the community). It does not cover all types of freedom (e.g. religious freedom). Some of the others may be very important, but not a part of the normal concept of the standard of living. Indeed, the living standard may be seen as corresponding to positive freedom in general in the way that Pigou's 'economic welfare' may be seen as corresponding to welfare as such (see Section 1 and 3 above). It is in this sense that living standard can be seen as 'economic freedom'.

It may, of course, be pointed out that the rejection of opulence or utility as the basis of assessing standard of living, does not establish the relevance of freedom as such. There is scope for ambiguity in the arguments presented. We may well value what a person *does* (or actually *achieves*) rather than what he *can do* (or *can achieve*), which is what freedom has to be concerned with. Should we not, for example, look directly at *nourishment* as such rather than the *capability to be nourished*?

There is, I believe, substance in this line of questioning, but it is not as persuasive as it may first appear. What about the ascetic who decides to fast and becomes undernourished despite his being rich and having the means of being excellently nourished? It seems rather odd to see him as deprived, with a low standard of living. He has chosen to fast; he was not forced to fast.

Capability *is* of importance. To take another example, the *capability* to visit friends and relatives may be important for standard of living. However, a person who chooses not to make use of that capability, and curls up instead with a good book, may not be sensibly seen as being deprived and having a low standard of living.

It does seem plausible to concentrate on a person's capabilities and freedoms as indicators of living standard. Variations of tastes can be accommodated more easily in a format that focuses on the capability to function in different ways rather than just on particular functionings. Also, uncertainty about our own future tastes makes us value freedom more. But on top of that some importance may be attached to the power a person has over his or her own life—that a person is not forced by circumstances to lead a specific type of life and has a genuine freedom to choose as he wants. The standard of living has much to do with what Marx described as 'replacing the domination of circumstances and chance over individuals by the domination of individuals over chance and circumstances'.[12]

5. Difficulties

I am not under any illusion that the capability approach to the standard of living would be very easy to use. It is particularly difficult to get an idea of a person's positive freedom of choice—what he or she could or could not have done or been. What we observe are the actual choices and realizations. But the case for using the capability approach is not, of course, logistic convenience but *relevance*.

In some practical exercises with the capability approach, the logistic problems have not proved to be quite so hard as to make the effort to use existing data worthless. For example, in an exercise on checking the nature and extent of 'sex bias' in living standards in India (see Kynch and Sen (1983)), the approach has proved to be quite convenient. In fact, even the informational problems have been, if anything, eased by moving attention away from food consumption data of *particular members* of the family (almost impossible to get) to observed nutrition, morbidity, mortality, and so forth. Indeed, the move from individual *commodity consumption* to individual *functioning* would often tend to make the data problem easier, even though to identify *capability sets* fully, much harder data requirements would have to be imposed.

I end by noting three important issues that are particularly difficult to deal with. First, when there is diversity of taste, it becomes harder to surmise about capability by simply observing achievement. For extreme poverty this problem is less serious. Valuing better nourishment, less illness and longer life tend to be fairly universal, and also largely consistent with each other despite being distinct objectives. But in other cases—of greater relevance to the richer countries—the informational problems with the capability approach can be quite serious.

Second, if capabilities of different sorts have to be put together in one index, the issue of aggregation may be quite a difficult one even for a given person. There is, in addition, the problem of group aggregation. I have tried to discuss these issues elsewhere (Sen (1976), (1979), (1984a)), and the picture is far from hopeless. But I must confess that they are indeed hard problems to tackle, requiring a good deal of compromise. It is, however, worth mentioning that for many problems, an *aggregate* ranking is not needed, and for most, a *complete* aggregate ordering is quite redundant.

Third, freedom is a set (rather than just a 'point'), in the sense that it refers to various alternative bundles of things one could have done and not just to the particular bundle one did do. This makes the evaluation of 'capability sets' rather unlike that of evaluating utility or indexing commod-

---

[12] See Marx (1846); English translation from McLellan (1977), p. 190.

ity bundles. Often it will indeed make sense to identify the value of the set of capabilities with the worth of the 'best' element in the set, and this reduces the set-evaluation problem to a derived element-evaluation exercise. But in other contexts, the value of the 'best' element does not capture the value of freedom adequately. For example, if we remove from the feasibility set all elements other than the best one, the utility level that can be achieved with a given utility function may not be affected, but in a very real sense the person's freedom *is* reduced. In interpreting standard of living in terms of feedom (related to material capabilities), a different range of complex issues have to be faced that do not quite arise under the utility or the opulence approaches.

Nevertheless, if standard of living is best seen in terms of capabilities (as positive freedoms of particular types), then these complexities simply have to be faced. The standard of living is one of the central notions of economics. And it is one of the subjects that do interest the general public, specifically in the context of policy. In directing attention to these questions, economists such as Adam Smith, Pigou, and Hicks have taken on issues that are complex *as well as* of deep and lasting importance.

Even if data limitations may quite often force us to make practical compromises, conceptual clarity requires that we do not smugly elevate such a compromise to a position of unquestioned significance. Hicks has explained his attitude towards welfare economics thus:

> I have been trying to show that 'welfare economics', as I would now regard it, is composed of a series of steps, steps by which we try to take more and more of the things which concern us into account. None of our 'optima' marks the top of that staircase. We must always be prepared to push one, if we can, a little further (Hicks (1981), p. xvii).

It has been argued in this paper that the capability approach to the standard of living will be a step foward—certainly conceptually and perhaps even in actual empirical application.

All Souls College, Oxford

REFERENCES

Arrow, K. J. (1951). *Social Choice and Individual Values*, New York: Wiley.
Bergson, A. (1938). 'A Reformulation of Certain Aspects of Welfare Economics', *Quarterly Journal of Economics*, 52.
Berlin, I. (1969). *Four Essays on Liberty*, Oxford: Clarendon Press.
Brandt, R. (1979), *A Theory of the Good and the Right*, Oxford: Clarendon Press.
Deaton, A. and Muellbauer, J. (1980). *Economics and Consumer Behaviour*, Cambridge University Press.
Douglas, M. and Isherwood, B. (1979), *The World of Goods*, New York: Basic Books.
Fisher, F. M. and Shell, K. (1968), 'Tastes and Quality Change in the Pure Theory of the True Cost-of-Living Index', in J. N. Wolfe, ed., *Value, Capital and Growth: Papers in Honour of Sir John Hicks*, Edinburgh University Press.

FISHER, F. M. and SHELL, K. (1972), *The Economic Theory of Price Indices*, New York: Academic Press.

GORMAN, W. M. (1956). 'The Demand for Related Goods', *Journal Paper J3129*, Iowa Experimental Station, Ames, Iowa.

GOSLING, J. C. B. (1969), *Pleasure and Desire*, Oxford: Clarendon Press.

GRAAFF, J. de V. (1957), *Theoretical Welfare Economics*, Cambridge University Press.

GRIFFIN, J. (1982). 'Modern Utilitarianism', *Revue internationale de philosophie*, 141.

HARE, R. M. (1981), *Moral Thinking*, Oxford: Clarendon Press.

HARSANYI, J. (1976). *Essays on Ethics, Social Behaviour and Scientific Explanation*, Dordrecht: Reidel.

HICKS, J. R. (1939a), *Value and Capital*, Oxford: Clarendon Press.

HICKS, J. R. (1939b), 'Foundations of Welfare Economics', *Economic Journal*, 49; reprinted in Hicks (1981).

HICKS, J. R. (1940), 'Valuation of Social Income', *Economica*, 7; reprinted in Hicks (1981).

HICKS, J. R. (1958), 'The Measurement of Real Income', *Oxford Economic Papers*, 10; reprinted in Hicks (1981).

HICKS, J. R. (1959). 'A Manifesto', in *Essays in World Economics*, Oxford: Clarendon Press; reprinted in Hicks (1981), to which the page references relate.

HICKS, J. R. (1975), 'The Scope and Status of Welfare Economics', *Oxford Economic Papers*, 27; reprinted in Hicks (1981), to which the page references relate.

HICKS, J. R. (1981), *Wealth and Welfare, Collected Essays on Economic Theory*, vol. I, Oxford: Blackwell.

HICKS, J. R. (1983), ' A Discipline Not a Science', in his *Classics and Moderns, Collected Essays on Economic Theory*, vol. III, Oxford: Blackwell.

KALDOR, N. (1939), 'Welfare Propositions and Interpersonal Comparisons of Utility, *Economic Journal*, 49.

KYNCH, J., and SEN, A. K. (1983). 'Indian Women: Well-being and Survival', *Cambridge Journal of Economics*, 7.

LANCASTER, K. J. (1966), 'A New Approach to Consumer Theory', *Journal of Political Economy*, 74.

LITTLE, I. M. D. (1950), *A Critique of Welfare Economics*, Oxford: Clarendon Press; 2nd ed., 1957.

MARX, K. (1846), *The German Ideology*, jointly with F. Engels; English translation, Moscow: Foreign Language Publishing Press, 1964.

MARX, K. (1858), *Grundrisse*; English translation, Harmondsworth: Penguin, 1973.

MARX, K. (1875), *Critique of the Gotha Program*; English translation, New York: International Publishers.

MCLELLAN, D. (1977), ed., *Karl Marx: Selected Writings*, Oxford: Oxford University Press.

MILL, J. S. (1859), *On Liberty*; republished Harmondsworth: Penguin, 1974.

MILL, J. S. (1869), *On the Subjection of Women*; republished London: Dent, 1970.

MIRRLEES, J. A. (1982). 'The Economic Uses of Utilitarianism', in Sen and Williams (1982).

PIGOU, A. C. (1952), *The Economics of Welfare*, Fourth Edition, with eight new appendices, London: Macmillan.

RAMSEY, F. P. (1926). 'Truth and Probability'; republished in his *Foundations: Essays in Philosophy, Logic, Mathematics and Economics*, London: Routledge, 1978.

SAMUELSON, P. A. (1947), *Foundations of Economic Analysis*, Cambridge, Mass.: Harvard University Press.

SCITOVSKY, T. (1976), *The Joyless Economy*, London: Oxford University Press.

SCRIMSHAW, N. S. (1977). 'Effect of Infection on Nutrient Requirements', *American Journal on Clinical Nutrition*, 30.

SEN, A. K. (1976). 'Real National Income', *Review of Economic Studies*, 43; reprinted in Sen (1982a).

SEN, A. K. (1979). 'The Welfare Basis of Real Income Comparisons', *Journal of Economic Literature*, 17; reprinted in Sen (1984c).

SEN, A. K. (1980). 'Equality of What?' in S. McMurrin, eds., *Tanner Lectures on Human Values*, vol. I, Cambridge University Press; reprinted in Sen (1982*a*).

SEN, A. K. (1981). 'Plural Utility', *Proceedings of the Aristotelian Society*, 81.

SEN, A. K. (1982*a*), *Choice, Welfare and Measurement*, Oxford: Blackwell, and Cambridge, Mass.: MIT Press.

SEN, A. K. (1982*b*), 'Rights and Agency', *Philosophy and Public Affairs*, 11.

SEN, A. K. (1983). 'Poor, Relatively Speaking', *Oxford Economic Papers*, 35; reprinted in Sen (1984*c*).

SEN, A. K. (1984*a*), *Commodities and Capabilities*, Hennipman Lecture, 1982; to be published by North-Holland, Amsterdam.

SEN, A. K. (1984*b*), 'Rights and Capabilities', forthcoming in T. Honderich, ed., *Ethics and Objectivity*, Essays in Memory of John Mackie, to be published by Routledge, London.

SEN, A. K. (1984*c*). *Resources, Values and Development*. Oxford: Blackwell, and Cambridge, Mass.: Harvard University Press.

SEN, A. and WILLIAMS, B., ed. (1982), *Utilitarianism and Beyond*, Cambridge: Cambridge University Press.

SIDGWICK, H. (1874). *The Methods of Ethics*; 7th edn., London: Macmillan, 1907.

SMITH, A. (1776). *An Inquiry into the Nature and Causes of the Wealth of Nations*. Republished, London: Home University Library.

SRINIVASAN, T. N. (1982), 'Hunger: Defining It, Estimating Its Global Incidence and Alleviating It', mimeographed; forthcoming in D. Gale Johnson and E. Schuh, eds., *Role of Markets in the World Food Economy*.

SUKHATME, P. V. (1977). *Nutrition and Poverty*, New Delhi: Indian Agricultural Research Institute.

TOWNSEND, P. (1979), *Poverty in the United Kingdom*, London: Penguin.

DARWINISM AND ECONOMIC CHANGE*

By R. C. O. MATTHEWS

AMONG the most inspiring characteristics of John Hicks's work are its range and its capacity to cast new light on old problems by bringing together ways of thinking normally regarded as separate. In that spirit I propose to consider a topic on which he has made outstanding contributions—the theory of enonomic change, more particularly the theory of long-run historical change—in the light of an approach which as far as I know he has *not* much used, that of evolutionary biology. I shall consider one possible part of the mechanism of economic change, namely competitive selection, the economic equivalent of Darwinian natural selection in biology. In so doing, I shall make comparisons at some points with the biological selection process, the study of which is much more advanced both theoretically and empirically (though it remains a highly controversial subject). I do not mean to imply that the economic and biological processes are exactly analogous.[1]

1. Optimization and competitive selection

1.1. *Basic concepts*

Suppose that, in a given type of situation confronting an economic agent, there exist two alternative modes of behaviour, A and B. The economic agent may, for example, be an entrepreneur, and A and B alternative techniques of production. What is the process, other than chance, that may cause A to become generally adopted? Two possibilities may be distinguished.

(1) *Optimization.* Economic agents are rational and well informed. Before acting, they correctly perceive that A is the preferable course, and they adopt it. A distinction may be drawn between two sub-cases.

(1A) The choice in favour of A is made by perfectly *rational foresight* as soon as the option becomes available.

(1B) The choice in favour of A results from *learning*, that is to say by inference from the consequences of A and B in the past, as practised either by the economic agent himself or by others whose experience he can observe. The choice is this sub-case is subject to lags.

(2) *Competitive selection.* Economic agents, or at least some of them, are unable to discern the relative merits of A and B ex ante. Some choose A,

* I am much indebted for helpful comments to M. M. Bray, F. H. Hahn, R. E. Rowthorn, A. K. Sen, and to the participants in a seminar at Churchill College, Cambridge. Responsibility for remaining faults is entirely my own.

[1] In particular, although reasonably appropriate parallels can be drawn between economic processes and Darwinian ones, there is no counterpart in economics to the Mendelian theory of sexual reproduction which lies at the basis of classical genetics. Nor is there anything in economics corresponding to the sharp distinction that exists between animal species. For a general survey of biological approaches in economics, see Hirshleifer (1977).

some *B*. Those who choose *A* out-perform those who choose *B*. In the ensuing competition, *B*-users are presently eliminated by *A*-users, and option *B* is eliminated with them. The choice is indirect in the sense that the social choice between *A* and *B* results from the relative overall success of their practitioners, just as selection between genes occurs through the relative fitness of the organisms that embody them. Optimization is direct choice by the economic agent, competitive selection is indirect social choice through changes in the relative weights of different decision-makers, brought about through the working of the system.

Many choices are, of course, quite easy. So it would be absurd to suppose that optimization is ever unimportant. Equally, there cannot be such perfect foresight that people never make mistakes. Thus, although optimization and competitive selection are in themselves quite different processes, the question about their relative importance in practice must always be one of degree. Moreover, although the difference between optimization and competitive selection may reflect a difference in the mental processes of economic agents, it need not necessarily do so. People may always be trying their best to make the right choices, but their best may not be at all good, either because their powers are so feeble or because the problems are so difficult. Their attempts at optimization may then have no more than random chances of success.

I shall throughout use the term optimization to refer to *successful* attempts to make the right choice, where the success, moreover, is not just a matter of chance, like guessing rightly between heads and tails (I shall revert shortly to the question of the meaning of the distinction between chance and non-chance success). Attempts at optimization are liable to be unsuccessful in so far as there is defective knowledge. In circumstances where defective knowledge prevents rational foresight and learning from achieving the right decisions, adoption of the right choice throughout the economy will come about only, if at all, through competitive selection.

It will be noted that the criteria of choice are not identical in the two mechanisms, in that optimization maximizes utility and competitive selection maximizes survival. For the time being I shall disregard this distinction. Some of its consequences will be encountered in Section 2.1 below. One consequence is that selection processes may affect the outcome even in the absence of defective knowledge, by selecting against the modes of behaviour of those economic agents who deliberately choose to maximize something other than their survival (e.g. because of indolence or moral scruples).

A distinction may be drawn between two sub-cases of situations where knowledge is defective and where there is therefore scope for competitive selection:

(2A) *Uniformly defective knowledge* prevails among economic agents. They are all equally liable to make mistakes. Competition rewards those who happen by chance to choose the right mode of behaviour and selects in favour of that mode. This is the sub-case closest to genetic selection.

(2B) *Differentially defective knowledge* prevails among economic agents. Some of them are regularly more likely to make the right choices than others are. This case perhaps corresponds more nearly to the popular (political) notion of competitive selection, in which the able prosper and the less able go to the wall, carrying their inefficient modes of behaviour with them. Optimization and competitive selection here interact, in that the right choices made by the more able may be the consequence of optimization rather than luck, with competitive selection being required over only part of the field of economic agents.[2]

Even the less able will make some correct decisions by chance (e.g. they may have located their operations in the right region), and even the most able will find that some choices are too difficult to get right except by chance (e.g. choices dependent on future mineral discoveries). So sub-case (2B) will always be combined to some extent with elements of the kind of selection that occurs in sub-case (2A).

Since competitive selection between modes of behaviour works indirectly through the economic agents who practise them, it will not be effective unless there is consistency over time in the choices made by individual economic agents (this has similar effects to the requirements of 'heritability of traits'). If you sometimes choose A and sometimes B, and so do I, with neither of us more disposed in one direction than the other is, competition between us will not serve to eliminate the less efficient mode. A chance run of wrong choices, or a wrong choice on an important occasion, may eliminate one of us, but it will not affect the direction of future choices. The hypothesis of consistency can be justified by the assumption of *inertia*. People tend to go on doing what they were doing before, subject to stochastic variation. The postulate of inertia is itself quite a plausible one, capable of being derived from a variety of assumptions about the underlying mental processes. Thus inertia may reflect risk-avoidance or bounded rationality or satisficing (some interesting anthropological instances are described in Lumsden and Wilson (1981), pp. 72–4). However, the postulate will not always be valid. The fact that it is a necessary pre-condition of competitive selection is one of the reasons why competitive selection may not always work. For the same reason, the fact that competitive elimination of firms is observed to occur does not necessarily mean that competitive selection is going on between modes of behaviour.

Stochastic inertia also serves to explain how a new mode of behaviour (equivalent to a mutation), if it happens to be introduced, is able to gain a foothold and does not instantly disappear. However, inertia by itself would allow a new mode of behaviour to persist only through the life of one individual economic agent (whether an individual or a firm or other collec-

---

[2] Other forms of interaction are possible. One form is that postulated in satisficing models, in which the degree of competitive pressure affects the amount of care that people put with choices between options. Many authors have developed this kind of model; an early example was Downie (1953).

tive body). Longer persistence and transmission require *imitation*. Imitation of the kind most familiar to economists—Schumpeterian imitation—amounts to conscious learning, the deliberate choice of a new mode of behaviour because it looks better than an old one, and it therefore needs to be left aside in considering what may happen in circumstances where optimization fails. There are other forms of imitation, however. The introduction of a new mode of behaviour increases the repertory of modes from which other economic agents may make their choices, whether those choices are themselves based on optimization or whether they are random. In the latter case we may speak of non-optimizing imitation. A major example from outside economics of imitation that has no optimization characteristics is provided by the development of a spoken language over time—Latin evolved into Italian without any one consciously thinking that it was an improvement.

1.2. *The background in economic thought*

In the history of economic thought, pride of place has sometimes been given, as an explanation of reality, to optimization, and sometimes to competitive selection. Notions of competitive selection were prominent in Marshall, whose admiration for Darwin is well known, as is that of Marx. As economic theory became more formal, optimization gained ground, particularly optimization in the form of perfectly rational foresight. Its assumption of perfect knowledge obviously required qualification, but its other assumption, perfectly rational utility maximization, was and is more tenaciously adhered to. Most often, the assumption of rational utility maximization is seen as a substantive, refutable, assertion about economic behaviour; particularly has this been so in the work of the so-called economic imperialists, who have extended the application of economic concepts to traditionally alien domains like crime and the family. Sometimes the assumption has been seen merely as the definition of the kind of behaviour that falls within the scope of economics (Knight (1942)). In that case non-economic considerations may have to be adduced for the explanation of behaviour that is 'economic' in the broader sense of Marshall, that is to say concerned with the ordinary business of life. Either way, the assumption of rational optimization is commonly viewed as a distinctive feature of the economist's approach—and this is sometimes seen as a weakness in economics. Thus a leading biologist, seeking to explain what he sees as the surprising fact that game theory has proved to be more readily applicable to biology than to economics, has commented, 'there are good theoretical grounds to expect populations to evolve to stable states, whereas there are grounds for doubting whether human being always act rationally' (Maynard Smith (1982), p. vii).

Reaction against the optimization hypothesis among economists has come mainly from concern about bounded rationality. It can scarcely be disputed that rationality *is* bounded, because of the limitations of our mental pow-ers.[3] Organization of individuals into teams for purposes of decision-making may overcome some of these limitations but introduces others. The effects of bounded rationality may be difficult to distinguish, even in principle, from the effects of incomplete information: if someone acts on incomplete infor-mation, what does it matter whether the reason is that the information is not in his mental files or that he is incapable of extracting it from the files at the moment of decision? Anyway, a central place has to be given to incomplete information, due to one or both of these causes, in order to explain some leading economic phenomena. Without it, the competitive struggle—what is meant by competition in popular parlance—would be over before it started (Kirzner, 1964). So would economic growth, except in so far as it consisted purely of capital accumulation or population increase.

These objections apply with less force to optimization by learning than they do to optimization by rational foresight. But they do still apply there to some extent. Learning about the relative merits of alternative options may be a good deal more difficult in practice than it looks in theory. A producer may know that his marketing or his industrial relations are not going well, but it is a long step from that of knowing what (if any) specific change in policy would improve matters. If he has a piece of equipment that is always giving trouble, is the reason that its design is fundamentally faulty or that it needs some minor adjustments? Learning from the experience of com-petitors is even more difficult than learning from his own experience. He may know that a competitor is doing better than he is, but unless he knows why he will not be in a position to learn and imitate. The costs of individual processes and the profitability of individual product lines are commonly treated as matters of commercial secrecy just for that reason, to keep rivals guessing. Independently of incompleteness of information, imitation may be hampered by sunk costs, either because they cause a firm to go bankrupt before it can adapt or because of the demolition costs of existing physical, human or organizational capital.

Economists have been led by considerations such as these to invoke competitive selection as a supplement to optimization. Some economists have sought in competitive selection an alternative route to the conclusions that would follows from optimization by itself, and thereby to reinforce those conclusions. This is what Friedman did in his famous essay on methodology (1953). Competitive selection tends to be invoked particularly in connection with modes of behaviour that are too complex to be plausibly attributable to conscious optimization by the economic agents in question. Thus the leader of the economic imperialists, in a book that postulates some

[3] More controversially, it is sometimes suggested that apparent manifestations of bounded rationality reflect not only limited intellectual power but also certain deep-seated psychological tendencies to act in a particular way—tendencies which may have been conducive to fitness during the millennia when *homo sapiens* was evolving but are not necessarily conducive to it now (Lumsden and Wilson, (1981) and (1983)). For an enumeration of tendencies that appear to imply systematic irrationality, see Tversky and Kahneman (1974), Reijnders (1978).

very complicated maximizing operations, writes that, while utility maximization is central to his approach, he does not assume that human beings
consciously maximize (Becker, 1981, p. x). A similar view is often taken,
with varying degrees of explicitness, by writers of the school of the 'new
economic history' (such as many of the contributors to Floud and McCloskey (1981)).

Quite different is the approach of such writers as Boulding (1981) and
Nelson and Winter (1982),[4] who have used competitive selection models in
order to arrive at results that differ in important ways from those of
mainstream orthodoxy. These writers have seen competitive selection as one
part of a broader evolutionary approach to economic change.

1.3. *Modes of behaviour*

The more formal applications of competitive selection to economics in
recent times at first had reference to the theory of the firm (Alchian (1950)).
More relevant to general economic change, however, and closer to the
biological analogy, is its application to modes of behaviour, embodied in the
firm or other economic agent in the same sort of way that genes are
embodied in an organism. The term 'modes of behaviour' has so far been
used in this paper without much explanation. The concept now needs to be
looked at more closely.

The concept of modes of behaviour is taken from the broader field of
cultural evolution. Various names have been used in that literature, with
broadly similar meanings—memes (Dawkins (1976)), culturgens (Lumsden
and Wilson (1981)), and, in the economic context, routines (Nelson and
Winter (1982)). I shall stick to the neutral sounding term modes of behaviour, or modes for short. Modes of behaviour are, of course, an abstraction, in a way that genes are not, and the use of this kind of abstraction to
break down behaviour into a bundle of characteristic attributes (rather
reminiscent of Hume's treatment of personal identity) has been considered
objectionable reductionism by some social scientists (Leach (1981)). This
objection is perhaps likely to be less strongly felt by economists, who are
quite accustomed to the notion of discrete activities or discrete innovations
and techniques of production. Mode of behaviour is a better term in the
present context than technique, because it is broader, not so exclusively
suggestive of engineering. According to the purpose in hand, a mode of
behaviour can be defined either very broadly, so as to allow scope for
sub-modes within it, or else very narrowly. Some modes of behaviour may
be directly equivalent to decisions about production or consumption: using
diesel locomotives, or working nights, or relying on frozen food. Others may
affect production or consumption decisions more indirectly, though not

---

[4] Nelson and Winter's book, which incorporates and develops earlier published work by its
authors, is a major contribution on the subjects treated in the present paper and my
indebtedness to it will be apparent in many places.

necessarily to a less important extent: having a multi-divisional corporate structure, being a member of a craft union, or using insurance. An important class of modes of behaviour, possibly the most important class, are those concerned with responses to externally originating stimuli or signals. Some modes, like some genes, are directly translated one for one into observable traits; other modes may influence a variety of observable traits (the biological equivalent is known as pleiotropy) or else may produce observable traits only when in conjunction with other modes (polygenic inheritance).

The consideration that modes of behaviour may have broad applications or narrow ones is related to the question mentioned earlier about how to distinguish between cases where success in attempts at optimization is or is not due merely to chance. Whether the adoption of a correct decision on a single occasion was due to chance or skill is an unanswerable question in practice, and perhaps even in principle. The same may be said of correct decisions that are habitually made, as a result of inertia, in respect of a single narrowly defined class of choices. However, to the extent that an economic agent habitually makes right choices in a number of different types of decision, or in a number of different types of environment, then it is reasonable to say that he manifests skill rather than good luck. He will be enabled to do this if he is using certain modes of behaviour that have a good effect over a wide area—whatever the reasons for his adopting them in the first instance. Such modes may relate to the individual (he uses double-entry book-keeping, he avoids alcohol at lunch-time) or to groups of people co-operating in an organization (they have a good committee system or good promotion procedures). Greater or less success in optimization may thus itself result from the adoption of the right or wrong choice among certain wide-ranging (pleiotropic) modes of behaviour. In so far as such modes exist, and firms differ in their use of them, the situation will conform to sub-case (2B), differentially defective knowledge, rather than to sub-case (2A), uniformly defective knowledge. One might even regard successful optimization as itself a mode of behaviour, but this is unlikely to be a helpful way of looking at things unless one can be more specific about what makes for the success.[5]

---

[5] Throughout this paper I disregard strictly genetic factors and assume that there are no changes that are economically significant in the genetic make-up of *homo sapiens* over the periods we are concerned with. This assumption is safe enough in relation to a period of, say, 250 years, though perhaps not quite so safe in relation to a period of, say, 2,500 years. In this connection, reference to the apparently contrary belief held by Marshall may be of interest, not least because Appendix A of the *Principles* ('The Growth of Free Trade and Enterprise') covers much the same theme as Hicks's *Theory of Economic History* to which I shall be referring below. Marshall's treatment has the same grand sweep as Hicks's and, like Hicks, he assigns large importance to changes in institutions and to liberation from the rule of custom. The peculiar feature is the stress that Marshall puts on national character, using frequently such words as race and natural selection. In some passages the meaning is clearly not intended to be genetic and refers rather to the set of modes of behaviour that have been fostered by a nation's historical circumstances (including particularly its geography and climate, rather than in the manner of Braudel's *La Méditerranée*). But he also makes such remarks as a 'a process of natural selection brought to [England's] shores those members of each successive migration

1.4. *Competitive selection and the evolutionary view of economic change*

We are interested in economic change rather than stationary equilibrium. Competitive selection is only one phase of the process of change. Three phases may be distinguished: the origin of a new mode of behaviour; its persistence beyond the moment of origin; and competitive selection between it and other modes. The following table shows how each of these phases is treated in an optimization model and in the kind of evolutionary model of which competitive selection forms a natural part, with the biological equivalent shown for comparison.[6] Optimization and evolution in this sense are, of course, to be understood as extreme cases, with reality always likely to be a mixture.

Phases in the process of change

| Phase | Economic change | | Biological change |
	Optimization	Evolution	
1. Origin		Chance	Chance (mutation, combination, random genetic drift)
2. Persistence	Ratiocination (including optimizing imitation)	Inertia + non-optimizing imitation	Intergenerational reproduction
3. Spread		Competitive selection	Darwinian selection (relative fecundity and mortality)

It should be noted at this point that economic change, in the present sense, is not the same thing as economic growth. Economic change means change in modes of behaviour, comparable to changes in the traits of a species brought about by evolution. Economic growth means increase in real national income (the conceptual ambiguities created by index-number problems, income distribution, income per head versus total income, and so on,

---

wave who were most daring and self-reliant' (p. 740). This can be interpreted as the perfectly tenable hypothesis that the individuals concerned made especially valuable contributions to shaping modes of behaviour, either themselves or through the education of their children, a hypothesis that could also be put forward for the United States (though Marshall does not choose to say so, rather surprisingly). But it is difficult in reading Appendix A to resist the conclusion that Marshall also had in mind that these people's superior qualities were transmitted to their descendants genetically. That hypothesis would be regarded as unsound by most present-day biologists, on the grounds that the relevant attributes are polygenic and would rapidly regress to the mean, in the absence of selective breeding in *each successive generation* of the kind practised by stockbreeders. It has to be remembered that, although Marshall was so much influenced by Darwin, his thought was formed at a time when genetics was in its infancy. There is a further ambivalent and visibly uneasy discussion in *Industry and Trade*, p. 163 n.

[6] This table may be compared, both for similarities and difference, with the more comprehensive table in Hirshleifer (1977), p. 50.

need not concern us in the present context). Its analogy is with an increase in the population of a species—enlargement of its niche—whether or not this is accompanied by changes in its traits. In principle, growth can occur without change and change can occur without growth. Growth can occur without change because of capital accumulation or simply because it takes time to reach the equilibrium level of income associated with any set of modes; also, of course, it can occur through changes in sub-modes if the modes are defined broadly. It is a little more paradoxical that change can occur without growth, since change in modes will on the face of it occur only if the change is in the interest of their practitioners, though interest is, of course, ambiguous (utility, survival, income). The reasons why it may do so, even disregarding that ambiguity, are off-setting adverse changes in the environment and externalities. Externalities and their significance are a major topic that will be considered at length presently; for the time being I shall disregard them.

My main consideration in this paper is with Phase 3, but, as will be seen presently, considerations relating to the three phases cannot be entirely separated from one another. The relative importance of optimization and evolution need not be the same at each of the three phases. But circumstances making for a predominance of the evolutionary process at one phase are likely also to do so at the others. Thus competitive selection will be important relatively to ratiocination at Phase 3 in circumstances where it is difficult to make *ex ante* judgements on the relative merits of alternative modes of behaviour. Such circumstances will also make difficult the application of ratiocination at Phase 1—they will make it more likely that chance should play an important part in that phase. Similar considerations apply in Phase 2.

It does not follow, however, that in an economy with a high degree of substantive and procedural rationality there is bound to be little scope left for competitive selection. Indeed, the opposite may hold. In such an economy the rate of innovation (Phase 1) is likely to be rapid. But since the future is unknowable, a lot of economic agents will make the wrong moves, or no moves, at Phase 1. The fast rate of innovation makes for a fast rate of change in everybody's environment. A high degree of rationality means that a high proportion of the adaptation process at Phase 3 will be achieved by optimization (imitation) rather than by competitive selection; but it also means there will be a large amount of adaptation to be done. Hence the prevalence of a high degree of rationality throughout the economy may serve to increase, rather than decrease, the absolute amount of competitive selection going on at any time.

I have focused attention on competitive selection, going on to consider what are its natural concomitants at the other phases of the process of economic change. It would be possible to approach matters from a different angle. For some purposes, the distinctive feature of an evolutionary view of economic change might be better thought of as the hypothesis of inertia, whether accompanied by competitive selection or not. Inertia means that the *status quo* has a unique importance as the starting point for further developments. This is to be contrasted with the consequences of out-and-out optimization, where economic agents are conceived of as surveying all the alternatives open to them, without treating the initial position as of any special significance. As far as change is concerned, the distinction is then equivalent to that between a technical progress function and a production function. The consequence of inertia is that each step starts where the last one stopped: *natura non facit saltum*. Each step is likely to affect subsequent changes, both their rate and their direction.[7] This approach would give a different emphasis from that of the present paper but would involve many of the same issues. Towards the end of the paper I shall refer to some aspects of the process of change that are certainly evolutionary yet can hardly be regarded as subject to competitive selection.

2. The selection process and its preconditions and speed

2.1. *Selective contraction and expansion*

How does the process of competitive selection actually work as applied to economic behaviour? It is not good enough to take it for granted, nor will it do to rely on vague Darwinian analogies, since the processes are quite different. Darwinian natural selection works through the relative ability of organisms with given characteristics to survive and reproduce themselves, as a result of differential mortality and fertility. It is true that much the same might perhaps be said of economic behaviour during much of the history of *homo sapiens*. But competitive selection between modes of behaviour, in even moderately advanced economies, is not literally a matter of life and death in the physiological sense. When we consider how the process may actually work, the main conclusion that emerges is that its speed and even its occurrence depend very much on circumstances.[8]

Consider first the negative side (equivalent to mortality). In the course of time competition will bring about a fall in the relative weight of users of an inefficient mode. The quantitative importance of the inefficient mode in the economy will thereby be reduced. The speed and extent of this decline will depend on a variety of circumstances. Some are obvious, such as the severity of competition (the amount of slack provided by rents) and the nature of bankruptcy law. Two, more basic, circumstances require comment.

The first is the division of labour. Many modes of behaviour are specific to particular activities, that is to say the production of particular goods or services. Thus handloom weaving is a mode of behaviour specific to the

---

[7] As is well known, this can result also from models that are not explicitly evolutionary at all but are based on learning processes (Atkinson and Stiglitz (1969)).

[8] How complex it may be to model the process exactly is shown by the treatment in Farrell (1970) of one of the examples cited by Friedman, the alleged tendency for competitive selection to ensure that speculation in net stabilizes prices.

textile industries. If competition forces an economic agent to give up an activity and take up another one instead, he loses the opportunity to practise the modes of behaviour specific to his old activity; as far as he is concerned, those modes disappear altogether instead of merely becoming less important quantitatively. The extent to which this happens will depend on the extent and nature of the division of labour. If everybody practises all activities, as under a regime without any exchange, there will be little scope for movement. Of course even if the scope does exist, an economic agent may choose instead to accept less pay or work harder, as the handloom weavers in the cotton industry actually did in nineteenth-century Britain, and in that case competitive selection will be correspondingly slow.

The second is the extent to which production is organized into firms, that is to say undertakings with hired factors and an internal command system. Internal command introduces an element of gearing into decision-making. Certain individuals—entrepreneurs or managers—control modes of behaviour relating to the use not only of their personal labour and capital but also of resources bought or hired from other people. The effects of their decisions are thus magnified. At the same time the employment of factors remunerated at a fixed rate increases the sensitivity of survival to the modes chosen. The firm needs to break even; if it ceases to do so, it will in due course cease to exist and so will the modes of behaviour embodied in it. In addition, scope exists for competitive selection of individuals within firms, by promotion, takeovers, and amalgamations. Space prevents this important aspect from receiving more than a mention here—the processes involved are not identical to those in competition in product markets.

All these circumstances may vary. They will affect not only the speed of selection but also the form that it takes—for example, whether the elimination of the less fit is confined to the very unfit or else applies according to some proportional rule to all economic agents of below-average fitness. There are some circumstances in which it will not operate at all. One important example is that the process will not have any tendency to eliminate inefficient modes of behaviour within a *country*, if those modes are general there and apply with equal effect in all activities (though it will diminish the weight of the country's distinctive modes in the world economy). Another is that it will not have any tendency to eliminate inefficient modes of behaviour relating to consumption, unless inefficiency as consumer is such that it leads also to inefficiency as producer or in the reproduction of surviving offspring. This is because inefficiency in consumption reduces utility rather than economic survival.

Now consider the other side of the coin, the position of the practitioners of the more efficient mode. How does their above-average prosperity cause them, and hence the mode they practise, to become more important? This side is not symmetrical with the previous one, because there is no equivalent to bankruptcy or to giving up an activity. One possibility is that their greater efficiency simply enables them to increase their market share, especially since the less efficient firms are withdrawing from the scene. Alternatively, or in addition, ploughing back of profits may be important. This indeed is the mechanism of competitive selection that is closest to Darwinism, with saving—reproduction of capital—taking the place of reproduction of offspring and operating symmetrically on gainers and losers. It presupposes that growth is capital-constrained.

The relatively unfit must be replaced by the more fit. The negative side and the positive side are both necessary in order for competitive selection to work, though their relative importance will depend on the rate of growth of the economy. The two sides are not fully symmetrical and the process will not work properly unless there is sufficient urge to expand. This condition may not be met to the same extent in all periods and places. Edith Penrose (1952) argued that although losses do indeed impose stringent imperatives, the urge to expand is less reliable; if successful firms are content to sit on their laurels, the space that might be created by the elimination of the unfit will not necessarily be filled.[9]

A strict Darwinist might reply that a propensity to sit on one's laurels, even if quite deliberately adopted, is itself a relatively unfit mode of behaviour that will be selected against. It is quite true that it *will* be selected against (a further consequence of the non-identity of utility and survival, and one which is in principle independent of defective knowledge). But what if firms that have an urge to expand are inefficient in other respects? This is a particular instance of an important general problem, to which we shall turn in a moment (Section 2.2).

How might one seek to measure empirically the relative contributions made by optimization and competitive selection to the diffusion of a given mode of behaviour, say a new technique of production? A first approximation might be sought in the relative magnitudes of intra-firm change and of changes in the relative weights of firms. Writing Q and q respectively for the proportion of output produced by the new technique in the industry and in the firm respectively, and w for proportion of industry's output produced by a firm, the sources of diffusion over a period are given by summing across firms:

$$\Delta Q = \sum w \, \Delta q + \sum \Delta w (q - Q) + \sum \Delta w \, \Delta q$$

The first term on the right hand side could be taken as the result of optimization and the second and third terms as the result of competitive selection (reflecting the gain in weight of firms that respectively employ the new technique to an above-average extent initially and shift towards the new technique in the course of the period).

Such measures can in principle be calculated quite readily from data of the Census of Production kind, at least in respect of unambigously identifi-

[9] The corresponding problem in biology is dealt with by the assumption that all species tend to multiply unless in some way constrained.

able techniques. But they are not necessarily an accurate measure, even apart from stochastic elements. On the one hand, the contribution of optimization will be underestimated in so far as Δw is itself the result of optimization rather than of past success—as most obviously if new entrants systematically choose to put resources into production by the new mode. On the other hand, the contribution of competitive selection will be underestimated in so far as (a) intra-firm changes reflect the outcome of competitive selection between individuals or sections within firms, or (b) some new entrants die as the result of competitive selection and so do not appear in the figures for either the opening or the closing year. For these and similar reasons a serious empirical study would be unlikely to get far without detailed industrial history.

2.2. Multiple loci and Haldane's dilemma

The overall behaviour of an economic agent is composed of a large number of different modes of behaviour; it is determined by the choices made in respect of a large number of different aspects of behaviour, just as the genetic composition of an organism depends on the 'choice' between alleles at a large number of loci. There is no necessary presumption that an economic agent who practises one efficient mode of behaviour also practises others: a firm that had good engineering practices may be bad at industrial relations, or a firm that is well located weak in design or marketing. The elimination of each of a number of inefficient modes separately is a much larger task for competitive selection to perform than the elimination of a single inefficient mode would be in a situation where fitness depended only on that one aspect of behaviour. If there is little or no correlation in efficiency between the different modes of behaviour adopted by a single firm, it is likely that competitive selection will not be able to work fast enough, relatively to the rate of change in the environment, to eliminate all the relatively unfit modes that exist at any particular time. The most that can then be reasonably expected is that it should eliminate those modes of behaviour that either are gravely unfit in a particular environment or else are to some degree unfit in all environments.

This problem and its biological counterpart can be considered further in relation to the social costs of the selection process.

Some of these costs are of an obvious kind. In so far as selection takes time, there will be a loss of potential output during the period while the unfit modes are being eliminated. Calling this a cost does not mean that it is necessarily avoidable: optimization may be an unattainable ideal. These are costs comparable to the costs of R & D. More relevant in the present context are the costs involved by the fact that economic agents are eliminated in the process of selection. In part those costs are a matter of the distribution of income between the economic agents who are in the course of being elimated and the rest. But account must also be taken of capital costs. Production uses physical capital, human capital, and also organizational capital in the form of the experience, information, contacts, and so on that enable people to co-operate effectively as a group. Competitive selection will cause some of this capital to be scrapped. In so far as the capital is inherently specific to unfit modes of behaviour, capital depreciation is admittedly not necessarily any greater under selection than under optimization. But competitive selection implies more *ex post* non-malleability of capital than does optimization, particularly in respect of organizational capital. It therefore requires more gross investment in order for any innovation to be diffused throughout the economy.

There is a corresponding problem in biology, and a serious one. J. B. S. Haldane (1957) defined the cost of a genetic change as the ratio of the sum of 'selective deaths', over all generations, to survivors. On reasonable assumptions this ratio turns out to be high, even in the case of a single genetic change (change at a single locus). If changes are required at many loci—the realistic case—the ratio becomes astronomical. The population will become extinct if there are more than a limited number of selective deaths in each generation. Hence the rate of genetic change seems to have to be exceedingly slow (even apart from continuing changes in the environment). This is known as Haldane's dilemma. It does not seem to have been entirely resolved by biologists, though various resolutions have been offered (Maynard Smith (1968); Hartl (1980), pp. 377–8, and references there).

The economic parallel may be illustrated by an extreme example. Productivity growth is commonly believed to come about more from a combination of small advances than for a few spectacular breakthroughs, and likewise, in econometric cross-section studies, differences in performance almost always have to be traced by a considerable number of variables (see, for example, Caves (1980)). So suppose that productivity improvement in a particular industry at a given time is available from improvements in ten modes of behaviour, that the choice at each of the ten loci is bipolar (right or wrong), and that there is no correlation between the choices that have initially been made at each locus. If the number of firms is small, it is unlikely that any one firm ever has the right mode at every locus. In that case, competitive selection can never get rid of all the inefficient modes. If there are many firms, a few of them may by chance have all the right answers. In order for the normal distribution to yield one such firm, the number of firms must be 2^{10}, i.e. 1024. The capital stock in this one firm will comprise only a tiny proportion of the capital stock in the industry. If all capital is specific to particular modes, almost the whole of the industry's capital will then have to be eliminated in order for competitive selection to do its job completely, even on the supposition that all the replacement investment takes place in the one best firm. If we suppose a capital-output ratio of 4, and a gross-investment ratio of $\frac{1}{4}$, the process will take 16 years. Not too bad, perhaps. But this greatly understates the problem. On natural assumptions, the replacement investment will be spread over all the firms of above-average fitness, and a large part of it will therefore be in firms that will themselves fail to be eliminated. The industry's capital stock will therefore have to be replaced several times over, probably taking many decades, far longer than the period for which the environment can be expected to remain unchanged.[10] Faster elimination of the unfit firms would lead to a decline in the size of the industry—equivalent to the second horn of Haldene's dilemma—on account of the constraint on gross investment.[11]

Haldane's dilemma will, of course, not exist in circumstances where the choice of mode of behaviour at a single locus is of overwhelming importance, as may sometimes happen, for example, in an industry at an early stage of its development where technology is still very unsettled and there are many one-product firms each trying to find a decisive breakthrough. In the more normal case, where more than one locus is important, the dilemma will be made less acute in so far as the modes of behaviour that matter are few in number, or there is correlation between choices at different loci, or the efficiency of a mode survives changes in the environment. All these are characteristic of sub-case (2B), where there is differentially defective knowledge and economic agents differ from one another in modes of behaviour that are pleiotropic. It will also help if capital is not too specific to particular modes of behaviour; the elimination of inefficient modes of behaviour can then be achieved by takeover, with the entrepreneurs being eliminated without the need to scrap their physical assets.[12] Notwithstanding these qualifications and the other unrealistic features of the arithmetic example, Haldane's dilemma does constitute an important reason why competitive selection is unlikely to produce the same results as optimization. The two processes cannot be regarded as equivalent.

2.3. Growth models

The foregoing relates to once-for-all adaptation towards a certain set of models of behaviour. Why does it come out so differently from the ordinary 'vintage' model of economic growth, in which, likewise, capital equipment is assumed to be wholly specific to particular techniques yet growth is not thereby constrained to a snail's pace? The underlying difference (details apart) is that the vintage model assumes that there is *a continuous change for the better* at an independently given rate in the techniques available for

[10] This may be compared with the very long periods found in growth theory to be needed to execute the 'traverse' called for by a once-for-all change such as the rise in the saving ratio (Sato (1963); Hicks (1965), ch. 16).

[11] There is evidence of something like this happening on the 1970s. Despite a much lower rate of investment than previously, the rate of increase in the proportion of output produced by means of certain new technologies turned out, surprisingly, to be no slower than before. This was achieved by a combination of more rapid than previous scrapping of old-technology plants and a decline (or slow-down in the rate of increase) of total capacity (Ray (1984), pp. 77–9).

[12] Agriculture is a prominent example. Not much scrapping of capital was involved in the takeover of neighbours' farms by kulaks in the USSR in the 1920s or in the takeover of East Anglian farms by Scottish farmers in the 1880s.

embodiment in new equipment. As a result, the rate of replacement does not affect the steady state growth rate, since if replacement occurs only after a long interval there is a correspondingly large improvement in productivity when it does finally occur. The continuous technical advance is a source of growth separate from competitive selection. To postulate that it occurs is an assumption about Phase 1 of the process of change, the phase relating to the origin of changes in modes of behaviour. Thus the working of competitive selection (Phase 3) is not independent of what is going on at Phase 1.

The hypothesis that chance-based competitive selection predominates at Phase 3 does not sit easily with the hypothesis that there is continuous exogenous improvement in the modes of behaviour available. The latter hypothesis would be analogous to continuous mutations all for the better (orthogenesis), an unlikely case. It is perfectly possible, however, to devise models in which a more congenial combination of assumptions—competitive selection plus random changes in the range of available modes of behaviour—does lead to continuous growth in productivity (whether such a model is realistic is a separate matter). The following is an example. Suppose that initially there exists a dispersion in the efficiency of firms and that proportional changes from one period to the next in each firm's efficiency are randomly distributed about a mean of zero (that is to say, some of the changes are positive, some are negative).[13] Because of these random changes, dispersion in efficiency has a tendency to become greater in period 2 than in period 1. Suppose, however, that competition imposes a limit on dispersion. The tendency to increasing dispersion will be checked by contraction or elimination of the firms nearer the bottom of the distribution in period 2 and relative expansion of those nearer the top. The average efficiency will thus come to be higher than in period 1. Random changes in the next round start from a higher base. So there is continuous growth, at a rate dependent on the severity of competition at the bottom and on the limits to gross investment at the top. In one limiting case, where competition is so weak that there is no selection at all, the tendency to increasing dispersion will remain unchecked and there will be no advance in the average. At another extreme, where, say because of low average profitability, there is severe selection at the bottom but a limited rate of expansion at the top, the average efficiency of the industry will rise but total capacity will diminish, with danger of extinction of the industry. Further complications may arise if the relative fitness of modes of behaviour is itself a function of the severity of competition (thus the mode of having industry run by accountants may conduce to fitness in a context of severe selection but to inefficiency in other contexts). Continuous growth is, however, at least a possibility.

Yet if the changes in modes of behaviour were entirely random, the scope

---

[13] Growth will be slowed but not prevented if, as supposed by Leibenstein (1976), changes in the negative direction tend to preponderate, on account of lethargy, in the absence of some specfic stimulus.

for further improvements might surely become exhausted after a while. Modes of behaviour would then settle into equilibrium, just as biological phenotypes settle into equilibrium in the absence of changes in the environment. Continuous economic change at a non-negligible pace appears unlikely without the interposition of some success in optimization [14] or else of some entirely separate process making for improvement in the range of modes available. Such a source of improvement might be the growth of scientific knowledge, subject to its own independent evolutionary process.

Over much the greater part of human history, of course, the average rate of increase of income per head—or of population, for that matter—*was* very slow; and it was punctuated by long periods of stagnation or retrogression. To explain that sort of growth largely in terms of competitive selection is not necessarily so absurd.

3. Externalities, institutions, and governments

3.1. *Non-invadability and optimality*

A mode of behaviour is evolutionarily stable if, in the language of biologists, it is uninvadable, that is to say if no alternative would have any tendency to displace it via competitive selection. Evolutionary stability thus corresponds to Nash-equilibrium in game theory. It is not necessarily an optimum, in any sense, for the population (species) as a whole. It may fail to be an optimum for either of two reasons: because it is only a local optimum, a concept familiar to biologists; or else because there are externalities, a concept not explicitly used by biologists, doubtless because they regard them as the rule rather than the exception. In this section I shall consider some aspects of externalities and how they affect economic change under a system of competitive selection.

Necessary conditions for externalities to be precluded in a competitive system are that there are complete markets and that all the effects of the actions of one agent on another are internalized by a complete system of property rights. The existence of property rights enforced by law (external compulsion) is unique to *homo sapiens*. It would appear to follow that nature must be full of non-optimalities, even if attention is confined to a single species and we disregard the raw externality that exists between predator and prey.[15] Admittedly evolution has produced some modes of behaviour that have the effect of internalizing externalities, most obviously in the relation between parents and their offspring; and property rights are also to some extent simulated e.g. by the propensity to fight more vigorously in defence of one's own territory than in attack on another's. But there are

---

[14] Corresponding to what Winter (1971) calls 'the innovating remnant'.

[15] 'A race of wolves that has well organized plans for hunting in packs is likely to survive and spread; because those plans enable it to catch its prey, not because they confer a benefit on the world' (Marshall (1923), p. 175). For treatment of non-optimalities in nature from an economic standpoint, see Hirshleifer (1978).

very large areas of behaviour in which the externalities remain. The result is that there are indeed very large non-optimalities, contrary to what was supposed by naive early Darwinists. The quasi-optimizing unit is the gene, or possibly groupings of genes, not the species. For example, traits may develop that are uninvadable because they are useful in competition for mates (and therefore confer negative externalities on other members of the same sex) but at the same time hamper foraging or escape from predators; stock examples are the peacock, with its inconvenient tail, and the so-called Irish elk, which apparently had antlers seventeen times the weight of its skull (Dobzhansky *et al.* (1977), p. 244). Likewise, the interests of the species may be prejudiced by fighting among its members; there is some reason to believe that evolution has been less effective in mitigating this than was once supposed.[16]

The consequences of such non-optimalities may be merely that the niche of the species is smaller, or less rapidly expanding, than it would otherwise have been. However, if the disadvantages are sufficiently great, the species may become extinct. Whether or not this happens depends on the severity of the environment. If it does, the traits are invadable in the large though not in the small. It is believed that some 90 per cent of all species that have ever existed are extinct, some of them, doubtless, for that kind of reason.

The human economic analogies are obvious. Groups of economic agents may get trapped in modes of behaviour which are collectively harmful, as in the Prisoner's Dilemma type of situation. The result may merely be that their income is lower or less rapidly growing than it would otherwise have been. In more extreme cases it may lead to absolute decline, say of a region or an industry, or even its extinction, notwithstanding that it is not in the interests of any individual economic agent to alter his mode of behaviour. Likewise, on the borderline of economics and politics: for example, corruption may merely make the organs of the state work inefficiently, or it may ultimately lead to the collapse of the state itself.

3.2. *The role of institutions*

The extent and nature of externalities in economic behaviour depend on a particular class of modes of behaviour that I shall call *institutions*. Institutions are defined as those modes of behaviour that (a) are concerned with inter-personal relationships and (b) are, and are understood and expected to be, generally adopted in certain types of situation. Property rights are a prime example. They may be enforced by law but they do not necessarily have to be: their sanction may instead lie in religion or morality, in custom, or simply in self-interest (long-term or short-term). In this sense even endemic Hobbesian war can be regarded as one kind of institution.

In the normal way, however, institutions regulate the grossest forms of

---

[16] It has been estimated that a quarter of all gorillas meet their death from other gorillas (Hrdy (1981), p. 91).

externality, such as arise from the use of force or threats (in the sense of Boulding).[17] At a more sophisticated level, they may, for example, permit the use of money, or insurance, enforce or prohibit slavery, provide for the operation of monasteries, or limit the liabilities of share-holders in joint-stock companies. They may regulate the mutual relations between people who have formed an alliance or organization for particular purposes (monks or shareholders); or they may regulate the relations between those groups and third parties. Institutions have varied over time and place both in the modes of behaviour they have prescribed and in the categories of people to whom those modes have been made applicable. The need for an adequate theory of institutions has been an increasingly common theme in economic literature in recent years.

It is at this point, rather belatedly, that there emerges the connection between the present paper and Hicks's *Theory of Economic History*. The contention advanced by Hicks there may be summarized, in vastly oversimplified outline, as consisting of two propositions. First, a major part in economic history was played by institutional changes, especially changes that facilitated or inhibited market exchange. Secondly, the institutional changes were themselves largely the product of the incentives offered by changing economic circumstances to certain classes of economic agents, including governments (rulers), though this process was not inevitable. Mutual feed-back occurred between the two causal relationships.

There are two separate ways in which institutions involve externalities. The first relates to the effects of given institutions, corresponding to the first of Hicks's propositions. The second relates to the evolution of the institutions themselves, relevant to Hicks's second proposition. Let us now consider the two sides, from the evolutionary standpoint adopted in the present paper.

3.3. *The effects of alternative institutions*

Institutions differ in the extent to which they internalize or otherwise regulate externalities in economic behaviour. As far as the institutions themselves are concerned, this is a matter of comparative statics. But alternative institutions will affect the way in which the economy grows under its own momentum and responds to other forces making for change.

Not all institutions, of course, are primarily concerned with the correction of potential externalities and the establishment of property rights. In many cases their chief function is informational, to reduce transaction costs by establishing standard terms of dealing between economic agents and so avoid the need to spend time and effort on working out everything from first

[17] A threat is a proposition of the form: if you do something nice to me, I shall refrain from doing something nasty to you. It is contrasted with the offer of exchange, which has the form: if you do something nice to me, I shall do something nice to you (Boulding (1962), pp. 223–8).

principles on each occasion.[18] Moreover, although a complete system of property rights would in theory eliminate externalities, it is impossible to conceive of a truly complete system, such as would govern literally every form of interaction between economic agents (Schelling, 1978, ch. 1). Hence a complete system of property rights may not be the most helpful yardstick by which to judge institutions. Indeed, for second-best reasons, it cannot be taken for granted that every (partial) expansion of the realm of property rights conduces to Pareto-efficiency. Alternative incomplete systems of property rights have each to be considered in detail before drawing any conclusions; and importance may attach to institutions that deal with the underlying problems otherwise than by property rights.

The comparative statics of institutions will affect the path of economic change whether the forces for change operate mainly through optimization or through competitive selection. But the effects will not necessarily be the same in the two cases. Change by means of competitive selection, as noted above, is achieved most readily if expansion and contraction in the activities of economic agents are closely tied to their success or failure. The following are some examples of the implications (intended to be suggestive rather than rigorously worked out). Under optimization, capital market imperfections that force firms to rely exclusively on internal finance hamper the process of change; but those imperfections might actually facilitate competitive selection, by trying future expansion or contraction tightly to past success or failure. By contrast, a land tenure system that makes it diffcult for individual cultivators to expand their holdings is a more serious obstacle to the diffusion of technical change under competitive selection than under optimization. Stringent bankruptcy laws facilitate competitive selection but may hamper change through optimization by inducing excessive caution. Institutionalized monopoly is a serious obtacle to competitive selection but does not as such prevent *technical* efficiency under optimization. And so on.

3.4. *Sources of changes in institutions.*

Externalities attend activities which, by compulsion, precept, or example contribute to bringing about changes in institutions (indeed the mere act of behaving in compliance with an existing institution may have externalities, by strengthening the hold of that institution). This is comparable to the externalities that attend technological innovation.

The evolution of institutions over time is part of cultural history and also, in so far as government is involved, part of political history. The externalities are so blatant that it scarcely seems plausible to postulate that institutions tend to an optimum, certainly not to a global optimum as opposed to a local one. The contrary belief has, however, been influential, as

---

[18] The two aspects are combined together by North (1981), whose interpretation of historical change is based on the postulate that zero transaction costs are a prerequisite of a complete system of property rights.

exemplified alike by the Whig theory of history and by the Marxist doctrine of the ultimate inevitability of communism.

At the same time it would obviously be wrong to overplay the externalities and to deny that institutions will evolve that do serve essential purposes, even in the absence of government. This is clearest in cases where the scope for co-operation in interpersonal interaction is large relatively to the scope for conflict—such cases as driving on a specified side of the road. It is to be noted that a limited amount of free-riding by some people does not make the rule cease to be worth following by others, i.e. the institution is not invadable in the small; at the same time the danger is apparent that such cooperative institutions will get stuck at local optima because it is in no one's interest to take the initiative in altering them. More interestingly, it has been shown theoretically that there is room for at least a limited degree of optimism about the probable outcome even of situations like the Prisoner's Dilemma, where the scope for conflict is large. Hobbesian war is not necessarily the outcome that will emerge from unrestrained self-interest. In the so-called Hawk-Dove problem in game theory, it is not the best strategy always to behave like a Hawk if the cost is large relative to the gain from winning a fight (Maynard Smith (1982), ch. 2). Closer to economics, perhaps, is the time-hallowed second-best institution that Hirshleifer (1978) calls the Silver Rule—return good-for-good and evil-for-evil. It was found in a laboratory experiment that the Silver Rule was the most successsessful strategy in long series of Prisoner's Dilemma games played between the same pair of opponents, the Silver Rule being defined as above but with the good-neighbourly supplement that the opening move in a game should be 'good' (Axerod and Hamilton (1981)).[19]

What role can competitive selection play in the evolution of institutions? Much of what was said in Section 2 about modes of behaviour generally continues to apply. If the gains from acting in accordance with one mode of behaviour are sufficiently great, those who adopt other modes will be tend to find their position eroded. The gains in question are those of the people whose actions shape the institutions, and if there are externalities these are not necessarily gains for the economy as a whole, or indeed even of those people themselves collectively. A mode of behaviour that is contrary to Nash-equilibrium will not have a chance to establish itself as an institution; in that sense competitive selection is largely the history of what did not happen. Once the mode of behaviour is established as an institution, however, it will be correspondingly difficult to alter; in order to act against it, an economic agent will not only have to overcome his own inertia but also will find himself swimming against the stream and upsetting other people's expectations. The auto-regressive properties of the system are thus

---

[19] Important contributions to the general theory of the internal evolution of institutions have been made by Schotter (1981) and, from the standpoint of moral philosophy, by Ullman-Margalit (1978).

especially pronounced where institutions are concerned. Special considerations are involved in relation to the kind of institution that takes the form of an alliance to overcome a potential conflict of interest. Alliances are vulnerable to free-riders, but if they become established and suitably reinforced by sanctions, they may be difficult to depart from (Olson 1965), (1982)). There are many possible groupings of economic agents between whom alliances may be formed and the particular alliance pattern evolving may therefore owe a good deal to chance.[20]

No consideration of the forces governing the evolution of institutions is likely to get very far unless it takes account of differences between the circumstances of different groups of economic agents, broadly equivalent to polymorphism in the biological context. Rather than attempt to pursue all the implications of economic polymorphism, I shall concentrate on the most extreme case, that involving governments—the difference between rulers and ruled that plays such a large part in Hicks's book. The compulsory powers of government remove it from the realm of voluntary exchange and make the presence of externalities almost inevitable. The externalities may be negative in so far as rulers use their powers to advance their personal interests; they may be positive in so far as rulers' laborious (and well-advised) efforts advance the public good. Governments play a major part in shaping economic institutions: by using their powers to reinforce institutions originating in the private sector, to prohibit or amend them, and to maintain institutions of their own, such as taxation.

There is no historical reason to suppose that governmental economic institutions tend to any equilibrium that is stable in the long run. Their evolutionary changes, moreover, are an aspect of economic life where competitive selection applies rather little. This conclusion is perhaps scarcely controversial. But it is worth indicating the reasons.

The distinctive feature of competitive selection is that competition between traits occurs indirectly through the fortunes of their carriers. In the present context this would mean that the choice between alternative governmental policies regarding economic institutions is shaped by their effects on the relative success of the governments that espouse them. This is an unpromising hypothesis, if only because so many of the main developments in governments' policies have historically continued irrespective of who happened to be in power (Hicks (1969), pp. 99–100). More specifically, there are two obstacles to the hypothetical process happening.

In the first place, competitive selection depends on there being a range of alternative modes of behaviour, embodied in different agents.[21] But there is

[20] An interesting example is given by Kocka (1981), who contrasts the historical solidarity of low-level white-collar workers in Germany with that of skilled manual workers in Britain. Neither phenomenon had much counterpart in the other country and both were directed to underlining the distinction between the group concerned and the generality of workers. Similar purposes have been and are served by alliances based on race, religion, language, sex, and so on.

[21] Compare the so-called fundamental theorem of natural selection: the rate of evolution is proportional to the genetic variance of the population.

only one government—that is of its essence, since the basic characteristic of government is that it has a monopoly, viz. a monopoly of the use of legitimate force. Admittedly, there are alternative governments, possibly numerous ones, but as they are not in power there is no opportunity for their policies to prove their fitness or otherwise. Alternative policies can be adopted only in sequence, as governments alter. Competitive selection could therefore work only if the environment remained unchanged for a sufficiently long period for the effects of alternative policies on the fortunes of successive governments to work themselves out.

In the second place, policies in the sphere of economic institutions are, at most, only one of the causes of the rise and fall of governments. Many other forces are involved, alike in palace revolutions and in electoral defeats, these being the main sources of fall of governments in non-democratic and democratic regimes respectively. Selection between economic institutions is thus gravely subject to Haldane's dilemma. This is well-known as an objection to the optimistic interpretation sometimes placed on 'social choice' theories of democracy, according to which vote-maximization will cause governments' policies to correspond exactly with the interests of the electorate (Downs (1957); Atkinson and Stiglitz (1980), pp. 307–10).

Of course, one should not exaggerate. The foregoing applies rather less strongly, for example, in forms of governments in which individual ministers or advisers have responsibilities for formulating specified parts of policy and are liable to dismissal if their policies turn out badly (this is an aspect of the question of competitive selection within bureaucracies, which I am not attempting to treat in this paper). Moreover, some governments and systems of government *have* fallen in consequence of their economic policies, either because they failed to attain their own objectives or else because the associated adverse externalities proved fatal. But, in general, policies relating to economic institutions have proved a poor discriminator between governments. And governments have proved unreliable vehicles of policies.

None of the above is intended to belittle the importance of the two-way connection between economic change and the institutions that are due to government. Nor do I mean to deny the evolutionary character of the connection, with each step in the process of change affecting all subsequent steps. The model remains that of a random walk. There is a difference, compared with the evolution of modes of behaviour that are not directly connected with government, that the direction of the walk is less likely to be guided by competitive selection. Sometimes the situation is sufficiently clear for optimization, including learning, by rulers to guide them in much the same direction in all countires that are similarly placed; some of the cases considered by Hicks are of that kind. In others, governments are free to diverge from one another and produce disparate national patterns. In all cases, the path is influenced by political dynamics, which, being expressed in the currency of power, do not necessarily resemble closely the dynamics of purely economic change.

The above relates to single countries taken in isolation. In a world of many countries, interactions between them introduce new considerations. The institutions created by the government of any one country may be invadable in the literal sense (war was recognized by Darwin himself as one possible instrument of natural selection). The institutions of the defeated country may then be displaced by those of its conqueror. There is no doubt that this constitutes competitive selection between alternative military arrangements; but whether it is competitive selection between economic institutions (governmental or non-governmental) depends on how far economic institutions are associated with military superiority. This has perhaps been most nearly true of colonial wars, where the antagonists have been at very different stages of economic development. However, military superiority has many sources other then economic institutions—not least the mere relative size of the antagonists—and history shows many examples of wars won by the economically less advanced contender. Military selection is therefore capable of being economically retrogressive.

At the same time, the rise and fall of dominant countries have obviously been among the most important sources of change in modes of economic behaviour in the world as a whole. The sources have not been exclusively military. Sometimes the effects have been felt through increase in the weight of an economically advancing country in world production, as with Great Britain in the nineteenth century and the U.S. in the twentieth—a straight case of competitive selection. Sometimes the effects have been felt through induced changes in modes of behaviour in the rest of world. The induced changes have in turn been brought about in a variety of ways (in addition to imposition of institutions by military force): imitation of the advancing country's institutions or its other modes of economic behaviour; adaptation by means of optimization to changes in comparative advantage brought about by events in the advancing country; adaptation by means of competitive selection to those changes in comparative advantage; and competitive selection achieved by emigration of entrepreneurship and management from the advancing country (Venetians in the Levant, multi-national corporations). All these effects may be brought about by the advance of a single country; they may also be brought about by improvement of transport and communications. Such improvement enlarges the scope both for optimization by imitation and for competitive selection, by enlarging the size of the world over which competition occurs and thereby increasing the relevant variance of modes of behaviour.

4. Conclusions

In briefest outline, the conclusions suggested by this paper may be summarized as follows.

The prevalance of limited information and bounded rationality restricts the scope for optimization. In some spheres, therefore, competitive selection—the economic equivalent of Darwinism—may be the only systematic mechanism directing the course of economic change. More typically, optimization and competitive selection will coexist and interact.

Competitive selection is an entirely different kind of process from optimization. A variety of considerations prevent them from leading to the same outcome, so they should not be regarded as equivalent. Competitive selection by itself is unreliable and stochastic and the movement it leads to has the character of a random walk.

A major characteristic of competitive selection is its slowness—slowness, that is to say, compared with optimization, not necessarily compared with the actual pace of historical change before modern times. It has often been suggested that processes of change can be arrayed in a hierarchy according to their speed. Thus genetic selection is very much faster than random recombination of the molecules that existed when the earth began, and cultural selection, in which traits can be transmitted non-genetically, is much faster than genetic selection. Competitive selection of an economic kind may, in favourable circumstances, be more rapid than other forms of cultural selection. Optimization, in turn, is likely to be much faster than competitive selection. A further conclusion suggests itself, that an important long-run contribution of competitive selection may be the extent to which it selects in favour of modes of behaviour that facilitate optimization.

Competitive selection, like optimization, is subject to externalities, though the effects of externalities do not work out identically under the two processes. Competitive selection therefore does not necessarily lead to social Pareto-efficiency, any more than natural selection, as nowadays understood, necessarily leads to the best possible outcome for the species as a whole. The extent and nature of externalities are affected by institutions, which constitute one class of modes of behaviour; institutions therefore affect the path taken by an economy in which competitive selection plays a part. Moreover, institutions themselves are subject to evolution over time, and their evolution may be affected by competitive selection of one sort of another. It is doubtful whether competitive selection of an economic kind will be very effective in shaping that part of the evolution of institutions— likely to be a significant part—that is determined by governments.

A complete model of economic change would have to take account of the nature of the different kinds of process that determine economic and political evolution and how they interact. It would also have to incorporate the effects of their interaction with yet another element, itself subject to evolutionary principles of its own, the development of ideas (both in ideology and religion and in science). As it requires computer simulation to work out random walks along even a single dimension, there is no prospect of actually constructing such a model in a way that would be intuitively understandable and have any claim to validity. The most one can do is to extract snippets, for particular purposes, from one's own notion of what it might look like.

Clare College, Cambridge

REFERENCES

ALCHIAN, A. A. (1950), 'Uncertainty, evolution, and economic theory', *Journal of Political Economy*, 211–22.

ATKINSON, A. B. and STIGLITZ, J. E. (1969), 'A new theory of technological change', *Economic Journal*, 573–8.

ATKINSON, A. B. and STIGLITZ, J. E. (1980), *Public Economics* (London).

AXELROD, R. and HAMILTON, W. D. (1981), 'The evolution of cooperation', *Science*, 1390–6.

BECKER, G. S. (1981), *A Treatise on the Family* (Harvard, Mass.).

BOULDING, K. E. (1962), *Conflict and Defense* (New York).

BOULDING, K. E. (1981), *Evolutionary Economics* (Beverly Hills, Calif.).

CAVES, R. E. (1980), 'Productivity differences among industries', in R. E. Caves and L. B. Krause (eds), *Britain's Economic Performance* (Washington, DC): 135–198.

DAWKINS, R. (1976), *The Selfish Gene* (Oxford).

DOBZHANSKY, T., AYALA, F. J., STEBBINGS, G. L. and VALENTINE, J. W. (1977), *Evolution* (San Francisco).

DOWNIE, J. (1958), *The Competitive Process* (London).

DOWNS, A. (1957), *An Economic Theory of Democracy* (New York).

FARRELL, M. J. (1970), 'Some elementary selection processes in economics', *Review of Economic Studies*, 305–19.

FLOUD, R. C. and McCLOSKEY, D. N. (eds.) (1981), *The Economic History of Britain since 1700* (Cambridge).

FRIEDMAN, M. (1953), 'The methodology of positive economics', in *Essays in Positive Economics* (Chicago).

HALDANE, J. B. S. (1957), 'The cost of natural selection', *Journal of Genetics*, 511–24.

HARTL, D. L. (1980), *Principles of Population Genetics* (Sundelland, Mass.).

HICKS, J. R. (1965), *Capital and Growth* (Oxford).

HICKS, J. R. (1969), *A Theory of Economic History* (Oxford).

HIRSHLEIFER, J. (1977), 'Economics from a biological viewpoint', *Journal of Law and Economics*, 1–52.

HIRSHLEIFER, J. (1978), 'Natural economy versus political economy', *Journal of Social Biological Structures*, 319–37.

HRDY, S. B. (1981), *The Woman that Never Evolved* (Harvard).

KIRZNER, I. M. (1973), *Competition and Entrepreneurship* (Chicago).

KNIGHT, F. H. (1942), 'Some notes on the economic interpretation of history' in *Studies in the History of Culture* (Menasha, Wisc.).

KOCKA, J. (1981), 'Competition and bureaucracy in German industrialisation before 1914', *Economic History Review*, 453–68.

LEACH, E. (1981), Review of Lumsden and Wilson (1981) in *Nature*, 267–8.

LEIBENSTEIN, H. (1976), *Beyond Economic Man* (Harvard).

LUMSDEN, C. J. and WILSON, E. O. (1981), *Genes, Mind, and Culture* (Harvard).

LUMSDEN, C. J. and WILSON, E. O. (1983), *Promethean Fire* (Harvard).

MARSHALL, A. (1920), *Principles of Economics*, 8th ed. (London).

MARSHALL, A. (1923), *Industry and Trade*, 4th ed. (London).

MAYNARD SMITH, J. (1968), 'Haldane's Dilemma and the rate of evolution', *Nature*, 1114–16.

MAYNARD SMITH, J. (1982), *Evolution and the Theory of Games* (Cambridge).

NELSON, R. R. and WINTER, S. G. (1982), *An Evolutionary Theory of Economic Change* (Harvard).

NORTH, D. C. (1981), *Structure and Change in Economic History* (New York).

OLSON, M. (1965), *The Logic and Collective Action* (Harvard).

OLSON, M. (1982), *The Rise and Decline of Nations* (New Haven).

PENROSE, E. T. (1952), 'Biological analogies in the theory of the firm', *American Economic Review*, 804–19.

RAY, G. F. (1984), *The Diffusion of Mature Technologies* (Cambridge).

REIJNDERS, L. (1978), 'On the applicability of game theory to evolution', *Journal of Theoretical Biology*, 245–47.

SATO, A. (1963), 'Fiscal policy in a neo-classical growth model: an analysis of time required for equilibrating adjustment', *Review of Economic Studies*, 16–23.

SCHELLING, T. C. (1978), *Micromotives and Macrobehaviour* (New York).

SCHOTTER, A. (1981), *The Economic Theory of Institutions* (Cambridge).

TVERSKY, A. and KAHNEMAN, D. (1974), 'Judgment under uncertainty: heuristics and biases', *Science*, 1124–31.

ULLMAN-MARGALIT, E. (1978), *The Emergence of Norms* (Oxford).

WINTER, S. G. (1971), 'Satisficing, selection and the innovating remnant', *Quarterly Journal of Economics*, 237–61.

PREDICTIONS AND CAUSES: A COMPARISON OF FRIEDMAN AND HICKS ON METHOD[1]

By DIETER HELM

1. Introduction

ONE way of presenting methodological arguments, and focusing on the issues which divide theorists, is to place the problems within the framework of broadly conflicting views. Two economists who have made important and conflicting claims about economic method are Friedman and Hicks, but the extent to which their two views differ has not been fully explored. Friedman's (1953) essay on 'The Methodology of Positive Economics',[2] with its overriding stress on economics as a predictive science, is perhaps the most famous article ever written on economic methodology. Hicks's 'Causality in Economics' (1979) represents a radically different viewpoint from Friedman's, stressing the explanatory importance of causality. Thus in comparing and contrasting these two, important issues are illustrated.

The purpose of this paper is threefold. The first intention is expositional: to outline the two approaches, and highlight the points of conflict. The second purpose is to demonstrate how confused some of the issues are, and to explore the central ones concerning the status of empirical evidence and causality. The third task is to consider what criteria, building on Hicks's work in particular, are appropriate for the appraisal of economic theories. It will be argued that neither causality nor prediction in themselves are sufficient criteria to judge between competing economic theories. To these must be added an account of how causal relations are derived from theoretical classifications, and of what is to count as an economic cause. I shall stress the importance of Hicks's claims about classification, and add my own claims concerning the content of economic causes, particularly regarding the role of human reason in causation.

The two views can be expressed as stressing on the one hand empirical testing and prediction, and on the other, causality, explanation, and classification. For Friedman the science of positive economics aims to 'provide a system of generalizations that can be used to make correct predictions about the consequences of any change in circumstances' (p. 4). For Hicks, economics is not a science, but rather a discipline: 'economics is in time, and therefore in history, in a way that science is not', (1984b). These two views then are based on different conceptions of the status of economic knowledge, and hence have roots in different philosophies of science. However,

[1] I should like to thank Amartya Sen, Jonathon Cohen, David Collard, Tony Courakis, John Vickers, and Christopher Gilbert for comments on an earlier draft. I must also gratefully acknowledge long and detailed conversations with Sir John Hicks while I have had the great privilege of being his research assistant.
[2] All references to Friedman are to this 1953 article, unless otherwise stated.

although in particular Friedman has positivistic leanings which will be identified below, neither fits easily into pre-existing categories, and for two reasons. The first is that neither was familiar with the detail of the relevant philosophical literature when they wrote; the second is that the categories of the philosophy of science are neither all-encompassing, nor easily applicable to economics.

PART I: FRIEDMAN

2. Friedman's essay in context

The problems with interpreting Friedman's paper rest in part in its context. The paper is difficult to relate either to the debate to which it was supposed to provide a solution, or to the philosophical literature. Very little reference is made either to philosophers, or to economists who had written on methodology (with the exceptions of Lange and Marshall).[3]

Friedman's essay appeared in 1953 at the end of the debate which had raged through the 1940s, in particular in the *American Economic Review* (1946–8), on the realism of marginalist assumptions about the behaviour of firms. Hall and Hitch (1939) had shown before the war that many firms did not understand the concept of marginal cost pricing, and made the further claim that this theory was therefore not a good explanation of what firms did. Rather they argued that their evidence was consistent with an alternative explanation: full or mark-up pricing. The central problem with this kind of evidence is that it is not decisive between the two rival hypotheses, and in two senses. Firstly, as Harrod (1939) in the same issue of OEP pointed out, marginalism does not require that participants consciously employ marginalist methods. Optimal decision-making does require that people do their best *ex ante*, but not necessarily that they choose the best *ex post*, where there exist search and administrative costs in a world of imperfect information. Hall and Hitch's study was not therefore sufficient to reject marginalist theories of firms' pricing behaviour. The second problem of decisiveness concerns the alternatives available and the problem of theory comparability and commensurability. To persuade economists to drop particular theories, or assumptions embedded in certain theories, typically requires that an alternative be proposed, and no rigorous alternative of the same kind was then available. Theories must be of similar levels of generality, involve similarly defined concepts, and cover the same data set, for strict comparisons to be made.

Into this gap, created in part by the indecisiveness of the Hall and Hitch

---

[3] It is hard to see what impact Hayek, who was at Chicago after the war, or Popper had on the paper. Subsequent evidence, like that provided by Frazer and Boland (1983), is based on Friedman's own memory and the relation between the arguments in the paper and others held at about that time. Simultaneity of argument does not establish connections; neither is memory entirely reliable over a thirty-year span.

evidence, came Friedman's article. It laid out apparently clear methodological principles for a 'positive' economics. It attempted to clarify the debate by pointing to the irrelevance of the realism of assumptions, rather than taking sides directly. Friedman wrote:

> The articles on both sides of the controversy largely neglect what seems to me clearly the main issue—the conformity to experience of the implications of the marginal analysis—and concentrate on the largely irrelevant question whether businessmen do or do not in fact reach their evidence by consulting schedules, or curves, or multivariate functions showing marginal cost and marginal revenue.

3. Friedman's inconsistent theses

In fact the article itself advances a series of theses, some of which are at best ambiguous; others are confused and, as we shall see, inconsistent. These include:

1. Positive economics can and should be separated from normative economics (pp. 3–4).

2. Positive economics 'is, or can be, an objective science, in precisely the same sense as any of the physical sciences' (p. 4).

3. Assumptions are to be chosen without regard to the correspondence between them and reality. The testing of assumptions is irrelevant. This is explicitly stated in the article, yet Friedman also tells us that they must be 'sufficiently good approximations for the purpose at hand' (p. 15).

4. The choice of assumptions is grounded in the ability to yield 'valid' predictions. 'Simplicity' and 'fruitfulness' of assumptions are relevant criteria for their choice, as well as their 'intuitive plausibility' (p. 26). 'The gains from further accuracy [of prediction] alone, which depend on the purpose in mind, must then be balanced against the costs of achieving it' (p. 17).

5. In general, the more significant the theory, the more unrealistic the assumptions (p. 14).

6. Predictions are testable by direct relation to empirical evidence which provides an independent and objective test. This can be either (a) positively by verification (strong claim); or (b) negatively by falsification.

7. The survival of predictive testing is modified by the 'frequency' of refutation with respect to alternative hypotheses (p. 9).

8. A theory is comprised of two parts: (a) a language or analytical filing-system, the theoretical categories, which can be shown to have meaningful empirical counterparts; and (b) substantive hypotheses.

9. Indeterminacy principle, according to which there exists a relationship both between the observer and the observed, and between the process of measurement and the phenomena being measured (p. 5 n).

10. 'A theory is the way we perceive "facts", and we cannot perceive "facts" without a theory' (p. 34).

11. If one hypothesis is consistent with the available evidence, then there are an infinite number which are (p. 9).

12. Empirical evidence is to be used in the construction (as well as in the testing of predictions) of hypotheses (p. 13).

13. The maximization of returns is a realist assumption, because 'unless the businessman in some way or other approximated behaviour consistent with the maximization of returns, it seems unlikely that they would remain in business for long.' Competition acts like natural selection to enforce maximization.[4]

Rather than take this set of theses as consistent, and claim it to represent a particular philosophy of science, it seems to me more appropriate to recognize that they are simply muddled and confused.[5] In particular it is not clear from propositions (3) and (4) above which are the relevant criteria of judging assumptions. Friedman adds additional criteria to predictive testing in 'fruitfulness' and 'simplicity', yet elsewhere places overriding importance of the predictive test in his (6) and (7). Elsewhere there is a confusion as to whether theories and theoretical terms can or cannot be reduced to empirical counterparts, since (8) is contradicted by (9) and (10). Finally, (11) directly undermines Friedman's 'predictive science', for if it is true, then a theory cannot be selected solely on predictive grounds.

Given this evident confusion and inconsistency in Friedman's theses, there is, contrary to much of the literature, no 'right' or unique interpretation of his methodological position. For my purposes I shall take Friedman to mean precisely what he says in the following quotation:

Viewed as a body of substantive hypotheses, theory is to be judged by its predictive power for the class of phenomena which it is intended to 'explain'. Only factual evidence can show whether it is 'right' or 'wrong' or, better, tentatively 'accepted' or 'rejected' ... the only relevant test of the validity of the hypothesis is comparison of its predictions with experience ... Factual evidence can never 'prove' a hypothesis; it can only fail to disprove it. (pp. 8–9).

This methodology of economics crucially depends on the possibility of testing, and the independent status of empirical evidence. I shall therefore next consider what kind of a philosophy Friedman's arguments represent, placing him within the broad church of positivism. Having done that, and indicated the lines of criticism to which he is then open, I then turn to the second view, that of Hicks, to carry through those criticisms.

4. Positivist and instrumentalist

The importance of empirical evidence and testing are central to a number of philosophies of social and natural sciences. However giving empirical

[4] For a critique of this assertion, see Helm (1984).
[5] Boland (1979) is perhaps the most emphatic amongst those who claim Friedman to be consistent. Rather I should want to say that the critics have disagreed because individual propositions have been abstracted from context, and taken fully to represent Friedman. They have therefore been open to counter-quotation.

evidence the central role by reducing theoretical terms to empirical meanings is unique to positivism, and in this broad sense, Friedman is a positivist. It is not merely a question of semantics in ascribing this title to him, for there are a number of well-known objections to this philosophy. Positivism involves a large subset of less well-defined beliefs deriving from and related to its emphasis on observations. Besides emphasizing observation over theory,[6] these beliefs include[7] reducing causality to temporal orderings and claiming that there is no necessary connection between cause and effect, regarding prediction rather than explanation as the goal of science, holding the analytic–synthetic distinction[8] and emphasizing verification and falsification.[9] Friedman believes in the unity of science, in the existence of a sharp distinction between theory and observation (the analytic–synthetic distinction), the possibility of reducing theoretical concepts to statements of empirical meaning, the central importance of prediction, and the timelessness of theory. In this broader sense, writers such as Wong (1973), Boland (1979), Caldwell (1982), and Boland and Frazer (1983) are not strictly correct to call Friedman an instrumentalist[10] *rather* than a positivist, since although he does claim that theories and assumptions are only instrumental to the production of predictions, Friedman is ambiguous as to whether theories themselves are true or false, whereas the instrumentalist claims that they are neither true nor false. Theory may be instrumental to the production of predictions; but there is for Friedman a relationship between the logical statements and observable reality involving their truth or falsity. Some instruments are better than others; and as we have seen above, Friedman employs a series of what Caldwell (1983) describes as conventionalist criteria. Caldwell (1982), pp. 176–77, has also pointed out that Friedman confuses the 'indirect testability hypothesis', according to which testing predictions can indirectly act as a check on the validity of assumptions, with the instrumental claim that the realism of assumptions is irrelevant.

A more charitable interpretation of Friedman, given the inconsistencies pointed out above, is that he asserts this more sophisticated view, rather than subscribing to naive instrumentalism. Furthermore, the positivist has epistemological claims to make about the status of predictions which are not equivalent to the instrumentalist view. Indeed it is on this issue that

---

[6] Strictly all theoretical terms have exact empirical counterparts. According to Hume's epistemological theory, what exists is limited to 'impressions' derived from sense-data. 'Ideas', and hence theoretical terms, are ultimately reducible to their empirical counterparts.

[7] See Hacking (1983), pp. 41–2, on the meaning of positivism.

[8] A synthetic statement refers to the world, what Hume described as matters of fact. The predicate of a synthetic proposition is attached to the subject but not contained in it. An analytic statement, by contrast, contains the predicate in its subject and refers to 'matters of reason'. The distinction is thus between claims about the world and claims which are matters of logical relation.

[9] Dispute continues as to whether falsification as proposed by Popper is anti-positivist in the sense that Popper himself claimed it to be.

[10] Instrumentalism is the thesis that a theory is merely an instrument for predicting observable reality, irrespective of its truth-content.

instrumentalism is incomplete.[11] It is not impossible to interpret Friedman's method as positivist on the status of empirical observations, and instrumental on assumption choice, though if the indirect testability hypothesis is what he has in mind then he is not even strictly instrumental on this. If, however, the instrumentalist were to claim that predictions are not directly testable, then the validity of assumptions on the empirical grounds of the predictions that they produce cannot be the criterion of choice. Friedman's empiricism and his commitment to predictive science is thus open to a series of objections, which stress the importance of theoretical concepts, their priority over observations, and the causal relationship between variables. At this point, let us turn to Hicks' position.

PART II: HICKS

5. Hicks's anti-empiricism

Hicks has both in principle and in practice objected to the widespread adoption of empiricist methods in economics, from his early days as a member of the LSE group, exposed to both Robbins's and Hayek's views on the subject.[12] His objections have been grounded on two propositions. The first stems from the observation that economic theories are time-dependent. Economic institutions and behaviour alter with the passage of time, and the more characteristic problems are not static ones, but are 'problems of change, of growth and retrogression, and of fluctuation' (1979, p. xi). It is for this reason that scientific methods are less applicable to economics, since in economics everything must be dated, whereas in science Hicks claims this is not the case. At the level of observations of actual human behaviour, what might be true in one period need not be true in another, even if the motives of the agents do not themselves alter. Furthermore, dynamic theories[13] of economic behaviour need to incorporate the passage of time into processes through the relations of participants in those processes to that change. Testing is then at best limited to periods when the relevant institutions and individual behaviour remains constant, and to what is going on in those periods.

Hicks's second objection focuses on the problems of prediction, and he

[11] It is incomplete in the sense that the instrumentalist is left with no way of justifying the importance of predictions or their usefulness without a criterion of truth or falsity. In other words the consequences of the position on truth and falsity can be addressed to their own claims.

[12] See for example Hicks (1956), ch. 1; 'LSE and the Robbins Circle' in (1981); 'A Discipline not a Science' in (1983); (1979); (1984a); and (1984b). Another member of the LSE group, George Shackle, has developed related points to Hicks on uncertainty, time, and predictability. See in particular his (1967).

[13] Hicks uses the term 'dynamics' in a particular way. See his 'Methods of Dynamic Economics' (1956), reprinted in id. (1982), for his definitions.

claims that economics can at best make only weak predictions.[14] These weak predictions are claims about what will happen if other things remain the same. Since *ceteris* is almost never *paribus*,[15] a particular set of observations can never, themselves, form the basis for testing an hypothesis. Hicks writes ((1983) pp. 371–2):

> Once it is recognised that economic theories (those which are not mere tautologies) can offer no more than weak explanations—that they are always subject to a *ceteris paribus* clause—it becomes clear that they cannot be verified (or 'falsified') by confrontation with fact. We are told that 'when theory and fact come into conflict, it is theory, not fact, that must give way'. It is very doubtful how far that dictum applies to economics. Our theories . . . are not that sort of theory; but it is also true that our facts are not that sort of fact.

Thus Hicks and Friedman diverge on the central issues of methodology, the one emphasizing the predictive content of economic science, the other stressing causality and the obstacles to testing and empiricist methods. Hicks argues that given two alternative assumptions, within a theoretical system, we cannot simply refer to the evidence, and so need to look for other additional criteria. Such a problem cannot be considered without tackling the wider question of what an economic theory and explanation consists of, what are its parts, and what such a theory is for. On the broad issue as well as the narrower one, Hicks and Friedman have very different views in principle, though not always in practise. The first crucial difference comes out in Hicks's account of causality, which is not limited to temporal priority and predictive content.[16] Next that account is outlined, improvements are made to it, and further criteria of appraisal are introduced.

6. Causality

Hicksian causality is the central building-block of his non-positivistic methodology,[17] which stands in contrast to that of Friedman. There are three components to his account of causality. The first relates to weak predictions and the *ceteris paribus* clauses mentioned above, and is his distinction between strong and weak causality. The second is his counterfactual account. The third is his relation between temporal ordering and his three possibilities: static, reciprocal, and contemporaneous.

[14] There are few if any explicit or strong predictions in economics. Not even the 'law of demand' makes clear predictions: negatively sloped demand curves are predicted only on a joint condition concerning the income effect.

[15] Friedman, p. 10, acknowledges this: 'no experiment can be completely controlled, and every experience is partially controlled'.

[16] In this respect Hicks immediately parts company with what have misleading been called Granger 'causality tests'. Granger and Newbold (1977), p. 225, themselves acknowledge these tests to be only temporal relation tests. See Zellner (1979), pp. 10–11, for an exposition of their causality definitions. Tony Courakis has pointed out to me that Friedman, in discussing the relationship between money and income has recently been careful to dissociate himself from these 'causality test' explanations. On this see Courakis (1981), pp. 287, 345.

[17] Indeed early positivists like Comte denied that causality had any meaning, discarding it as a remnant of metaphysics.

The distinction between strong and weak causality rests on the observation that in economics at least there are typically quite a number of causes operating together to produce an effect. We may consider these to make up a vector, say $(a_1, a_2, \ldots, a_n)$, producing the total effect, say B. Each component of the vector is a weak cause of B; only if the vector is a one-component vector or if background conditions remain unaltered can we say that strong causality exists. The relationship between the components may be either separable or non-separable, and there is no a priori reason in economics to suppose that the former necessarily holds in any particular case. So long as it is multi-membered, prediction is also weak, since it depends on nothing happening to the other components.

The second part of the Hicksian analysis concerns counterfactuals. Hicks claims that to say that A causes B involves positing that not-A produces not-B. This Hicks asserts is a theoretical matter:

> I have insisted that the assertion 'if not-A, then not-B' is theoretical; it is derived from something which in the most general sense may be described as a theory or model (1979 p. 22).

There are considerable problems with this definition to which I shall return below. Essentially while Hicks is correct to assert that a counterfactual is required, and that it is a theoretical and not empirical matter in at least the non-experimental subjects, the definition is insufficient. In itself it says nothing about the plurality of possible counterfactuals or the content of causality, and indeed to be fair, Hicks would not claim it to be sufficient.

However, let us now add the third component of the Hicksian theory of causality. Hicks points out that time and causality need to be related carefully. In particular he notes that Hume[18] and his followers typically think of cause and effect at moments in time, and describe a temporal ordering as causality. Hicks stresses that many economic causes and effects take time; they happen in periods rather than at points or moments in time. Sequential causality is the traditional view, where one event happens after another. Hicks wants to introduce two further possibilities: that cause and effect might reciprocate each other, and that they might occur simultaneously or, as he prefers to call it, contemporaneously. Much of his book is devoted to economic examples of these in economic problems.[19]

The Hicksian theory of causality and the status of empirical claims in economics bears a strong but not complete relationship to other philosophical writings, and the tangency between what philosophers and Hicks have said on the subject proves most enlightening. The two tangencies I have in

---

[18] For a discussion of Hume's two definitions of causality, see Stroud (1977), ch. 3.

[19] Temporal asymmetry is frequently stressed in defining causes, particularly in the econometric versions like that of Granger. Philosophers have, however, disagreed, arguing that this is not necessary. On this see Mackie (1975), and in the economics literature Tobin's famous (1970) critique of the money-income relationship.

mind are firstly that between Hicks's *ceteris paribus* clauses and Mackie's INUS conditions, and secondly between Hicks's general anti-empiricism and Quine's famous critique of empiricism. I shall take each in turn.

7. Mackie and Hicks

The counterfactual definition which Hicks has proposed receives powerful support in the definition of causality put forward in John Mackie's article 'Causation and Conditionals' (1965), and his later book *The Cement of the Universe* (1975). Mackie (1975) suggested that:

> when we take A to be ... a partial cause of B, we can say that if A had not occurred, B would not; a cause is to be taken in this counterfactual sense necessary in the circumstances for B, though sometimes also sufficient in the circumstances as well, or perhaps only sufficient in the circumstance and not necessary: we have alternative counterfactual concepts of causation. But these counterfactual conditional relationships do not exhaust our concept of causation, for this concept includes also the notion of symmetry between cause and effect ... (p. xi).

Mackie's famous INUS condition for causality is

> an *insufficient* but *necessary* part of a condition which is itself *unnecessary* but *sufficient* for that result.

We can then assign A to be the cause of a dated event E if A is an INUS condition of E. As Sosa (1975), p. 4, pointed out, there is in fact very little difference between this condition and *ceteris paribus* sufficiency, excepting only in the question of unique sufficiency on a particular date.[20]

If causality were limited to the INUS condition, then this would be the end of the matter.[21] But the importance of causality arises after its counterfactual representation has been recognized, and recognized as a matter of theoretical rather than empirical epistemological status. In particular the importance of Hicks's work on causality is less the definitional second chapter of his book, but rather what he has to say about the content of causes. Hicks has considered, firstly, the way in which we arrive at causal statements, by way of the use of classifications, and secondly what the consequences of *ceteris paribus* limitations are. The former we will return to in Section 9 below, the latter concerns the extent to which weak causality limits empiricism and econometric methods. I shall next, therefore, relate

[20] As Sosa defines the difference: 'the only significant difference is that if C is an INUS condition of E then C is an essential part of a condition that is *uniquely* sufficient for E on that occasion, whereas C may be *ceteris paribus* sufficient for E in circumstances where there are several sufficient conditions for E, including some that do not contain C as a part.'

[21] It should be noted in passing that the Granger 'causality' concept, being limited to temporal relations (see n 16 above) is not to be confused with the Mackie or Hicks conditionals, both of the latter admitting of the possibility that causality is not unidirectional. Furthermore, counterfactuals, being theoretical assertions which cannot be observed, cannot be 'causality tested'.

Hicks's critique of predictions and testing to the more general philosophical critique of empiricism.

8. The Quine–Duhem thesis

The Quine–Duhem thesis, concerning the relation between theory and empirical evidence, has recently received attention from economists.[22] While Hicks has stressed the weakness of predictions, the difficulties of testing, and thus the primacy of theory, philosophers have focused on the relationship between theoretical terms and empirical observations, *within* the network of logically related terms which go to make up theories. Above, we saw that Friedman held the essentially positivistic view that theories were mere filing systems, and that the terms within them could be reduced to empirical counterparts. The critique of such empiricism, of which the Quine–Duhem thesis is an important part, concentrates on this relationship.

The Quine–Duhem thesis has in fact been seperately advanced by Duhem (1914) and by Quine (1953). In its latter formulation, Quine presented the thesis as the conclusion of his now classic critique of empiricism—'Two Dogmas of Empiricism'. In that article, he was concerned to criticize the analytic–synthetic distinction and the proposition that theoretical terms could be reduced to meaningful empirical counterparts, i.e. precisely the foundations of the position which Friedman's appears to have adopted. The thesis itself is founded on two propositions. The first concerns the network of theories and beliefs[23] which we hold and their relation to experience:

> The totality of our so-called knowledge or beliefs . . . is a man-made fabric which impinges on experience only along the edges. Or, to change the figure, total science is like a field of force whose boundary conditions are experience. A conflict with experience at the periphery occasions readjustments in the interior of the field ((1953), p. 42).

Thus a theoretical statement, such as that permanent consumption is a function of permanent income, to take an example from Friedman's work, involves a host of beliefs or theoretical propositions. These include, for example, the notion of consumption, the relation between different concepts of consumption, the concept of income, of permanent income, their determinants, as well as the relation between permanent income and permanent consumption. These form a nest of supporting hypotheses, which are themselves supported by deeper theoretical views about measurement and language. A conflict then between observation and theory is thus a conflict with this network of supporting beliefs. The problem then is to discover which observations relate to which parts of that network. Quine next presents his

[22] See especially Cross (1982).
[23] Quine argues not only that theories come not in isolation but in packages, or what Kuhn (1970) and Lakatos (1970) would call respectively paradigms and research programmes, but also that the theoretical terms are themselves interconnected in their meanings.

second premise, that:

> The total field is so undetermined by the boundary conditions, experience, that there is much latitude of choice as to what statements to reevaluate in the light of any single contrary experience. No particular experiences are linked with any particular statements in the interior of the field, except indirectly through considerations of equilibrium affecting the fields as a whole' (p. 43).

Thus in our example, an empirical conflict with Friedman's own permanent-income hypothesis could relate to any one or more of the nest of propositions which make up the theory. A particular problem here which illustrates this relational difficulty is that permanent income and consumption are theoretical terms requiring correspondence rules with actual observations, and there is no agreed method of making this translation.[24]

Indeed Quine points out that 'it is misleading to speak of the empirical content of an individual statement' and that 'it becomes folly to seek a boundary between synthetic statements, which hold contingently on experience, and analytical statements, which hold come what may' (p. 43). Therefore Quine claims what has become known as the Quine–Duhem thesis, that:

> Any statement can be held true come what may, if we make drastic enough adjustments elsewhere in the system... Conversely, by the same token, no statement is immune to revision (p. 43).

The claim as it stands is open to different interpretations. In particular Lakatos (1970), p. 184, has pointed out that it may either mean that targeting observations onto specific theoretical terms is impossible, or it may much more radically be taken as a denial of any empirical check on theory. In its weaker form, the thesis powerfully supports Hicks's caution on empiricism, but while he concentrates on the change in background conditions over time, Quine focuses his critique on the interconnectedness of theoretical terms. The two are thus complementary critiques of the positivist position, which Friedman at least at times expounds.[25]

We have then two views of economic method, supported by different philosophical positions on the relation between theory and evidence, and on the notion of causality. The first stresses the importance of prediction and testing, and the irrelevance of the realism of assumptions and the content of

---

[24] Friedman (1957), p. 20, himself notes that 'the magnitudes termed "permanent income" and "permanent consumption" cannot be directly observed... They are ex ante magnitudes; empirical data is ex post', thus recognizing the further complication of expectations being unobservable.

[25] The relation between the Quine–Duhem thesis and the F-Twist/S-Twist debate, following Samuelson's (1963) attempt to propose an operationalist theory, (which amounted to the claim that predictions were logically related to assumptions, such that they provided an 'indirect test'), is that Quine would want to deny that a particular prediction could be related to a particular assumption. It should also be noted that Samuelson's claim is false: because $A \Rightarrow B \Rightarrow C$, it does not follows that $A \Leftrightarrow B \Leftrightarrow C$. On this see Wong (1973) and Hoover (1984).

theory. The other stresses economic explanation and causal relations, and emphasizes that the understanding of behaviour is essentially theoretical, since counterfactuals are not themselves observable. But the question remains as to the choice and selection of assumptions, and in this respect there are two further components to a theory which need to be considered: first classification, and secondly the role of reasons in causality, what I shall call feasibility. Let us now look at classification and come back to feasibility later.

9. Classification

Friedman asserts that theories act as 'filing systems' and, retreating from the pure instrumentalist case, admits that there is a relationship between theories and facts. Hicks is much clearer on the implications of this relationship, arguing that when theory and fact conflict, as they often do, fact rather than theory might give way.[26] But if prediction cannot uniquely inform us, how are we to select our simplifications at this more general level; how are we to classify? The Hicksian answer is that selection depends on the problem at hand.[27] The choice of a theory depends on the sort of problem we want to solve, and that choice is at two levels: at the grand level of paradigms or research programmes,[28] and at the narrower level of particular assumptions.[29] Large theory-set changes, revolutions, occur with problem-shifts. These are not normally 'revolutions' in the violent sense, but much more natural evolutions. And Hicks claims that these Kuhnian changes are better understood as changes in classification. When two large sets of theories are appraised, say Ricardian and Keynesian, we ask what were the problems that they tried to solve, and what were the characteristics of the economies to which they referred. Common elements are checked for, to see whether, in our example, there are Ricardian traces in Keynes's writings. To ask whether one is better than another is strictly meaningless unless the problem and the time period are specified. We cannot, on the Hicksian view, compare their predictions. Economics is not that sort of science. In contrast for example, Hicks would argue that scientific theories like those of Einstein and Newton can be compared at least in principle, since they are not dated.[30] Classifications are, for Hicks, problem and time-period dependent because background conditions alter, and it is only if two rival sets of theories claim to refer to the same period and answer the same questions that they are strictly commensurable. Predictions are appraised only if the

[26] See quotation p. 124 above.
[27] Hicks writes ((1979), p. x): 'one must classify according to the kinds of problems (of real problem) to which they claim to have relevance. Many of the disputes amongst theorists can then be referred to the interests of those who construct them, in different problems.' See also Machlup (1967), p. 240, who makes a similar point.
[28] Hicks would prefer not to use these terms, but rather writes of 'blinkers'. See his (1976).
[29] See on assumption choice, Hicks (1939), pp. 83–4.
[30] Hicks calls these theories 'static'; and essentially his claim is that whereas science is essentially static, economics is dynamic ((1979), p. 24); see also note 13 above.

same *ceteris paribus* clauses apply. Unfortunately, however, the set of such cases is limited. The example of marginal and full cost pricing, discussed at the beginning of this paper, might at first glance appear to be of this type; but it runs up against the further point that these two theories do not necessarily predict different outcomes. It is the interpretations of the outcomes in this case which is at stake, not different empirical predictions. Friedman, in his confusion, admits this in his thesis about an infinite number of possible theories covering the same data set, point (11) of my list on p. 120 above.

PART THREE: REASONS AND CAUSES

10. Feasibility

The last points brings us to the final methodological criterion which I shall here discuss. It relates to a distinction Hicks uses in his account of causality between what he call the 'Old' and 'New Causality', and also to the dispute between those like Hall and Hitch on the one hand, and Friedman on the other, as to whether the reasons and motives for behaviour influence or cause particular outcomes. The central question concerns whether the purposeful or teleological nature of human behaviour implies a special and distinct social science notion of causality, including reasons as being causal in actions, and thus additionally whether they are a necessary part of human behaviour.

In what Hicks describes as the 'Old Causality' causes were considered as the action or agency of some one or more individuals whether human or supernatural. In contrast, the New Causality permitted causal explanation free from the necessity of agency (Hicks (1979), (1984a)). Friedman argues that reasons for an action are not necessary to theory construction. He writes that in the same way as a billiard player does not calculate the forces and resistances of a billiard ball in planning a particular shot, the inability to calculate marginal values does not invalidate marginalist theories of decision-making.[31] The confusion in Friedman concerns prediction and explanation. Because it is quite plausible that a good billiards player chooses close to optimal shots, it follows that a good predictor of his behaviour might be what he would have done if he had calculated the forces and resistances. But that in itself does not explain *how* he plays. The marginalist case is different from the billiards example in two respects. First, predictability is complicated by the possibility that both theories may predict the same outcomes. Secondly, the possibility that behaviour in the absence of marginal calculation is predictably the same as in its presence is more contentious, in the sense that it does not follow that it can be similarly *explained*. The

---

[31] Machlup (1967), in support of Friedman, calls this criticism 'the fallacy of misplaced concreteness'.

reasoning process of managers causes certain behavioural outcomes. The way in which this happens brings together reasoning and causality.

Feasibility, whether an individual is actually capable of assumed acts, and causality thus come together. To explain an action involves positing causes. Human actions, unlike scientific observations, are partially or weakly caused by the reasons that the person has in carrying out the act.[32] Feasible actions are those of which the human mind is capable of formulating reasons for. This claim concerning the content of causality has been formally presented by Davidson (1963). He asserts that only certain types of reasons can act as causes. These he calls 'primary reasons', and defines this term as follows ((1980), p. 5):

> R is a primary reason why an agent performed the action A under the description d only if R consists of a pro attitude of the agent towards actions with a certain property, and a belief of the agent that A, under the description d, has that property.

The inclusion of primary reasons as causal factors in explanation still leaves the substantive problem of how these might be in practice identified. A principle of charity is typically invoked, whereby the reasons an agent gives are taken to be *the* reasons for that act, unless the observer has good reason himself to think contrarily. Such a procedure is imperfect, but so are the alternatives. Now one of the restrictions placed on primary reasons is that they be feasible, and this is one of the limitations or constraints to be placed on the principle of charity. The implication of this criterion of feasibility is most clearly seen in the debate which sparked off Friedman's article, the maximization of profits, or more generally the maximization of utility. How are we to decide whether this assumption is justified? If Hicks is right, the issue is, firstly, a non-empirical one. The defenders of maximization argue that it does not matter whether people are capable of calculating appropriately. These are associated with Friedman as we have discussed above, with Becker (1976), Muth (1961), and Boland (1981). The opponents of maximization generally argue that maximization is not feasible. Feasibility refers both to the capacity of the brain to process information, and the quality of potential information. Simon (1955) claimed that humans are biologically limited by the capacity of the central nervous system, in their ability to compare alternatives, and proposed that individuals satisfice rather then maximize. Shackle (1949) has emphasized that it is not feasible to form probability judgements under a wide variety of uncertainty situations. Cyert and March (1963) argue that the problem of conflicting objectives of managers and workers leads to bargaining and trade-offs which

---

[32] This is the point which Addison *et al.* (1984) stress in their comment on Hicks's Old or New Causality distinction. They write: 'Causality in human beings operates through the mind of an agent'. The difference between their view and my own turns on whether *the set* of reasons constitute *weak* or *strong* causes of actions. Others who have also stressed the role of reasons include Hayek (1937) and Shackle (1967).

yield non-maximizing objectives for firms.[33] Our two views of methodology come down on different sides on this issue. Friedman, we have seen, denies that feasibility matters. Hicks is ambiguous, as one would expect given his problem-solving methodology, which depends on the importance of uncertainty and the costs of information for the problem at hand. Nevertheless, as early as 1939, he stressed the importance of considering the limitations of human behaviour (p. 337):

> for the understanding of the economic system we need something more, something which refer back, in the last resort, to the behaviour of people and the motives of their conduct.

He quite naturally accepts that information about probability is not always defined, and that maximization may not always be pursued ((1983), p. 139, 371). But our two views represent different tasks: the one to predict, the other to explain and thus to find causes for actions.

If feasibility counts, it is because the mental processes employed by decision-makers affect the outcomes of their actions. In this sense, causality and feasibility are linked. For a causal account to count as an explanation of an act it should thus include an account of the reasons for the act.

11. Conclusion

The search for a single method of theory appraisal has proved to be unsuccessful, and methodologies which advance such principles fail. Those parts of Friedman's article which are most positivistic in their emphasis on prediction to the exclusion of all other criteria fail in the face of the philosophical difficulties with testing predictions outlined above. The more reflective parts of Friedman's article deviate from this methodology, and hence are more acceptable. It is also worth noting that Friedman rarely, if ever, employs his procedures in his more practical work. In the theory of the consumption function (1957), for example, he carefully devotes the first part of the book to specifying (irrelevantly if the realism of assumptions is irrelevant) the micro-foundations of consumer theory, and then develops theoretical concepts without immediate empirical counterparts.[34]

But because a single principle like prediction is inadequate, it does not follow that unbridled pluralism is either permissible or desirable. Hicks's conception of causality is undoubtedly to be included as a basic explanatory criterion. But it needs to be extended to include some restrictions on the content of causes. Hicks has already carried out some of this exercise, with respect particularly to classification. I have added feasibility, and shown how that feasibility is related to causal accounts, by virtue of the causal effects of

[33] Other important critiques of maximization include Leibenstein (1976) and Winter's infinite regress argument proposed in his 1964 paper.

[34] In Friedman's monetary theory, another striking example of his ambivalence to the prediction criterion is to be found with regard to the unitary elasticity of the demand for money. On this see Courakis (1984).

reasons on actions. Economics is, Hicks asserts, 'a discipline not a science'. As in all disciplines, however, there are limitations on what is permissible, and what is not. Feasibility, I have argued, is one such limitation.

The Queen's College, Oxford

REFERENCES

ADDISON, J. T., BURTON, J. and TORRANCE, T. S. (1984), 'Causation, Social Science & Sir John Hicks', *Oxford Economic Papers*, NS xxxvi (1).

BECKER, G. S. (1976), *The Economic Approach to Human Behaviour*, University of Chicago Press.

BOLAND, L. A. (1979), 'A Critique of Friedman's Critics', *Journal of Economic Literature*, xvii, 503–22.

BOLAND, L. A. (1981), 'On the Futility of Criticizing the Neoclassical Maximization Hypothesis', *American Economic Review*, lxxi. 1031–6.

CALDWELL, B. (1982), *Beyond Positivism*, George Allen & Unwin, London.

CALDWELL, B. (1983), 'The Neoclassical Maximization Hypothesis: Comments', *American Economic Review*, lxxiii, 824–7.

COURAKIS, A. S. (1981), 'Monetary Targets: Conceptual Antecedents and Recent Policies in the US, UK and West Germany' in id. (ed.), *Inflation, Depression and Economic Policy in the West*, Mansell, London.

COURAKIS, A. S. (1984), 'The Demand for Money in South Africa'. *South African Journal of Economics*, lii, 1–41.

CROSS, R. (1982), 'The Duhem–Quine Thesis, Lakatos and the Appraisal of Theories in Macroeconomics', *Economic Journal*, xcii, 320–40.

CYERT, R. M. and MARCH, J. G. (1963), *A Behavioural Theory of the Firm*, Prentice–Hall. Englewood Cliffs, NJ.

DAVIDSON, D. (1963) 'Reasons as Causes', reprinted in id. (1980), *Essays on Actions and Events*, Oxford University Press.

DOBB, M. (1973), *Theories of Value and Distribution since Adam Smith*, Cambridge University Press.

DUHEM, P. (1914), *The Aims and Structure of Physical Theory*, Riviére, Paris, translated by P. Weiner, Princeton University Press (1954).

FRAZER, W. J., Jr and BOLAND, L. A. (1983), 'An Essay on the Foundation of Friedman's Methodology', *American Economic Review*, lxxiii, 129–44.

FRIEDMAN, M. (1953), 'The Methodology of Positive Economics', in id., *Essays in Positive Economics*, University of Chicago.

FRIEDMAN, M. (1957), *A Theory of the Consumption Function*, Princeton University Press.

GRANGER, C. W. J. and NEWBOLD, P. (1977), *Forecasting Economic Time Series*, Academic Press.

HACKING, I. (1983), *Representing and Intervening*, Cambridge University Press.

HALL, R. L. and HITCH, C. J. (1939). 'Price Theory and Business Behaviour', *Oxford Economic Papers*, NS ii, 15–45.

HARROD, R. (1939), 'Price and Cost in Entrepreneur's Policy', *Oxford Economic Papers*, NS ii, 1–11.

HAYEK, F. VON (1937) 'Economics and Knowledge', *Economica*, NS, iv, 33–54.

HELM, D. R. (1984), *Enforced Maximisation*. D. Phil thesis, Oxford.

HICKS, J. R. (1939), *Value and Capital*, Oxford University Press.

HICKS, J. R. (1956), *A Revision of Demand Theory*, Oxford University Press.

HICKS, J. R. (1969), *A Theory of Economic History*, Oxford University Press.

HICKS, J. R. (1976), '"Revolutions" in Economics' in S. J. Latsis (ed.), *Method and Appraisal in Economics*, Cambridge University Press, and reprinted in Hicks (1983).

HICKS, J. R. (1979), *Causality in Economics*, Basil Blackwell, Oxford.

HICKS, J. R. (1981) *Wealth and Welfare*, Basil Blackwell, Oxford [including 'LSE and the Robbins Circle].

HICKS, J. R. (1982), *Money, Interest and Wages*, Basil Blackwell, Oxford [including 'Methods of Dynamic Economics'],

HICKS, J. R. (1983), *Classics and Moderns*, Basil Blackwell, Oxford [including 'A Discipline not a Science'].

HICKS, J. R. (1984a), 'The "New Causality": an Explanation', *Oxford Economic Papers*, NS xxxvi (1).

HICKS, J. R. (1984b), 'Is Economics A Science?', *Interdisciplinary Science Review*, forthcoming.

HOOVER, K. (1984) 'Comment on Boland', *American Economic Review*, forthcoming.

HUME, D. (1738), *A Treatise on Human Nature*. Modern Edn., by L. A. Selby-Brigge (1978), Oxford University Press.

KUHN, T. (1970), 'The Structure of Scientific Revolutions', *International Encyclopedia of Unified Science*, vol. ii, no. 2; 2nd enlarged edn., Chicago University Press.

LAKATOS, I. (1970), 'Falsification and the Methodology of Scientific Research Programmes', in Lakatos and Musgrave (eds.), *Criticism and The Growth of Knowledge*. Cambridge University Press.

LEIBERSTEIN, H. (1976), *Beyond Economic Man*. Harvard University Press.

MACHLUP, F. (1967), 'Theories of the Firm: Marginalist, Behavioural and Managerial', *American Economic Review*, lvii, 1–33.

MACKIE, J. L. (1965), 'Causes and Conditions', *American Philosophical Quarterly*, ii (4), 245–64.

MACKIE, J. L. (1975), *The Cement of the Universe*, Oxford University Press.

MUTH, J. F. (1961), 'Rational Expectations and the Theory of Price Movements', *Econometrica*, xxix, 315–35.

QUINE, V. (1953), 'Two Dogmas of Empiricism' in id; *From a Logical Point of View*, Harvard University Press.

SAMUELSON, P. A. (1963), 'Problems of Methodology—Discussion', *American Economic Review*, P & P, liii, 231–6.

SAMUELSON, P. A. (1972), 'Maximum Principles in Analytical Economics', *American Economic Review*, lxii, 249–62.

SEN, A. K. (1980), 'Description as Choice', *Oxford Economic Papers*, xxxii, 353–69.

SHACKLE, G. L. S. (1949), *Expectations in Economics*, Cambridge University Press.

SHACKLE, G. L. S. (1967), *Decision, Order and Time*, Cambridge University Press.

SIMON, H. A. (1955), 'A Behavioural Model of Rational Choice', *Quarterly Journal of Economics*, lxix, 99–118.

SOSA, E. (ed.) (1975), *Causation and Conditionals*, Oxford University Press.

STROUD, B. (1977), *Hume*, Routledge and Kegan Paul, London.

TOBIN, J. (1970), 'Money and Income: Post Hoc Ergo Propter Hoc', *Quarterly Journal of Economics*, lxxxiv, 301–17.

WINTER, S. (1964), 'Economic "natural selection" and the Theory of the Firm', *Yale Economic Essays*, iv, 225–72.

WONG, S. (1973), 'The F-Twist and the Methodology of Paul Samuelson', *American Economic Review*, lxiii 313–25.

ZELLNER, A. (1979), 'Causality and Econometrics', in K. Brunner and A. H. Meltzer (eds.), *Three Aspects of Policy Making*, North Holland.

RICARDO AND HAYEK EFFECTS IN A FIXWAGE MODEL OF TRAVERSE

By STEFANO ZAMAGNI

1. On the scope of Hicksian traverse analysis

A FUNDAMENTAL characteristic of productive activity involving the use of durable means of production is that of causally linking events in temporal sequences. This implies that, to be useful, a study of the evolution of the material structure of an economy must, on the one hand, visualize production as an essentially joint process and, on the other hand, pay due attention to the complementarity relationships among technical possibilities belonging to different moments of time. Two main approaches to the problems posed by the presence of durable capital inputs can be found in the economic literature, the dividing line between the two being traceable back to the way the temporal element is dealt with.

According to the first—nowadays the dominant one—time is handled in such a way that it is reduced to a dimension of space. The activity-analysis model à la Malinvaud–von Neumann is the most rigorous and general expression of the 'synchronic' heterogeneity of capital—as one may call it—emerging from a horizontal representation of productive activity: the productive process is analyzed from one point in time to another over a series of time units, with no attention being paid to when things happen within the unit time. A noteworthy consequence of this spatial conception of time is that the latter enters economic analysis only in a quite restricted way, in the sense that the equations are invariant with respect to time inversion $(t \rightarrow -t)$.[1] According to the view of time as motion, future and past play essentially the same role and change is merely reduced to a sequence of substantially equivalent states.[2]

The other approach, on the other hand, explicitly recognizes that both duration of production and timing of production are essential features of capitalistic production. An immediate consequence of this is that the intermediate products, which characterize the various stages into which the productive process can be decomposed, are intertemporal complements to one another. What emerges is therefore a 'diachronic' heterogeneity of capital, quite different from the heterogeneity of buildings, equipment, tools,

---

[1] It will be recalled that D'Alembert was the first to remark that time appears in dynamics as a mere 'geometrical parameter' unaffected by the transformation that it describes. And Lagrange went so far as to call dynamics a four-dimensional geometry.

[2] In economics this view of time is well expressed by E. Malinvaud when he writes: 'The introduction of time does not seem to imply any new principle. Choices between commodities available at different times raise essentially the same problem as choices between different commodities available at the same time' ((1953), p. 233) and by E. Burmeister: 'If we have n distinct types of commodities and T periods it is evident that there is an exact correspondence to a static model having different commodities equal in number to nT' ((1980), p. 2).

and stocks of commodities. This was the view taken by the classics, by the early Jevons—the Jevons of 'A Serious Fall in the Value of Gold' of 1863—and in a more systematic way by the Austrian writers. According to these latter, time enters production in two distinct ways: as duration of the process by which original inputs are transformed into final outputs, and as duration of the 'machine' generating a temporal joint supply of goods stretching over a certain period of time.

For various reasons,[3] the vertical representation of the productive structure has so far received little attention within the profession. Recently, Sir John Hicks has come to call attention to the potentialities of this approach for the study of non-steady state growth paths. *Capital and Time* is primarily and essentially aimed at laying the foundations of a descriptive theory of disproportional growth by exploiting the Austrian insight of vertical integration of productive processes. A major concept of *Capital and Time* is the 'impulse'—the impact of a technical innovation, consisting in a new method for making a given final commodity, on historical processes. Technical change is not only a major growth stimulus but also a source of many adjustment problems. After a structural change, a new steady state equilibrium—defined with respect to the particular composition of the capital stock appropriate to the new technology and compatible with the labour and savings flows—can only be achieved, if ever, when the 'transmutation' of the capital stock to the proportions required by the new steady state has been completed.

It is precisely the focus on transitions that leads Hicks to a representation of the productive system in which intersectoral transactions are forgotten, in order not to be disturbed by the physical changes in the capital stock under the influence of the new invention. In his words: 'it is here undesirable that these goods should be physically specified, since there is no way of establishing a physical relation between the capital goods that are required in the one technique and those that are required in the other. The only relation that can be established runs in terms of costs and of capacity to produce final output'.[4]

It would therefore be out of place to try to establish the 'superiority' of one approach over the other: each one enjoys a sort of comparative

---

[3] It is beyond question that the unfortunate association between the Austrian approach to capital theory and the work of Böhm–Bawerk not only has prevented a thorough evaluation of the many differences among the Austrian authors themselves but has also contributed to propagate the idea of a sort of coextensivity between the Austrian capital theory and the analysis of a stationary economy with circulating capital only. On this, cf. F. von Hayek (1941), pp. 47 ff.

[4] Cf. Hicks (1977), p. 193. It is not without interest to note that vertical integration also forms the basis of the theory of structural dynamics recently developed by Pasinetti. Concerning the rationale of framing a dynamic analysis in terms of vertically integrated sectors, he writes: 'Of course, at any given point in time, the input-output model gives us more information... But, over time, the input–output coefficients change and the inter-industry system breaks down... Then it is only the vertically integrated model that allows us to follow the vicissitudes of the economic system through time' (1981), p. 115.

advantage in dealing with different fields of enquiry. And the field where the vertical approach shows all its potentialities concerns the study of the effects (not the causes) of those kinds of innovations which consist in new methods for producing a given commodity. The last qualification is important, since it reminds us that the approach under consideration is not equally well suited for studying other kinds of traverse, such as those generated by innovations introducing new goods, nor for dealing with all other aspects of innovation, such as those related to the effects of innovation upon the industrial structure.[5]

Two further points should be kept in mind for a correct assessment of traverse theory, in its Hicksian form. First, we might say that its main role is the study of the 'turbulent' short periods if this expression were not surrounded by a penumbra of ambiguity. As is well known, in the classics the distinction between short and long period corresponds, vaguely, to that between phenomena which are changeable and temporary and phenomena which are structural and permanent. Yet, between 'the immediate and temporary effects of particular changes' and 'the permanent state of things which will result from them',[6] there is a territory where phenomena occur which are less 'temporary' than those characterizing the classical adjustment process of market prices to natural prices, but less 'permanent' than those through which the accumulation process takes way. Well, traverse analysis deals precisely with phenomena of this kind, constituting a whole territory which has been left so far largely unexplored.

The second point refers to a particular utilization of traverse theory on methodological grounds. By drawing attention on the deviations between the actual position of the system and its corresponding long-period position—which in the most simple applications is identified with a steady state—traverse theory provides a case for the counterfactual approach to sequential causality:[7] the cause being a change in technology occurring at a certain point of time, the effect being the entire difference between the traverse or actual path and the path the economy would have followed in the absence of the disturbance.[8]

[5] In a recent and very interesting contribution, Belloc has generalized the Hicksian neo-Austrian method to take into consideration the inter-industrial relationships. By allowing a certain degree of sectoral interdependencies, he shows how it is possible to deal with intermediate products. Cf. B. Belloc (1980).

[6] Cf. Ricardo to Malthus (1817), in Ricardo (1951–1973), vol. vii, p. 120.

[7] Cf. J. Hicks (1979). It goes without saying that the counterfactual approach to causality is not without its own difficulties. Suffice here to mention the celebrated 'Bizet–Verdi paradox' due to O. Quine and the more recent 'fundamental paradox of counterfactuals' due to J. Elster (1978), p. 184. It may be interesting to remember that in the *Treatise*, where he first talks about 'causal processes', Keynes writes: 'The real task is to treat the problem dynamically ... in such a manner as to exhibit the causal process by which the price level is determined and the method of transition from one position of equilibrium to another' (vol. v, p. 120). As can be shown from a textual analysis, Keynes's argument runs in terms of deviations of actual magnitudes from long-period counterparts: an exercise methodologically very close to Hicksian sequential causality.

[8] However, as we will mention in the final section, the use of traverse analysis for the study of sequential causality undergoes an important qualification.

In the sequel, I shall discuss a fixwage model of traverse where the temporal structure of the elementary process is of the continuous input–continuous output type. Instead of aiming at a 'widening' of the basic model, the purpose here is that of taking a fresh look at certain vexed questions of economic theory with the intention of showing the potentialities of the Hicksian traverse as a method for dynamic analysis. Indeed, if the criteria for a method to qualify as dynamic are that it should be capable of dealing with both the process in which the economy is moving and the state at which it finds itself during this process, then traverse analysis is such a method.

2. The model

2.1. Let $\{l(t); b(t)\}_{t=0}^{t=\hat{\theta}}$ represent the generic elementary process, where $l(t)$ denotes the instantaneous flow rate of primary inputs in fixed proportions—labour, for short; $b(t)$ the instantaneous flow rate of final output; t the time measured from the start of the process and $\hat{\theta}$ the physical life of the process. Denoting with T the historical or calendar time—a continuous variable—the sequence $\{x(T-t)\}_{t=0}^{t=\theta(T)}$, where $x(T-t)$ stands for the rate of starts of processes at $(T-t)$, tells us about the age structure of the capital stock. We shall assume that elementary processes can be activated at any level under conditions of constant returns to scale and that no process has value as scrap when it is terminated. Finally, $\theta(T)$ represents the optimal life of the process of time T, which presupposes the possibility of truncation.[9]

Under steady-state conditions, $x(T-t) = x(0)e^{g(T-t)}$ where $g > -1$ is the growth rate. Let $B(T)$ denote the total amount, at time T, of final output and $L(T)$ total employment at time T. Therefore:

$$B(T) = \int_0^{\theta(T)} b(t)x(T-t)\,\mathrm{d}t = \int_0^{\theta} b(t)x(0)e^{g(T-t)}\,\mathrm{d}t$$

whence $\dot{B}(T) = gB(T)$ and

$$L(T) = \int_0^{\theta(T)} l(t)x(T-t)\,\mathrm{d}t = \int_0^{\theta} l(t)x(0)e^{g(T-t)}\,\mathrm{d}t$$

whence $\dot{L}(T) = gL(T)$.

As far as the valuation side of the economy is concerned, under the assumption of a fixed wage rate, w^*, exogenously given, we have:

$$\begin{cases} \int_0^{\theta(r)} [b(t) - wl(t)]e^{-rt}\,\mathrm{d}t = 0 \\ W = W^* \end{cases} \tag{2.1}$$

where final output is our *numéraire*, r is the rate of profit, and $\theta(r)$ remains

---

[9] As is known, truncation assures the monotonicity of the capital value of the process and therefore uniqueness of its internal rate of return. However, whereas with intertemporal geometrical prices truncation is a sufficient but not necessary condition to assure monotonicity to the capital value of the process, it becomes a necessary and sufficient condition whenever the profit rate changes over time. Cf. S. Ross, C. Spatt, P. Dybvig (1980). See also A. Sen (1975).

constant over time. Solving with respect to w, equation (2.1) gives the familiar efficiency curve for the economy. It is immediately seen that as $w \to 0$, $r \to \infty$, which shows the absence of basic goods in the Sraffa sense. Moreover, it can be shown that under the conditions for the Hicksian 'fundamental theorem' to hold, the efficiency curve is downward sloping.[10]

The temporal profiles of the process are endowed with the following obvious assumptions:

(i) $l(0) > 0$, $l(t) \geq 0$ $\forall t \in [0, \hat{\theta}]$; $\displaystyle\int_{\tau}^{\theta(r)} l(t) \, dt > 0$, $\theta(r) \leq \hat{\theta}$

where τ stands for the time at which the utilization phase of the process begins. Unlike θ, τ is a technical parameter.

(ii) $b(t) = 0$ $\forall t \in [0, \tau)$; $b(t) > 0$, $\forall t \in [\tau, \hat{\theta}]$; $\displaystyle\int_{0}^{\theta} b(t) \, dt > 0$;

which expresses the essentiality of time in the productive activity: while the 'machine' is being constructed, final output is zero.

(iii) functions $b(t)$ and $l(t)$ are continuous and a.e. differentiable. Hence, also the net output function $q(t) = b(t) - wl(t)$ shares the same properties.

2.2. A technical innovation, occurring at time $T = 0$, is the causal factor which, by upsetting the steady state equilibrium, pushes the economy onto the traverse path. The form of technical change we shall consider is the mechanization one, undoubtedly the most interesting form.[11] To avoid useless formal complications, we characterize the case of mechanization as follows (starred variables refer to the old technique):

$$\begin{cases} l(t) > l^*(t) & \forall t \in [0, t') \\ l(t') = l^*(t') & \text{where } t' \text{ stands for the time at which the input profiles of the} \\ & \text{two techniques intersect each other;} \\ l(t) < l^*(t) & \forall t \in (t', \theta^*], \text{ i.e. we are assuming that } \theta > \theta^*: \text{ the lengthening} \\ & \text{case;}^{12} \\ b(t) = b^*(t) & \forall t \in [\max(\tau, \tau^*), \min(\theta, \theta^*)] \end{cases}$$

In words, the new process is more mechanized than the old one if the output profiles are the same over their common interval of time and the former employs more labour during the construction period and less labour during the utilization period than the latter.

Naturally, the switch to the new technique will be effective if and only if, at the steady state prices, the following condition is met:

$$\int_{0}^{\theta(r^*)} b(t) e^{-r^* t} \, dt > w^* \int_{0}^{\theta(r^*)} l(t) e^{-r^* t} \, dt$$

[10] There is no difficulty in obtaining the other steady-state properties of the model, which do not vary from those of the parent models.

[11] It has been shown that the evolution of technologies through time presents some significant regularities, including the mechanization of production processes. Cf. R. R. Nelson, S. Winter (1977). See also L. Pasinetti, op. cit.

[12] Needless to say, in general the optimal durations need not be unique.

i.e. if and only if the introduction of the new process implies at the old prices and given static expectations, extra-profits. In view of the Hicksian fundamental theorem, this means that $r > r^*$.[13]

3. The Hayek effect

3.1. We are now ready to work out the fixwage path the economy will follow starting from $T = 0$. The introduction of the new process primes a double adjustment mechanism. On the one hand, from $T = 0$ onwards, the old-type processes will no longer be started since they have become obsolete—this is the direct effect of the change. On the other hand, it might become profitable to truncate the old-type processes still in operation at $T = 0$, and this as a consequence of the fact that at the higher rate of interest $(r > r^*)$, the capital value of these processes may be negative—we will refer to this as the indirect effect of the change.[14]

The upshot is that the rate of starts along the traverse path depends on both the savings generated within the system—we are in fact assuming full performance—and the resources which are set free by the truncation decisions. In order to isolate the direct from the indirect effect, we will first suppose that the net output profile of the old technique is such that no truncation can occur at $T = 0$.

In full performance, at any $T \geqslant 0$, the following condition must be met:

$$B(T) = C(T) + c_w w^* L(T)$$

where $C(T)$ denotes the capitalists' consumption during the traverse, c_w $(0 < c_w < 1)$ stands for the marginal and average propensity to consume of workers, and w^* is the wage rate carried over from the old steady state and remaining inflexible.

To simplify, but with no loss in generality, assume:

$$K^*(t) \equiv b^*(t) - c_w w^* l^*(t) > 0 \quad \forall\, t \in (t_2^*, \theta^*]$$
$$K(t) \equiv b(t) - c_w^* l(t) > 0 \qquad \forall\, t \in (t_2, \theta]$$

where the dates t_2 and t_2^* are defined by the following conditions:

$$\int_0^{t_2} K(t)\, dt \quad \text{and} \quad \int_0^{t_2^*} K^*(t)\, dt = 0 \qquad t_2, t_2^* \in (0, \theta^*)$$

and their existence is assured by the non-negativity of the internal rates of return associated with the old and the new processes.

The following Volterra integral equations of the first kind describe the

---

[13] It should be noted that the rise of the rate of profit which accompanies the introduction of the new process is here the effect and not the cause of the innovation. Moreover, it is implicit in the above argument that the criterion for the choice of technique remains that of the maximization of the profit rate, even outside steady states. We shall come back on this point in the final section.

[14] Cf. J. Hicks, (1973), ch. V.

successive phases of the traverse:

$$\int_0^T K(T-t)x(t)\,dt + \int_{T-\theta^*}^0 K^*(T-t)x^*(t)\,dt = C(T) \quad \forall\, T \in [0, \theta^*]$$

(3.1)

$$\int_0^T K(T-t)x(t)\,dt = C(T) \quad \forall\, T \in [\theta^*, \theta]$$ (3.1')

$$\int_{T-\theta}^T K(T-t)x(t)\,dt = C(T) \quad \forall\, T > \theta.$$ (3.1'')

On the other hand, along the reference path, which we take to be the continuation of the old steady-state path, we have:

$$\int_{T-\theta^*}^T K^*(T-t)x^*(t)\,dt = C^*(T) \quad \forall\, T \geq 0.$$ (3.2)

We focus attention on the early phase of the traverse, which extends from time 0, when the new technique is introduced, up to the moment when the last of the old processes is terminated. After the substitution of (3.2) into (3.1) we get:

$$\int_0^T K(T-t)x(t)\,dt = \int_0^T K^*(T-t)x^*(t)\,dt + C(T) - C^*(T) \quad \forall\, T \in [0, \theta^*].$$

(3.3)

Since we assume the functions $C^*(T)$, $C(T)$, $x^*(T)$ to be analytic, we can seek the solution of (3.3) in the form of series of powers:

$$C^*(T) \equiv \sum_{n=0}^{\infty} C_n^* T^n; \qquad x^*(t) \equiv \sum_{n=0}^{\infty} x_n^* t^n;$$

$$C(T) \equiv \sum_{n=0}^{\infty} C_n T^n; \qquad x(T) \equiv \sum_{n=0}^{\infty} x_n T^n.$$

It is easily demonstrated that

$$x_n(T) = \left\{ \Delta C_n T^n + x_n^* \int_0^T K^*(t)(T-t)^n\,dt \right\} \left\{ \int_0^T K(t)(T-t)^n\,dt \right\}^{-1},$$

$$n = 0, 1, \ldots \infty. \quad (3.4)$$

On the other hand, since $x_n^* \geq 0$ $(n = 0, 1, \ldots \infty)$ and

$$\int_0^T K^*(t)(T-t)^n\,dt = \int_0^T du_n \int_0^{u_n} du_{n-1} \int_0^{u_{n-1}} \ldots \int_0^{u_1} K^*(t)\,dt$$ (3.5)

and

$$\int_0^T K(t)(T-t)^n\,dt = \int_0^T du_n \int_0^{u_n} du_{n-1} \int_0^{u_{n-1}} \ldots \int_0^{u_1} K(t)\,dt$$

in the special case where $\Delta C(T) \equiv C(T) - C^*(T) = 0$, equation (3.4) shows that the evolution of $x(T)$ depends on the time shape of the profiles characterizing the old and the new technique. The assumption $\Delta C(T) = 0$ implies that consumption out of profits is unaffected by the change in technique, hence by the change in profits. While this may be considered a fair approximation to what is likely to happen in the neighbourhood of time 0, it is not without interest to enquire about the impact of a change in the capitalist consumption pattern on the rate of starts. To this end, we calculate the following derivative:

$$\frac{\mathrm{d}x_n(T)}{\mathrm{d}(\Delta C_n)} = T\left\{\int_0^T K(t)(T-t)^n \, \mathrm{d}t\right\}^{-1} \qquad n = 0, 1, \ldots, \infty \qquad (3.6)$$

whose sign, in view of the supposed analyticity of the functions involved, is the same as that of the following derivative in the Fréchet sense:

$$\frac{\partial x(T)}{\partial(\Delta C(T))} \quad \forall \, T \in [0, \theta^*]. \qquad (3.7)$$

We can now summarize the major results concerning (a) the sign of $x(T)$; (b) the relation between the rates of starts on the reference path and on the traverse; (c) the impact of changes in $\Delta C(T)$ on $x(T)$, as follows:[15]

$$x(T) \leqslant x^*(T); \qquad \partial x(T)/\partial[\Delta C(T)] < 0; \qquad x(T) > 0 \quad \forall \, T \in [0, t_1]$$
$$(3.8)$$

$$x(T) \geqslant x^*(T); \qquad \partial x(T)/\partial[\Delta C(T)] < 0; \qquad x(T) > 0 \quad \forall \, T \in [t_1, t_2^*]$$
$$(3.9)$$

$$x(T) < x^*(T); \qquad \partial x(T)/\partial[\Delta C(T)] < 0; \qquad x(T) < 0 \quad \forall \, T \in [t_2^*, t_2]$$
$$(3.10)$$

$$x(T) > x^*(T); \qquad \partial x(T)/\partial[\Delta C(T)] > 0; \qquad x(T) > 0 \quad \forall \, T \in [t_2, \theta^*]$$
$$(3.11)$$

where the date t_1 is defined by the condition:

$$\int_0^{t_1} K(t) \, \mathrm{d}t = \int_0^{t_1} K^*(t) \, \mathrm{d}t, \, t_1 \in (0, \theta^*)$$

and $t_1 \leqslant \min(t_2^*, t_2)$.[16]

3.2. We may briefly comment on the above results. First of all, inequalities (3.10) single out an interval of time $[t_2^*, t_2]$ in the course of the traverse during which the rate of starts becomes negative. The economic interpretation is straightforward: in an economy such as the present one, where the labour force poses no contraint on productive activity, the only

---

[15] For a proof, see the appendix at the end of the paper.
[16] From the definition of the dates t_1, t_2, t_2^*, it follows that:

$$\int_0^T K(t) \, \mathrm{d}t \geqslant \int_0^T K^*(t) \, \mathrm{d}t; \quad \forall \, T \in [t_1, \theta^*].$$

bottleneck is constituted by lack of resources. This might not only prevent the starting of new processes $(x(T)=0)$, but it might also impose that processes, which have been started, be stopped $(x(T)<0)$. Such a phenomenon, which signals the emergence during the early phase of the traverse of an incompatibility between the level of consumption of capitalists, the fixed wage rate, and the time-shape of the new process on the one side and the full performance condition on the other, we call the *Hayek effect*.[17]

Indeed, as Hayek wrote in 1931: 'What they overlook is that durable means of production do not represent all the capital that is needed for an increase of output and that in order that the existing durable plants could be used to their full capacity it would be necessary to invest a great amount of other means of production in lengthy processes which would bear fruits only in a comparatively distant future. The existence of unused capacity is, therefore, by no means a proof that there exists an excess of capital and that consumption is insufficient: on the contrary, it is a symptom that we are unable to use the fixed plant to the full extent because the current demand for consumers' goods is too urgent to permit us to invest current productive services in the long processes for which ... the necessary durable equipment is available'.[18] The importance for industrial fluctuations of the temporal structure of productive processes was a major contribution of Hayek. The present analysis, by confirming his insight, sets the boundaries—hence, the conditions—within which the Hayek effect is operative.[19]

It is important to stress that the underutilization of productive capacity is due, in the present context, not to a deficiency of effective demand, but to the fact that technical change has taken a form which is hard to accommodate. In fact, as can be seen from (3.8)–(3.11), over the period $[0, t_2]$ and therefore over the sub-period $[t_2^*, t_2]$ during which the Hayek effect is in operation, an increase in effective demand, here representable as an increase of $C(T)$ above $C^*(T)$, has an adverse impact on $x(T)$, worsening that effect.

The present finding reminds us that accumulation of capital never takes the form of a mere multiplication of the elements already in existence but rather that of a change in its composition. If capital were a homogeneous aggregate, then the only possible factor explaining, under the present conditions, under-functioning of the economy would be a lack of effective demand.[20]

[17] To avoid misunderstandings, the Hayek effect we are talking about is not to be confused with the 'Hayek effect' considered by J. Schumpeter (1939), pp. 345, 812, 814. The latter refers to the influence of factor prices on the introduction of a new productive technique.

[18] Cf. F. von Hayek (1931), p. 96.

[19] Obviously, there will be a certain asymmetry between the case where the new process has a longer constructional period and a shorter utilizational period vis-à-vis the old process and the case where the opposite is true.

[20] In his 'A reply to Dr. Hayek', J. M. Keynes writes 'Dr. Hayek complains that I do not myself propound any satisfactory theory of capital and interest ... He means by this, I take it, the theory of capital accumulation relatively to the rate of consumption and the factors which determine the natural rate of interest. This is quite true, and I agree with Dr. Hayek that a development of this theory would be highly relevant to my treatment of monetary matters and likely to throw light into dark corners' (Vol. xiii, pp. 252–3). The above result can be seen as throwing some light into a 'dark corner'.

3.3. What, now, of the truncation at $T=0$ of the old-type processes? First of all, why is it that it pays to truncate at $T=0$? Simply because at the new and higher internal rate of return $(r>r^*)$, the continuation of old processes might generate capital losses. Formally, denote the capital value of the 'tail' of the process as

$$v^*(t, r) \equiv \int_t^{\theta^*} q^*(u)e^{-r(u-t)} \, \mathrm{d}u.$$

In view of the following properties:

$$v^*(t, r^*) \geq 0 \quad \forall \, t \in [0, \theta^*]; \qquad v^*(0, r) < 0; \qquad v(0, r) = 0$$

and from the continuity of $v^*(t, r)$, it follows that there is a date

$$s_1 \in (0, t_2^*) \quad \text{s.t.} \quad v^*(s_1, r) = 0.$$

The population of old processes still in operation at $T=0$ can now be split into two classes: the class of those processes whose age falls in $[0, s_1]$, which will be truncated, and the class of those processes whose age falls in $[s_1, \theta^*]$ which will be continued as originally planned.[21]

By defining the index function

$$\sigma(t) = \begin{cases} 1 & \forall \, t \in [s_1, \theta^*] \\ 0 & \forall \, t \in [0, s_1] \end{cases}$$

and in view of (3.2), the equation of the early phase now becomes:

$$\int_0^T K(T-t)x(t) \, \mathrm{d}t = \Delta C(T) + \int_0^T K^*(T-t)x^*(t) \, \mathrm{d}t$$

$$+ \int_T^{\theta^*} K^*(t)(1-\sigma(t))x^*(T-t) \, \mathrm{d}t. \qquad (3.12)$$

Focusing on the case where $\Delta C(T) = 0$, express the solution of (3.12) in terms of power series:

$$x_n(T) = \left\{ \int_0^T K^*(t)(T-t)^n \, \mathrm{d}t + \int_T^{\theta^*} K^*(t)(1-\sigma(t))(T-t)^n \, \mathrm{d}t \right\}$$

$$\times \left\{ \int_0^T K(t)(T-t)^n \, \mathrm{d}t \right\}^{-1}, \qquad n = 0, 1, \ldots, \infty. \qquad (3.13)$$

Equation (3.13) differs from (2.4) only by the second integral occurring in its numerator. It is easily seen that this integral is positive for $T \in [0, \min(s_1, t_2)]$ which means that, over this interval, the rate of starts will be higher than that which would have occurred in the absence of truncation. Now, whenever $s_1 < t_2$, from the fact that, as we already know, $s_1 < t_2^*$, it follows that truncation mitigates, momentarily, the Hayek effect, partly

---

[21] It can be proved that capitalists will always suffer a capital loss on old-type processes during the early phase of traverse. Indeed, the total amount of profits the capitalists would have reaped along the reference path is higher than that obtained during the early phase. What truncation achieves is to mitigate this capital loss.

offsetting its impact. All this makes perfect economic sense: under full performance conditions, the resources which are left free by the truncation must be utilized to start processes of the new type.[22]

4. The Ricardo machinery effect

4.1. We pass now to consider the effect on the level of employment of the introduction of a new technique. The literature on technological unemployment is huge.[23] Nevertheless, it is a fact that the analysis of the Ricardo effect[24] continues, quite often, to be carried on within a comparative static framework. This is methodologically wrong, for the very simple reason that the issue at stake is not that of ascertaining whether or not there will be a drop in employment as a consequence of the introduction of machinery—a task which can properly be accomplished by comparing two steady-state equilibria—but that of finding out the moment when this will occur and, above all, the period of time during which the adverse effect on employment will remain effective. One should not forget, in fact, that it was Ricardo himself who carefully stated that the harmful effect cannot persist indefinitely. Therefore, only a study of the path of transition will give proper answers to the problems of technological unemployment.

Passing to the formal side, we note that at any instant T along the traverse, the following condition must be satisfied (whenever $\Delta C(T) = 0$):

$$B(T) - B^*(T) = w^*[L(T) - L^*(T)]c_w \quad \forall\, T \in [0, \theta^*]. \tag{4.1}$$

This implies that the change in the volume of final output is the factor determining, in the present context, the change in employment. In view of our definition of mechanization we can rewrite (4.1), after expansion in power series of $x(T)$ and $x^*(T)$, as follows:

$$L(T) - L^*(T) \equiv \Delta L(T) = \frac{1}{c_w w^*} \sum_{n=0}^{\infty} [x_n(T) - x_n^*] \int_0^T b(t)(T-t)^n \, dt. \tag{4.2}$$

Since the integral appearing in (4.2) is positive, the study of the sign of $\Delta L(T)$ reduces to that of the sign of $[x_n(T) - x_n^*]$. It will be noticed that when $\tau = \tau^*$, $\Delta L(T) = 0$ $\forall\, T \in [0, \tau]$: the impact on employment becomes effective only after the new "machines" have started producing final output.

---

[22] From a formal point of view, truncation at $T = 0$ of old processes determines a discontinuity in the function $x(T)$, occurring only at $T = 0$ in view of the fixwage assumption. Obviously, another jump in $x(T)$ will occur at $T = \theta$ when a larger number of new processes will reach the end of their economic life. It is proper to note that there is nothing inconsistent between the present analysis and that developed by Hicks in chapter XI of his *Capital and Time*: the latter being a special case—the "simple profile" case—of the farmer.

[23] It may suffice here to refer to M. Berg (1980), ch. 4, where a thorough historical interpretation of that question is also offered.

[24] To be sure, the Ricardo machinery effect here investigated should not be confused with the 'Ricardo effect' considered by Hayek (1939), p. 10. The former concerns the employment *effects* of the introduction of a different method of production; the latter deals with the *causes* of its introduction, in particular with the impact of factor prices on the introduction of new technologies.

From inequalities (3.8)–(3.11) we get:

$$\Delta L(T)\begin{cases} >0 & \forall\ T\in[t_1, t_2^*]\cup[t_2, \theta^*] \\ <0 & \forall\ T\in[0, t_1]\cup[t_2^*, t_2]. \end{cases} \quad (4.3)$$

The economic interpretation of (4.3) vindicates the famous Ricardian conclusion according to which a 'transformation of circulating capital into fixed capital' causes an adverse, but temporary, effect on employment. The novelty here is that this statement holds true even in the case of the introduction of a less mechanized method of production. To see this, we simply need to reverse the signs of the inequalities (3.8)–(3.11).

Before we draw an interesting implication of this 'discovery', let us note that truncation at $T = 0$ originates two opposing influences on employment: on the one hand, it determines a reduction of employment whenever $\tau^* < s_1 < \theta^*$; on the other hand, it produces an increment of employment thanks to the processes which have to be started at $T = 0$ in order that the full performance condition be satisfied. Now, by substituting (3.13) into (4.2), it can be seen that the net effect on employment of truncation over the period $[0, \tau^*]$ is always negative, irrespective of the particular form taken by technical change—a result which clearly reinforces our general proposition.[25]

4.2. It will be recalled that, in his celebrated chapter 'On machinery', Ricardo, answering to Barton, recognizes that the introduction of improved machinery may operate in such a way as to 'transfer capital from its effective occupation as circulating capital' to its employment as fixed capital. In turn, this might determine a decrease of gross revenue, hence of the fund for the employment of labour.

But what exactly does Ricardo mean by the distinction between fixed and circulating capital? At first sight (and according to many interpreters) it might be thought that Ricardo based his distinction on the length of time a commodity keeps a particular physical form.[26] However, if this were the case, i.e. if one keeps to the durability criterion in order to distinguish between fixed and circulating capital and if one adheres to the classical idea according to which the adverse effect on employment is associated with a transformation of circulating into fixed capital, then the introduction of a less mechanized technique should not cause any drop in employment, contrary to our finding. Indeed, if one wants to continue to associate the Ricardo effect with that transformation, the only thing one can do is either

---

[25] Contrast this with the conclusion arrived at by T. Ito, who, in a recent paper, develops a simple one-sector neoclassical growth model whose production side is represented by a standard production function. Concerning the possibility of the Ricardo effect he writes: '... for a sufficiently small value for the elasticity of substitution, it is possible that technological spurt causes temporary technological unemployment if the wage is sluggish'. (1980), p. 399.

[26] 'According as capital is rapidly perishable and requires to be frequently reproduced or is of slow consumption, it is classed under the heads of circulating or of fixed capital' (Ricardo ch. I, sect. iv, p. 31). However, in the footnote we read: 'A division not essential and in which the line of demarcation cannot be accurately drawn'.

to change or to supplement the traditional criterion to distinguish between fixed and circulating capital.

In this regard, a possible solution is that of supplementing the durability criterion with that of the 'distance' of a capital good from final consumption, as Ricardo himself[27] seems to have hinted at and as Hayek explicitly proposed.[28] More specifically, if we define circulating capital as that part of capital stock which will be transformed into consumer goods during the current period—including those durable goods which will cease to exist within the same period—and fixed capital all the other means of production, it then becomes clear that any change in the composition of a given stock of capital in favour of the fixed component (so defined) will result in a decrement of the rate of final output and therefore of employment, and this irrespective of the form taken by technical change.

The main lesson to be drawn from the above argument is that the complexities of capital structure are such that no single classification of its elements based on a unidimensional criterion—be it durability or distance from consumption—can be deemed fully satisfactory for all purposes. In situations like the present one, a mere dichotomy such as that between fixed and circulating capital cannot but yield misleading results: once we leave the mythical world of steady states, it is the entire temporal articulation of the various elements of the capital stock which should be taken into careful consideration.

5. The late phase and sequential causality

5.1. What happens during the late phase—the phase of the traverse where the only processes in operation are those of the new type? In particular, under which set of conditions is it possible to prove the convergence of the traverse path to the steady state equilibrium compatible with the new technique introduced at $T = 0$? In another paper[29] it has been proved that only under very special conditions is convergence assured (e.g. this is the

[27] 'On account then of the different degrees of durability of their capitals, or, *which is the same thing*, on account of the time which must elapse before one set of commodities can be brought to market...' (Ricardo, Ch. I, sect. iv, p. 34; italics added) and a few pages later '...the superior price of one commodity is owing to the greater length of time which must elapse before it can be brought to market' (id., p. 37).

[28] '...The proposition that a conversion of circulating capital into fixed capital will bring about a reduction in the rate of output due to that capital is not strictly correct if we define fixed capital as durable goods and circulating capital as goods in process, but becomes true if we define the two kinds of capital... according to their final distance from consumption' (Hayek (1941), p. 428). It may be interesting to note that a very similar criterion is proposed by Marx when he writes that, since fixed capital never enters directly in circulation as use value, it is proper to distinguish between fixed capital and circulating capital 'from the perspective of individual consumption' (Marx (1973), p. 716) And it is on the basis of such a criterion of distinction that, according to Marx, it is possible to explain that '...in the constant under- and overproduction of modern industry, constant fluctuations and convulsions arise from the disproportion, when sometimes too little, then again too much circulating capital is transformed into fixed capital'. (Id., p. 708, Notebook, vii).

[29] Cf. S. Zamagni and G. Gozzi (1982).

case when the input and output profiles of the process are of the point input-continuous output type). This should not surprise: a similar conclusion has been arrived at within the framework of analysis dealing with growth models with heterogeneous capital goods—the so-called saddle-point instability.[30]

However, what also emerges from traverse theory is the substantial irrelevance of the problem of convergence as such. At best, the convergence of the late phase to a new equilibrium would take a long time and before the economy had entered the late phase and before that time had elapsed, a myriad of phenomena of various kinds would certainly have occurred to modify the basic relations of the economy. Indeed, the rate at which technologies, endowments, and institutional constraints change is so rapid in modern times, relative to the rate at which an economy adjusts to any set of underlying institutional and structural factors, that any inherent convergence tendencies are of very secondary importance and interest. In a world of continuing but only dimly foreseeable change, the notion of an economy in steady state equilibrium disappears, but that of process acquires a central role both in understanding the phenomena and in drawing out their implications for policy. This is to say that while a process not approaching an equilibrium can be of great interest in itself, an equilibrium that is not approached by any process is certainly of no interest. Here lies the basic difference between stability analysis and traverse analysis: since it is only in the late phase that any question of convergence to equilibrium can arise, traverse analysis is in any case capable of telling us about the short-run effects of a technical change, a task which cannot be accomplished by stability analysis.

5.2. This brings us to the above mentioned qualification concerning the possibility of employing traverse analysis to study sequential causality. There is, indeed, a difficulty and this is due to the fact that in economics the immediate cause of an effect is nearly always a decision followed by an action taken by someone. 'But it is not enough in economic analysis', Hicks writes, 'to refer the effect to the decision; we are also concerned with the reasons for the decisions, the causes of the decision. Thus even the simplest case of sequential causation in economics has two steps in it: a prior step, from the objective cause to the decisions that are based on it . . . and a posterior step, from the decision to their (objective) effects . . . Each of these steps may take time, so the total *lag* between cause and effect consists of two parts, prior and posterior.'[31]

Well, the analysis we have so far developed refers only to the 'posterior lag': innovation at $T = 0$ is our objective cause, and the evolution of the rate of starts and of employment are its effects. There is no room in our model for the 'prior lag'. At time 0, capital markets adjust instantaneously to the new conditions and capitalists—all of them—decide at that very instant how

[30] Cf. M. Kuga (1977) and E. Burmeister (1980).
[31] Cf. J. Hicks (1979), p. 88.

and how much to invest. The technical change in no way modifies the economic behaviour of agents, who exhibit during the traverse exactly the same mode of behaviour as that manifested in the old steady state. Our entrepreneurs do not react, but simply adapt themselves, to the new situation which has been created at time 0.

This is clearly unsatisfactory. The innovative process has some rules of its own which cannot be described as simple and flexible adaptations to changes in market conditions. Why is it that capitalists should continue to choose the optimal technique only on the basis of profit rate maximization, without paying any attention to the volume of profits accruing to them over a certain time span? Why should capitalists maintain during the entire traverse the same consumption pattern as that on the reference path, when it is known that they will meet capital losses and gains? Finally, why is it that all capitalists are able, instantaneously and simultaneously, to introduce the innovation which becomes available at $T = 0$? After all, the emergence of an innovation is only a signal, the indication of a new opportunity which must be perceived and then interpreted before it can materialize in an action. And nobody would dispute that not all entrepreneurs are innovators in Schumpeter's sense.

It will be apparent that a proper consideration of the prior lag would bring us very close to some of the most important themes of Schumpeter's reflection on economic development viewed as a morphological transformation of the economic system.[32] It is a remarkable feature of Hicks's traverse theory that it provides a vantage point allowing us to put the historical dynamics of technical change into perspective.

University of Bologna

APPENDIX†

In order to prove the results listed under (3.8)–(3.11), we apply the Laplace transforms‡ to equation (3.3) with $\Delta C(T) = 0$. We get:

(i)
$$L[x] = \frac{L[\hat{K}^*]}{L[\hat{K}]} L[x^*] \quad \text{where} \quad L[f] \equiv \int_0^{+\infty} f(t)e^{-st} \, dt$$

for a generic function $f(t)$.

Obviously

$$\hat{K}^* = \begin{cases} K^*(t) & \forall t \in [0, \theta^*] \\ 0 & \forall t \in (\theta^*, +\infty) \end{cases} \quad \text{and} \quad \hat{K} = \begin{cases} K(t) & \forall t \in [0, \theta] \\ 0 & \forall t \in (\theta, +\infty) \end{cases}$$

By putting $1/s \equiv T$ and by developing the integrals in (i), we obtain:

(ii)
$$L[x^*] = \left(\sum_{n=0}^{\infty} \hat{K}_n^* T^n n! \Big/ \sum_{n=0}^{\infty} \hat{K}_n T^n n! \right) L[x^*]$$

---

[32] For an initial exploration of a 'Schumpeterian traverse', where the assumption of static expectations is relaxed and where entrepreneurs are dichotomized into innovators and imitators, see R. Violi (1983).

† I owe this demonstration to R. Violi.

‡ We are assuming that the functions here implied possess such a transform. For the conditions which are required, see R. Bellman and K. Cooke (1963).

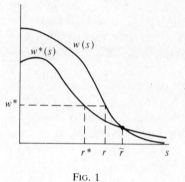

FIG. 1   FIG. 2

where

$$L[x^*] \equiv \sum_{n=0}^{\infty} x_n^* \frac{n!}{s^{n+1}} > 0.$$

As can be seen, equation (ii) expresses equation (i) in terms of historical time, T. Keeping in mind that the Hicksian fundamental theorem holds also for $K^*(t)$ and $K(t)$, we proceed geometrically. To this end, put:

$$g(s) \equiv \frac{L[x]}{L[x^*]} = \frac{L[\hat{K}^*]}{L[\hat{K}]}.$$

We have:

$$g(s) = \frac{1 - \dfrac{c_w w^*}{w^*(s)}}{1 - \dfrac{c_w w^*}{w(s)}} \quad \text{where} \quad \begin{cases} w^*(s) = \dfrac{\int_0^{\theta^*} b^*(t)e^{-st}\,dt}{\int_0^{\theta^*} l(t)e^{-st}\,dt} \\[4mm] w(s) = \dfrac{\int_0^{\theta} b(t)e^{-st}\,dt}{\int_0^{\theta} l(t)e^{-st}\,dt}. \end{cases}$$

As can be seen from Fig. 1, the relation between the two curves $w(s)$ and $w^*(s)$ depends on the postulated form of technical change (mechanization).§

In particular we have:

$$w^*(r^*) \equiv w^* < w(r^*); \qquad g(\bar{r}) = 1; \qquad w(s) \geq w^*(s) \quad \forall\, s \in [0, \bar{r}];$$

$$w(s) \leq w^*(s) \quad \forall\, s \in [\bar{r}, +\infty).$$

Fig. 2 describes the behaviour of $g(s)$. It allows us to derive the relation between $x_n(T)$ and $x_n^*(T)$ and therefore between $x(T)$ and $x^*(T)$. As can be seen:

$$x_n(s) \leq 0 \quad \forall\, s \in [r_2^*, r_2]; \qquad x_n(s) \geq 1 \quad \forall\, s \in [0, r_1]$$

$$x_n(s) \in [0, 1] \quad \forall\, s \in [r_1, r_2^*] \cup [r_2, r_1'] \cup [r_1'', +\infty), \qquad (r_2^* > r^*; \bar{r} \geq r_2)$$

Finally, to establish the sign of (3.6), we apply the Laplace transforms to obtain:

$$\frac{dx_n(T)}{d(\Delta C_n)} = \frac{s^n}{L[K]n!} \begin{cases} \geq 0 & \forall\, s \in [0, r] \\ \leq 0 & \forall\, s \in [r, +\infty) \end{cases}$$

and therefore:

$$\frac{dx_n(T)}{d(\Delta C_n)} \begin{cases} \geq 0 & \forall\, T \in [t_2, +\infty) \\ \leq 0 & \forall\, T \in [0, t_2] \end{cases}$$

§ Cf. B. Belloc, (1980).

BIBLIOGRAPHY

BELLMAN, R. and COOKE, K. 1963, *Differential-difference equations*, New York, Academic Press.

BELLOC, B. 1980, *Croissance économique et adaptation du capital productif*, Paris, Economica.

BERG, M. 1980, *The Machinery Question and the Making of Political Economy*, Cambridge, Cambridge University Press.

BURMEISTER, E. (1980), *Capital Theory and Dynamics*, Cambridge, Cambridge University Press.

ELSTER, J. (1978), *Logic and Society*, New York, J. Wiley.

VON HAYEK, F. (1931), *Prices and Production*, London, Routledge and Kegan Paul.

VON HAYEK, F. (1939), *Profits, Interest and Investment*, London, Routledge and Kegan Paul.

VON HAYEK, F. (1941), *The Pure Theory of Capital*, London, Macmillan.

HICKS, J. (1973), *Capital and Time*, Oxford, Oxford University Press.

HICKS, J. (1977), *Economic Perspectives*, Oxford, Clarendon Press.

HICKS, J. (1979), *Causality in Economics*, Oxford, Basil Blackwell.

ITO, T. (1980), 'Disequilibrium Growth Theory', *Journal of Economic Theory*.

KEYNES, J. M. (1973), *The Collected Writings of John Maynard Keynes*, London, Macmillan.

KUGA, M. (1977), 'General Saddlepoint Property of the Steady State of a Growth Model with Heterogeneous Capital Goods', *International Economic Review*.

MALINVAUD, E. (1953), 'Capital Accumulation and Efficient Allocation of Resources', *Econometrica*.

MARX, K. (1973), *Grundrisse*, Penguin Book, Harmondsworth.

NELSON, R. R. and WINTER, S. (1977), 'In Search of a Useful Theory of Innovation', *Research Policy*.

PASINETTI, L. L. (1981), *Structural Change and Economic Growth*, Cambridge, Cambridge University Press.

RICARDO, D. (1951–1973), *The Works and Correspondence of David Ricardo*, ed. P. Sraffa with the collaboration of M. Dobb, Cambridge, Cambridge University Press.

ROSS, S., SPATT, C., and DYBVIG, P. (1980), 'Present Values and Internal Rates of Return', *Journal of Economic Theory*.

SEN, A. (1975), 'Minimal Conditions for Monotonicity of Capital Value', *Journal of Economic Theory*.

SCHUMPETER, J. (1939), *Business Cycles*, New York, McGraw-Hill.

VIOLI, R. (1983), 'Disequilibrium in traverse analysis', Mimeo, Department of Economics Discussion Papers, University of Bologna.

ZAMAGNI, S. and GOZZI, G. (1982), 'Crescita non uniforme e struttura produttiva: un modello di traversa a salario fisso', *Giornale degli economisti e annali di economia*.

REAL WAGE RESISTANCE: EIGHTY
YEARS OF THE BRITISH
COST OF LIVING[1]

By J. F. WRIGHT

THE best-known elements of John Hicks's genius are those displayed in his main contributions to economic theory: the ability to follow-through and develop his mathematical discoveries combined with a continual striving to make a sense of mathematical results that can be expressed in words; and the perception of what is centrally important that has led to a lifetime struggle to elucidate basic economic concepts like capital and liquidity. But there is another element that contributes to the distinctive quality of his writing: a relentless search to make ordered sense of his experience—an experience which is the product of intense commonsense observation applied to his wide reading and travelling and everyday business. This element dominates *The Theory of Economic History*; but it is an ingredient of a great deal of his work, even that ostensibly concerned with pursuing the pure logic of theory. The instinct is very visible in his first published paper 'Wage-Fixing in the Building Industry' (1928);[2] and well developed in his first book *The Theory of Wages* (1932).[3]

Thus, though remaining in these areas pre-eminently a theorist (for he wants to make *systematic* sense of his experience), Hicks does not confine himself to extending the body of deductions from assumptions of pure economic rationality. In the general history of mankind he sees economic activity in its most pure market forms as having been confined to certain political and technological environments. This is the central theme of *The Theory of Economic History*. Political and social forces working through the legal framework, or simply through social pressures, will prohibit or inhibit the pursuit of economic objectives. Normally this will suppress or delay the operation of economic mechanisms, though on occasion where it leads to an increasing disequilibrium it might eventually cause an explosion.

[1] Thanks are due to Paul Fenn, Roderick Martin, Maurice Scott, and Jean Wright for their helpful comments on earlier drafts.
[2] *Economica*, viii (1928) 159 ff.
[3] He himself has said quite enough about the imperfections of some of the pure theory of that book; and too little about its other qualities. In detail it tried to incorporate into its analysis the facts of the institutions of the British labour market. A central theme was the effect on unemployment of the rigidity produced by the post-First World War system of British labour institutions. He has restated, in his Nobel Lecture, the theory of the effect of excessive real wages on employment in a way that does not contradict the possibility of unemployment due to deficient demand. There remains the question of correctness of diagnosis. That in inter-war Britain there was some, perhaps much, unemployment due to deficient demand of the type subsequently diagnosed by Keynes in *The General Theory* does not imply that it was misguided for a British economist in the 1920s to be worried about the effect of high real wages on employment. Few Keynesians can claim to have predicted the astonishing growth in labour productivity that, coupled with the maintenance of the net barter terms of trade of industrial countries, makes the concern in the 1920s with the level of real wages now seem misdirected.

It is in his approach to labour economics that this rejection of a pure economic approach is most consistently demonstrated.

> ... we must conceive the wages of labour (at least over a very large part of the labour market) as a 'system', a system with very considerable internal stresses of its own. As economic conditions vary, they bring about changes in the system, but the external changes have to reach a certain magnitude and a certain duration before they can break down the internal resistance.[4]

This was a view developed as a result of his early graduate research, which involved him in both extensive reading on the history of industrial relations and close observation of the working of the British labour market in the 1920s.[5] The research led him to attach great importance to two historical factors: the growth during the previous century of 'regular' (as opposed to 'temporary' or 'casual') employment;[6] and the rapid growth since the beginning of the twentieth century in determination of wages by collective bargaining, so that by the 1920s it was possible to characterize collective bargaining (much of it national) as being the normal method of wage determination.[7]

When he turns to a more formal analysis this perception of the nature of the labour market has led him to emphasize two characteristics. The first is that the labour market has in it substantial elements of monopoly and, quite probably, bilateral monopoly. This comes not only from the institution of collective bargaining but also from factors leading to 'regular' employment: namely, the importance of non-marketable skills including simple experience of the working of a particular organization. Bilateral monopoly is potentially very volatile, but it will be in the interests of both sides either to have long-term agreements or at least to develop long-term understandings that have a stabilizing effect.[8]

The second characteristic of the labour market is that the quality of the services provided by an employee may be affected by his feelings about the justice of his treatment.

> It is quite wrong to think of the labour market as being similar to a primary product market, in which price is set by demand and supply. Even the more sophisticated versions of wage theory, which attribute the rate of rise in wages to variations in the balance between unemployment and unfilled vacancies, are on the wrong track. The contract of employment, at least in so far as the more important parts of the labour market are concerned, is an arrangement under which people have to work together; they will not work together efficiently unless the terms of employment are felt to be fair, by both sides. [*Economic Perspectives*, p. 102]

Again we may note that the importance of this characteristic depends as

---

[4] *Theory of Wages*, p. 86; see also 'Economic Foundations of Wage Policy' (*Economic Journal*, 1955) retitled 'Inflation and the Wage-Structure' in *Collected Essays*, ii. 195.

[5] The published products of this work were the article on building wages in the 1920's cited above and 'The Early History of Industrial Conciliation in England' *Economica*, x (1930) 25 ff.

[6] *TW*. 69; see also *Theory of Economic History*, pp. 155–6.

[7] *CE* ii. 194.

[8] *TW*, pp. 70–1; *CE* ii. 199.

much on the nature of the employment as on the existence of collective bargaining.[9]

In the continuation of the passage cited, Hicks uses the argument about the need for 'fairness' in the employment relation to underpin his contention that 'real wage resistance' is a fundamental factor in the inflationary process; and, by implication, is a factor that policy-makers have to take into account.

> The pursuit of fairness in labour relations has many difficult aspects (differentials for instance); but one of the clearest and least controversial of the demands which it makes is for continuity in the standard of living. Thus, when there is a considerable rise in the cost of living, it is felt, by both sides, that a rise in money wages is fair. That is the reason for indexation of wages, whether formal or informal. Whether or not it is formal it must be expected to be present.

This view, expressed several times in the 1970s,[10] is very much the same as that underlying his 1955 British Association lecture where it is related to what he termed the Labour Standard; and it is consistent with his concern about real wages in his papers on post-war recovery.[11]

In a footnote to the passage cited Hicks comments on the origin of cost-of-living compensation:

> It did evidently happen, in former times.... that there were sharp increases in the cost of living, in particular years, associated with harvest failures; but these do not appear, in those times, to have led to rises in money wages.

He suggests that on these matters it is likely that:

> ... there has been a long-term change of the climate of opinion, in a more 'socialist' direction. If it was this last, the two wars would have been decisive catalysts. Wage-indexation, so far as Britain is concerned, seems to make its first appearance in World War I.

The main purpose of the remainder of this paper is to trace the development of this cost-of-living consciousness in Great Britain during the past eighty years.[12]

[9] *Economic Perspectives*, p. 102. We should be cautious about taking the use of the word 'contract' here as being the same as that fashionable in current wage theory. It would be paradoxical to take a remark from a passage that is denying that the essence of the employment relationship can be reduced to a market bargain as an unconditional endorsement of a type of analysis that, for all its sophistication, attempts to do just that. Moreover, Hicks's point about the self-interest of the employer in fair dealing does not seem fundamentally different from his views about the prudent conduct of masters in domestic slavery in *TEH*, pp. 124–5, and it would clearly be a very extended use to apply the word 'contract' to this.

[10] *The Crisis in Keynesian Economics*; 'What is Wrong with Monetarism?', *Lloyds Bank Review* (Oct. 1975).

[11] 'World Recovery after the War' and 'Full Employment in a Period of Reconstruction' in *CE* ii. chs. XIII and XIV.

[12] The paper will make no econometric contribution but it may be noted here that the period covered roughly coincides with that which provided the data for A. W. Phillips, 'The Relation Between Unemployment and the Rate of Change of Money Wage Rates in the United Kingdom, 1861–1957' *Economica*, NS XXV, 283ff. On the role of prices, R. G. Lipsey's comment on Phillips ('Further Analysis', *Economica*, NS ii, 1ff) is particularly relevant. For the period 1862–1913 Lipsey found that changes in the cost of living had a little explanatory power (pp. 8–12) but that for the period after 1920 changes in the cost of living had much greater explanatory power (pp. 25–6) even when the years of greatest change in price were omitted.

II. Cost of living consciousness before 1914

A close relationship between the cost-of-living and wages is not possible until a more or less precise measure of the level of relevant prices is available within a short period of the time to which it refers. It was not until autumn 1914, after the First World War had started, that such an index came into existence, and then in a very incomplete form.[13]

The previous ten years had seen developments in official statistics that provided some of the foundations needed for a cost-of-living index. In 1903 a tentative annual estimate of the retail price of food for 1877–1901 had been published; but this was a retrospective exercise making the best of the sparse official statistics and depending, for its budgets, primarily on data collected by others. The first new official work was the survey in 1904 of the food budgets of 1944 working-class families followed by a survey of rents and prices in 1905, repeated in 1912. The 1904 budgets provided the weights for the estimates of the level of prices in the reports on the two surveys and for a new index of the price of food in London that was published annually immediately after the end of the year.[14] This index, calculated more frequently, became the main, food, component of the cost-of-living index. Other information from the 1904 survey was the principal basis of the weightings adopted for the broader categories of the index; and survived in use until 1947.

The improvement of labour statistics had been a very important strand in the late Victorian concern with the conditions of labour. Marshall, writing in 1887, had even advocated wage indexation:

> Government could easily publish from time to time the money value of a unit of purchasing power which would be far more nearly constant than the value of money is. I think that it ought to do that. And then nearly all wage arrangements,

[13] E. H. Phelps Brown, *The Growth of Industrial Relations*, p. 336, refers to the pre-1914 period as an age of statistical darkness. The absence of any contemporary price index or much other information about retail prices is an obvious explanation for the relatively poor explanatory power of prices in the period before 1914 in Lipsey's study. Some wholesale prices were widely publicized and changes in price could directly impinge on employer and employee and produce some effect; but untutored impressions of price changes are likely to be very unreliable and so the correlation might be expected to be less than if knowledge of an index had been available at the time.

[14] *Memoranda on British and Foreign Trade and Industrial Conditions*. The first 'Fiscal Blue Book' (PP 1903, ii, 203) must have been hurriedly assembled by the Board of Trade to meet Balfour's request for information relevant to the Tariff Reform controversy. It revealed the poverty of the Board's own stock of information: fragmentary budgets that had been collected in 1888 had to be supplemented with material from budgets collected privately in the early 1890s as well as from a United States survey of 1891 of British conditions. But the request coincided with Llewellyn Smith taking charge of all the Board's statistics. He proceeded to organize the official collection of British budgets which were included in the Second Fiscal Blue Book in 1905 (PP 1905, lxxxiv, 1); and the *Enquiry by the Board of Trade into Working-Class Rents, Housing and Retail Prices*. Although the main information in this related to October 1905 it was not published until 1908. (PP 1908, xlvi, 319). It was clearly intended to be a thorough job and included comparisons of wages and prices in the principal industrial areas as well as with some foreign countries; it did also include some supplementary information on prices in 1906 and 1907 intended to bring it up to date. The 1912 Inquiry, though almost on the same scale, was completed by July 1918 (PP 1913, xlii, 393) which may indicate a greater consciousness of the speed with which prices changed.

but especially all sliding scales, should be based on that unit. This would at one stroke make both wages and profits more stable, and at the same time increase the steadiness of employment. It would perhaps be a further improvement if a special unit could be made for wages that should be based on the general unit but differ from it by giving greater weight to the prices of commodities chiefly used by the working classes. . .[15]

But this was not typical. The measurement of the cost of living had been an item in the programme for statistical improvement (see Appendix); but it was given little attention before 1904. Over a period in which prices, particularly of foodstuffs, had fallen dramatically, and made a great contribution to the improved standard of living of working men, the concern was whether the absolute *level* of some wages was adequate, not whether it was being adversely affected by price changes. It was indeed (and would remain) a problem for official statisticians that in collecting budget data to derive an average pattern of expenditure by which to weight an index of prices they might seem to be defining a standard of sufficiency. It needs to be remembered that in establishing a Labour Department in the Board of Trade it was always envisaged (by both supporters and critics) that the statistics it published would be given wide popular circulation and might decisively affect opinion (as health statistics had a generation before). On top of this the Department had acquired a central role in the conciliation of industrial disputes within a short time of being established in 1893. In seeking to protect this role it had to be careful to avoid seeming to endorse any principles of wage-determination including the concept of a 'living wage'.[16]

---

[15] From a preface to L. L. F. R. Price, *Industrial Peace, its Advantages, Methods and Difficulties* (London, 1887). Price's work was based on an inquiry financed by the Toynbee Trustees and Marshall's preface was intended as a tribute to Toynbee. But he used the occasion to provide a substantial statement of his own views on wage negotiations of which this proposal on wage indexation is only a small part. The preface, shorn of the tribute to Toynbee, was reprinted in A. C. Pigou (ed.) *Memorials of Alfred Marshall.* It was written at much the same time as 'Remedies for Fluctuations of General Price', which appeared in the *Contemporary Review* for March 1887, advocating a more comprehensive indexation. This was (and was acknowledged to be) in a longer tradition from Joseph Lowe and Poulett Scrope via Jevons of searching for a standard of value. What is interesting about the Price Preface is its modification specifically for use in wage determination. Price's book was mainly about a different type of sliding-scale that came into fashion in this period and was to be important until 1939, the automatic linking of wages with the market price of the product. The device was adopted quite widely in the Iron and Coal industries and replaced a situation in which there had been long periods of industrial strife, usually in the downswing when, faced with falling product prices, employers tried to claw back concessions that they had made to avoid interruptions in the boom. Prices in the industries concerned moved sharply over the cycle and though the wage-rates related to them by the scale might usually move in the same direction as the cost of living, they would move in much greater proportion both up and down. If anything, this sort of scale should be seen as a crude device for profit-sharing.

[16] Developments in this period deserve a separate paper. What needs to be noted here is that Llewellyn Smith, who gained full charge of all statistics at the Board of Trade in 1904 and who was Permanent Secretary from 1907 until Labour statistics were passed to the new Ministry of Labour in 1916, had taken charge of the Labour Department in 1893 and had grasped an opportunity to develop the central role of the Department in industrial conciliation several years before the Conciliation Act of 1896 gave it this role officially. See R. Davidson, 'Sir Hubert Llewellyn Smith and Labour Policy 1886–1916' (Cambridge Ph.D. thesis, 1971).

There had been concern since the 1880s with the low absolute level of wages of the 'sweated trades', where, as Marshall put it, the businessman might 'endeavour to make his profit not so much by able and energetic management of his business as by paying for labour at a lower rate than his competitors . . . taking advantage of the necessities of individual workers . . . and of their ignorance', making it difficult for other employers.[17] The Trade Boards Act of 1909 established bodies to set minimum wages in some of these industries. This would have had wider implications if it had been accompanied by the setting of a common minimum 'living' wage independent of the situation of the particular industry. For such a system would have involved revising the minimum wage should any considerable increase in the cost of living occur.[18]

The Tariff Reform controversy and a concern to find out how real wages had changed over the previous generation and how they compared with those in other industrial countries led to the important surveys of 1904 and 1905. Those who sought this information were not primarily concerned with accurate measurement of the effects of shorter-term changes in prices. The repetition of the 1905 survey in 1912 and the more regular publication of some annual estimates in the intervening years must be evidence of an official concern with the increase in prices that occurred after 1905.

In the years after 1905 prices rose fairly persistently. On the average, increases in money incomes matched the rise but there were many specific occupations, where trade and profits were less buoyant, where this did not happen. An outstanding example was the railways where G. W. Askwith, long the leading official industrial arbitrator, wrote of the cause of the dispute of 1907 simply that 'the cost of living had been going up, but the payment of grades had not increased proportionately'. This identifies cause but contains no presuppositions about employers' obligations. After 1909 the increase in prices accelerated and it is generally accepted that this pressure on real wages contributed to the explosion of industrial unrest in 1911. On this occasion the comment of Askwith is more explicit: 'Prices had been rising, but no sufficient increase in wages, and certainly no general

---

[17] Preface to Price, *op. cit.*

[18] British developments contrasted with those in Australia, where the judicial determination of wages and their linking to the cost of living was taken much further in the pre-1914 period. In 1906 the Commonwealth Parliament had imposed a tariff on imported manufactures with a similar excise duty on home-produced goods unless the producer was paying 'a fair and reasonable wage'. In 1907 Mr Justice Higgins, on application by the Harvester Corporation that their minimum wage of 6 s a day was reasonable, stated that in defining 'fair and reasonable' that he 'could not think of any other standard more appropriate than the normal needs of the average employee regarded as a human being living in a civilized community'. He estimated this as 7 s. a day. In 1908 this view was incorporated in the body of arbitration law. Subsequently the Federal Court asked the Commonwealth Statistician to measure changes in the cost of living so that it might revise its standard for the minimum wage which was done from 1912. See E. Aves, *Report to Home Department on The Wages Boards and Industrial Conciliation and Arbitration Acts of Australia and New Zealand*, (Cd 4167 of 1908); H. Heaton, 'The Basic Wage Principle in Australian Wages Regulation', *Economic Journal* xxxi (1921), 309. H. Phelps Brown, *The Origins of Trade Union Power* (Oxford, 1983), 274.

increase, had followed the rise. It may be said that employers had waited too much upon each other.'[19] Askwith became in 1911 the head of a new Industrial Relations department within the Board of Trade (with the rank of Permanent Secretary) and was to play a key role in the War. His comment may therefore be an indication of the presuppositions that official conciliators were now bringing to disputes.

Thus it is possible to discern before 1914 development of a consciousness of the concept of the cost of living, and perhaps of a social obligation to maintain some minimum standard of living of the working classes. The relevant statistical base had been partially established; actual legislation had involved public control over some low wages (though no definition of them in absolute standards); and there were some slight indications of an official acceptance that the cost of living had some relevance to wage disputes. Less tangibly, it may be that the political debate that began in 1903 and focused on living standards had reinforced the natural disposition of a large part of the electorate to expect from society a maintenance of those standards.

The factors listed above correspond to the Hicksian label 'socialistic', but it should be recognized that there were other very important factors, in the situation and structure of industry, that would delay any ready acceptance of formal or informal indexation. Marshall's argument in favour of indexation depended on an assumption that the price change that adversely affected the employee was caused by some general (monetary) factor that would benefit the employer. This might have been applicable to some cyclical movements but it failed to recognize that value added by British industry probably accounted for less than 20% of working-class budgets.[20] The main cause of change in the cost of living were changes in the prices of agricultural goods, which were increasingly determined in the world market. Thus many employers would be likely to resist a concession of the principle, even though they might often grant wage increases on specific occasions.

Virtually all employers were at that time very conscious that they were making their sales in a competititve market. In part this was because of the proportion of products exported (or subject to foreign competition in the home market); but it was also a consequence of the competition of other British producers. Hicks pointed out[21] that for many industries this situation had changed by the 1920s because of the introduction of industry-wide bargaining; for after that change firms would be less unwilling to make concessions that would increase their labour costs if the change would have an identical effect on the costs of their closest competitors.

The rapid extension of collective bargaining constitutes a clearer differ-

---

[19] G. W. Askwith, *Industrial Problems and Disputes* (London, 1920) 115–6, 175.

[20] The percentage weights in the index used in the occasional pre-war estimates were: Food 58; Rent 17; Clothing 17: Fuel 8. (PP 1905, lxxxiv) In the index eventually used in the war the weights were: Food 60; Rent 16: Clothing 12: Fuel 8; Other 4 (*Ministry of Labour Gazette*, February 1921).

[21] *TW*, pp. 172–3.

ence between the 1900s and the 1920s than the growth of regular employment. Though the latter was a very important trend, it operated more continuously over a much longer period. It was already a factor affecting employers' relations with their skilled labour forces long before 1914 (and contributed to the relative stability of money wages in that period).[22] It is difficult to see that it reached some crucial level between 1900 and 1920.

III. The cost of living and the First World War

The war and its immediate aftermath brought a wider recognition of increases in the cost of living as grounds for increases in wages. This was clearly seen as significant by observers like Barbara Wootton at the end of the war. She refers to 'the new departure in the practice of adding a bonus, warwage, or cost of living advance to the basic rate of wages'.[23] There were several stages in this development.[24] In the first part of the war awareness of an increase in prices led to many employers giving flat war bonuses. But there was no uniformity of size of these increases, or of the increases consequential on the acute demand for labour in the munitions industry as the scale of government orders increased. Because of the latter a Committee on Production (chaired by Askwith) was established by the Munitions of War Act 1915, and this body acquired the role of central arbitrator for the munitions industries. For a time there was a government attempt to resist cost-of-living increases in order to slow down inflation; but by 1916 wage rates had fallen a long way behind the cost-of-living and from then onwards changes in the cost of living became the primary ground for giving increases. In 1916–17 the rate of inflation accelerated and in early 1917 it was agreed that in the engineering industry there might be meetings every four months to consider what further alterations would be appropriate. At the same time some steps were taken to limit the extent of price rises on essential goods with the result that in the final year of the war wages caught up a little.

Anticipating that there might be a glut of labour in the immediate post-war period the Wages (Temporary Regulation) Act was passed in November 1918 forbidding employers to pay lower rates than at 11 November 1918 without application to an Interim Court of Arbitration. In the event the Court took over the role of the Committee on Production and continued to award increases related to the cost of living until November 1919. At that stage it was replaced by a new Industrial Court under the Industrial Courts Act. Though an obligation on employers to pay the current rates remained until October 1920, the new Court had no power to award increases. The role intended for the Court was essentially that of a panel of

[22] *CKE*, pp. 66–8.

[23] B. Wootton, 'Classical Principles and Modern Views of Labour', *Economic Journal*, xxx (March 1920), 46.

[24] Askwith, *op. cit.*; H. Wolfe, *Labour Supply and Regulation* (Oxford, 1923); A. G. B. Fisher, *Some Problems of Wages and Their Regulation in Great Britain Since 1918* (London, 1926).

expert arbitrators operating in the pre-war voluntary tradition. When matters were referred to it over the next few years its decision veered from qualifying the cost of living principle by reference to the state of trade to more positive rejection.[25]

What was the longer-term significance of the experience of the war? Labour had almost unlimited bargaining power because it was vital to avoid interruption of output in industry. Simultaneously, rapidly rising prices were giving cause for universal complaint. It was therefore natural for those attempting to introduce some sort of order to grasp at the principle of recognizing changes in the cost of living to provide a method of adjudication that would widely appeal to a sense of justice in the labour force. Because it was wartime and most industries were operating on cost-plus contracts, and because the government had to solve the problems it encountered without giving much thought whether the expedients were sustainable in the longer term, discussion of the conflict between wage costs determined on this basis and the need to price competitively was put on one side. But the question was not totally forgotten. Justification of the increases by reference to the cost of living and describing them as war bonuses clearly identified them as being justified by the abnormal conditions of the war and left scope for their subsequent reversal.[26] Thus, though cost-of-living compensation was a basis that some (perhaps including some of the arbitrators) would have been inclined to accept on grounds of principle, its inception should be regarded as an expediently devised concession to the temporary bargaining power of labour. That it was adopted no doubt contributed to expectations on the part of the workforce that it would be continued; and to its legitimation for a wider sector of public opinion. But the formula in which it was embodied reflected some doubts about its indefinite sustainability.

The index of cost of living was published in a rough and incomplete form until 1919; and cost-of-living bonuses given during the war were in very round amounts. Generally there was a feeling that the standard of living to be protected should relate to some minimum standard only. Increases given to time-workers were therefore usually in amounts not percentages; and this practice was an important factor leading to the narrowing of differentials that occurred over the period.[27]

---

[25] B. Wootton, *The Social Foundations of Wage Policy* (London, 1962), 92–3.

[26] The increases in wages given during the war were consistently described as bonuses, clearly implying that they might not be permanent. As late as 1920 the Industrial Court granted increases in wages with the phrase: 'The amounts here granted are to be regarded as war advances, due to and dependent on the existence of the abnormal conditions prevailing in consequence of the War' (Fisher, *op. cit.*, p. ix).

[27] The possibility of precise indexation depended on the development of a usable cost-of-living index. *The Historical Abstract of Labour Statistics* contains a table giving the monthly index of the cost of living from August 1914; but this is a retrospective compilation. Inspection of *The Labour Gazette* shows that the evolution of a published index in its fully developed form was much slower. Until August 1914 the only monthly return had been of wheat and bread prices; as early as September 1914 this had been replaced by a monthly version of the wider

On the face of it the incomplete form of publication reflected lack of relevant information. But the extension to a more comprehensive form involved calculations that might have been made on the back of an envelope: it depended on a few very simple weights virtually identical to those used in the isolated estimates of the previous ten years and some very broad assumptions about the prices of non-foodstuffs. It may well be, therefore, that production of the wider index was deferred until its publication became advantageous to dispel the notion that the cost of living as a whole was rising as fast as foodstuffs. There also seems to have been some moderately sophisticated discussion of the proper basis of the index.[28]

In 1919 the *Gazette* made its first report of an agreement that automatically tied wages (of wool and worsted workers) to the Index of the Cost of Living. Successive surveys of December 1920, August 1921, and July 1922 estimated that similar sliding-scales affected 1.5, 2.75, and 3 million workers.[29] The details of trades affected provided by some of the returns give a picture of sliding-scales spreading from wool to other textiles in 1919; to the civil service, railways, police, and various other public employees in 1920; to building and civil engineering in 1921; and finally to miscellaneous trades like boot-and-shoe and flour-milling in early 1922; together with several of the Trade Board industries. The latter had been prompted to adopt the system by the Ministry of Labour;[30] and many of the other industries

Reference 27 (*continued*)
index of food prices that had hitherto been produced annually. For two years that was all that was provided visibly in the Gazette (though the Ministry told the Balfour Committee in 1925 that they had been compiling a more comprehensive index from 1915). In 1916 the reporting of food prices began to be accompanied by a note that their increase was not representative of all prices, but these were not tabulated, presumably to emphasize their lack of quality. This rough format continued until 1919. See Department of Employment *British Labour Statistics Historical Abstract 1886–1968* (London 1971), Table 89 and p. 11; Committee on Industry and Trade, *Survey of Industrial Relations* (1926), p. 94, Memorandum on Wages and the Cost of Living furnished by Ministry of Labour; A. L. Bowley, *Prices and Wages in the United Kindom 1914–1920* (Oxford, 1921), 97–8. The *Gazettes* of March 1920 and February 1921 provided full details of the construction of the index.

[28] There are signs of an interesting internal debate. Eventually it seems to have been accepted that labour should be compensated for the whole rise in the cost of living, even though a part of the increase was caused by increases in indirect taxes. Initially, in the estimates that appeared from 1916, two estimates were provided distinguishing between increases from indirect taxation and increases from other causes which might be taken as implying a view that labour should accept some real burden. From Bowley, *op. cit.*, it is clear that there was also a discussion whether a constant basket of goods should be used, especially as the full quantities of some of the goods included were not available in the war. An alternative index using a basket providing constant nutrition was calculated by the Ministry of Food. A committee was appointed in 1918 to consider whether the index was the best measure of the increase in the cost of living since 1914. It calculated that if the index had been calculated on the basis of the actual pattern of expenditure in 1918 the increase would have been 74% and not 108% over the period since 1914. PP 1918, iii, 825.

[29] The *Gazette* surveys of the coverage of cost-of-living sliding scales appeared irregularly from 1919 to 1947 in November 1919, December 1920, August 1921, July 1922, July 1933, June 1944. In addition totals were reported for 1925 and 1939 (retrospectively at the next survey) and in 1947.

[30] Dorothy Sells, *The British Trade Boards System* (London, 1923).

adopting the practice were identified in relation to their Joint Industrial Councils. By this stage therefore it appears to have been thought particularly appropriate to many of the industries identified by the Whitley Committee as having either very imperfect or not completely adequate organizations for the normal processes of collective bargaining; and it was the adherence of these groups that extended the coverage of the system in 1921–2 by which time some industries, like wool textiles, were discontinuing the practice.

The sliding scales were not indexation in its simplest sense, i.e. proportional changes in wages identical to the proportionate change in prices: they were usually stated in amounts of money per point change in the index for a band of grades; and they often were contrived so that the maximum movement was less than in full proportion to the percentage change in prices; furthermore there might be a floor below which wages might not fall. Despite these various breaks the agreements often produced wage reductions; and, if the Ministry returns are to be taken at face value, accounted for quite a lot of the wage reductions that did take place in some years between the Wars.

After 1922 the numbers subject to a sliding-scales fell to 2.5 millions in July 1925 and to 1.25 in 1933, by which time they had been discontinued in the civil service. Only 0.75 to 1 million wage-earners were actually affected in 1933 because in many cases wages had reached a floor below which the agreement did not apply; and in other cases employers chose not to enforce a reduction. The only major groups left were building and civil engineering, and the railway clerks; the others were Trade Board industries and miscellaneous JICs.

After 1933 the number affected by cost of living agreements rose slightly to one-and-a-quarter million in 1939 because of greater employment in the trades affected. During the war there was an extension of coverage to mining, steel, and cotton; the number affected increased to 2.5 millions in 1944, at which level it remained until 1947. Thereafter for many years the existence of a significant number of workers who would automatically obtain cost-of-living increases was an anomaly for the devisers of plans of income restraint. There were still two million in 1965. The policy of wage restraint in 1966 did not recognize the practice as a vested interest and the largest group (building) and several others gave up the practice in the late sixties.[31] In the previous fifteen years the practice had lost much of its attraction: it did not provide full compensation for the rise in the index; and in most years other manual unions were obtaining in the annual wage bargain markedly more than the index (because of rising productivity). It became more attractive to abandon automatic compensation, join in the annual pay round, and be confirmed in the same moral claim to informal indexation possessed by other workers.

[31] H. A. Clegg, *The System of Industrial Relations in Great Britain* (2nd edn. Oxford, 1972).

A symptom of the interwar decline in general concern about the cost-of-living index was the prolonged delay in reforming its basis, although from the early twenties this was widely acknowledged to be unsatisfactory. Eventually, in 1937–8, a departmental survey was undertaken of working-class budgets to provide the weights for a new index; but although the survey was completed by 1939, the index was not revised before the War began. From June 1947, on the recommendation of the Cost of Living Advisory Committee,[32] the weights of 1937–8 were used to establish the *Interim Index of Retail Prices;* and a new comprehensive enquiry into family expenditure was carried out in 1953–4, which was used from January 1956 in a new *Index of Retail Prices.* Subsequently, from 1962, the expenditure weightings underlying the index derived from the Family Expenditure Survey were revised annually.[33] Thus it ceased to carry in its name any connection with the Cost of Living of the Working Class; and with its revised constituents from 1956 it ceased to be particularly associated with the prices of necessities.

It is clear from the above account that the formal indexation of wages is a relatively minor element in British wage history of the past sixty years.

Trade unions, though not averse to making claims on the grounds of increases in the cost of living, were suspicious of indexation because it might in some way weaken the pressure for increasing real wages. Their distrust was probably increased by the experience of 1920–1 when prices turned downwards and the operation of sliding scales may have contributed to the ease with which the level of money wages was reduced.[34] They were hostile to the actual index because its name, and the weights it used, seemed to imply a mere subsistence wage.[35]

Thus consideration of the cost-of-living seemed to disappear from the early 1920s until the beginning of the Second World War. But in other ways consciousness of the cost-of-living may have been developed. As Clay noted in 1923,[36] the prolonged public debate in the early twenties on the economic state of the country in which the index was used to test how real incomes had changed since 1913 reinforced a notion that real incomes should not fall. And when subsequently in the inter-war period the further fall in the price of goods was given as a reason why wages should be more flexible

---

[32] *Interim Report of the Cost of Living Advisory Committee* (PP 1946–47, x, 683).

[33] The *Gazettes* of August 1920 contain a report of a Joint Committee on the Cost of Living of the TUC and the Labour Party.

[34] If the categorization of causes of wage change provided annually by the Ministry of Labour is to be relied on, cost-of-living scales did not make as great a direct contribution to the reduction of wages in 1921–2 as that stated in G. Routh, *Occupation and Pay in Great Britain* 1906–79 (2nd. ed., 1980), p. 141. A more important cause was the operation of scales attached to the price of the product.

[35] '... it places the whole of the workmen as one distinct class on the basis of an amount, basing their livelihood on food alone...' (Ernest Bevin when appearing for the dockers before the Industrial Court in 1920, from Fisher, *op. cit.*, 156).

[36] H. Clay, 'The Post-War Wages Problem', paper read before British Association, 1923, reprinted in the *The Problem of Industrial Relations*, (London, 1929).

downwards than they proved to be, or as a reason why it would not be as harsh as it seemed to reduce social benefits, the principle of the preservation of the purchasing power of wages received a further implicit endorsement.

That cost-of-living remained an important factor was to be more dramatically illustrated in late 1939. The outbreak of war brought a sharp increase (12%) in prices in the second half of the year; and between September and December 1939 some four and three-quarter million workers were granted increases mainly because of the cost of living—an event that seems to have caused surprise and concern to the government, which was still toying with the possibility of finding real resources for the war effort by persuading the manual workers to accept some reduction in real incomes. With the advent of Bevin to the Ministry of Labour any hopes of holding down real wage rates had to be abandoned: eventually the rise in the prices constituting the index was brought to a dead stop by use of subsidies and, with a lag, the rise in wages slowed though it did not halt.[37]

In retrospect the behaviour of the cost-of-living has been an inescapable fact of life during the past forty years. The main questions have been how immediate reactions would be; and how far, as inflation accelerated, wage-pressure might begin to relate to expectations rather than experience. On these large and essentially quantitative matters the narrative approach of this paper can cast no light.

However, the significant change over the past 40 years has been in the expectations and reactions of salary-earners. The extent of the destabilization of prices produced by a given exogeneous disturbance is very sensitive to the proportion of national income that is thought to be entitled to revision.[38] By the end of the 1970s the use of changes in the retail price index to determine the minimum increase in money payment that could be offered or accepted in normal circumstances had extended to a very large proportion of earned incomes; thus extending the coverage of informally indexed entitlements to 70–80% of national income as compared with something like 40% in the First World War.

One element in this change is the increased importance of salaried employments brought about by the increasing proportion of employment in the public sector and by the increased relative importance of non-manual

---

[37] See *Gazette*, January 1940; W. K. Hancock and M. M. Gowing, *British War Economy* (London, 1949); H. M. D. Parker, *Manpower* (London, 1957). In effect an elaborate compromise was reached: the measured cost of living was held back artificially; and wage rates were allowed to rise a little in relation to it. It was known that a more widely based index of prices would have risen considerably more quickly; but actual earnings were rising faster than that. But the command of consumers over resources was limited by rationing and shortages so the extra income went either into savings or into expenditure (on drink, cinema, and cigarettes) that was highly taxed.

[38] Some salary- as well as wage-earners may have received cost-of-living bonuses in the First World War, but the bonus was a flat rate, so that it was received on considerably less than the total wage bill. In 1970 we take the total of wages and salaries as a proportion of *Net* National Product. On the simplest assumptions; a 40% share gives a multiplier of 1.67, and an 80% share a multiplier of 5.0.

jobs in both the private as well as the public sector. But it is also a product of a change in attitudes.

The Hicksian emphasis on the need for 'fair' treatment to ensure continuity in the quality of service provided has at least as much force in considering salaried as wage-earning occupations. The jobs done are often of the type where close and direct control of the quantity and quality of the employee's output is infeasible. In these jobs, therefore, absence of employee grievance is very important. If a decline in real income is accepted without grievance developing it must be because the salary earner more closely identifies himself with the long-run interests of his employer—because he is in a position to perceive his employer's situation or because of greater security and stability of employment and possibilities of advancement or perhaps because, in times of emergency, he has a different sense of social obligation.

A partial explanation of the change in attitude may lie in the increasing size of firms and of employing units which has produced a greater distance between salaried employees and their ultimate employers so that relations became more formalized (in some cases this has also resulted in unionization) and, in the case of business, the employees have became less sensitive to financial limitations of the firm. But a major reason must lie in their perception of their long-run situation.

Some salary earners had been affected by cost-of-living adjustments at an early stage; and it is not always clear that, in the period immediately after 1918, these were always given on a completely flat-rate, rather than proportionate, basis. As argued above, the existence of a cost-of-living index led to discussions in the 1920s about what the war had done to differentials, and this may have heightened the consciousness of non-wage earners. Nevertheless no expectation of quick, or full, indexation had developed in the inter-war period. As a result salaries fell sharply in real terms during the Second World War.

In the ten years after the War, when it gradually became clear that the experience of the 1920s would not be repeated, at various times groups of salaried employees obtained retrospective settlements. Subsequently, in the long period of relative calm when most manual wages were advancing as a result of productivity growth and simple comparability arguments, it was nevertheless the case that, because of persistent though slow inflation, salaried employees had to have further reviews of their remuneration from time to time; and in such reviews, further checks on the change in the real value of payments played a part—thus contributing to the legitimizing of the assumption that real standards should be maintained for all classes of person. For a long time the reviews of all salaries tended to be less frequent than reviews of wages but the increasing rate of inflation increased their frequency. Finally, the experience of policies of pay restraint, which tended to adopt formulae that assumed an annual wage round, made the annual salary round virtually universal.[39]

Pensioners were another class to receive increasingly frequent reviews; though in their case the process of revision converged on more or less formal indexation. This applied not only to the basic state pensions but also to the whole pensions of state servants. With the Pensions (Increase) Act of 1972 the apotheosis was complete: what had been the cost of living to working men had become the expenses in retirement of the Permanent Secretary of the Board of Trade.

Real-wage resistance is unlikely to be as fundamental a fact of life as the downward inflexibility of money wages. Moreover, after the experience of recent years it would be rash to say that real wages cannot be squeezed if employers are given enough cause for resolution and that cause is made visible to the employees.

Nevertheless, admission of the possibility that real wages may be squeezed in special circumstances is not to deny that 'real wage resistance' is a very important fact of an economy like our own. An admission that when companies are visibly in desperate situations their workforces will accept real cuts is not inconsistent with an expectation by both sides that, in less abnormal times, such a reduction will not be possible—thus providing a mechanism for the amplification of imported inflation and for the squeezing of profitability.

APPENDIX: THE MEANING OF 'COST OF LIVING' IN THE 1880s

As stated above the measurement of the cost of living had been an item in the programme for statistical improvement. In a prepared paper at the Industrial Remuneration Conference in 1885, (*Report of Proceedings of Industrial Remuneration Conference* London, 1885, p. 8), Sir Thomas Brassey maintained that 'the government should take in hand the collection of statistics . . . with regard to the remuneration of labour and the cost of living, the Board of Trade should issue publications similar to those put forth by the Bureau of Labour'. The same general proposal was embodied in a resolution passed by the House of Commons on 2 March 1886. In response, the Board of Trade extended its statistics (inter alia) 'To collect information on prices, production and cost of living'. (memorandum in PP. 1886, LXXI, 205). It may therefore seem mysterious that so little progress was made in the next seventeen years with that last objective.

But what exactly was the objective? The first use of the term 'cost of living' by the Massachusetts Bureau of Statistics of Labor was in a circular dated 1 October 1869, reproduced in *The First Report of the Bureau* 1869–70 (Boston, 1870). The circular earnestly solicited correspondents to provide information about labour including 'their average earnings and their average cost of living per year'; the latter expression makes most sense as a simple return of expenditure. Though in *The Second Report* (1871) the Bureau included a whole section headed 'The Cost of Living', which was an extended table by locality of the prices of a selection of 38 foodstuffs and 23 other items (soap, clothing, fuel, rent), this was not repeated. The term was certainly used in the sense of total annual expenditure in the fifth (1874) and sixth (1875) reports (see particularly page 354 of *The Sixth Report*). These were years when Carroll

---

[39] In the case of the salaries of staff in predominantly wage-earning businesses the annual round may have come earlier. The National Board for Prices and Incomes in *Salary Structures*, Report No. 132, Cmnd. 4187, (1969) reported that the chief factor in changes in the salaries of firms was changes in the wages of their own employees.

Wright[40] had taken charge; and the absence of any subsequent regular statistics on prices (or budgets) between 1876 and 1884 seems to confirm that the material had not been collected from any concern with price levels and their changes through time.

There were examples of what is recognizably the modern use. Thus the British trade unionist George Howell, in *The Beehive* 12 February 1876, called for the establishment of an English Bureau of Statistics of Labour which would deal with, *inter alia*, '8. Cost of Living, proportionate cost compared with wages for any given number of years. Have wages moved in the same proportion as the cost of living? Variations in different localities.' More notably in the *The Fifteenth Report* (1884) Carroll Wright included a section entitled 'Comparative cost of living in Massachusetts and Great Britain' which involved the combining of all the information about prices by weights derived from proportions of expenditure in order to produce a ratio by which the comparision might be made. In the following the sense is the same as the strict modern usage: 'In making comparisons the reader must remember that it is impossible to bring into comparison in all cases, goods identical in quality with those for which prices have been obtained. . . The articles are those used by workingmen . . . and a higher rate in one country may denote not simply a higher cost of living, but may indicate also an advance in the standard of living.'

However, it seems probable that neither Brassey nor Giffen were using the term in the modern sense. Thus Brassey, in the speech cited, said '. . . with more skill in the use of materials it is certain that much might be done to diminish the cost of living without diminishing the standard of comfort'; 'cost of living' here only makes sense as 'expenditure'. Giffen in 1893. in *Memorandum on the Progress of the Labour Department of the Board of Trade* (PP 1893–4, lxxxii, 263), referred to as a 'Report on Cost of Living by Mr Burnett' what had been published in 1889 as 'Returns of Expenditure by Working Men' (PP 1889, xxxviii, 97) and was certainly no more than that.

[40] For a fuller account of this great man see E. H. Phelps Brown and M. H. Browne, 'Carroll D. Wright and the Development of British Labour Statistics', *Economica* NS xxx, 280.

INDEX